Born in 1936 in Japan, Audrey Sansbury Talks spent the first five years of her life in Tokyo with her family. There her father taught at a theological college and became chaplain to the British Embassy. After four years in Canada, during the Second World War, she came to England. She attended Cheltenham Ladies' College and St Andrew's University, where she received an MA in Modern and Medieval History. After marrying and having four sons, she worked part-time as an English teacher at Rugby School, where her husband taught French and Russian. While at Rugby she studied for a postgraduate MA in English at Warwick University. She finally returned to the Far East in 1990, and again in 1995.

A TALE OF TWO JAPANS

Ten Years to Pearl Harbor

Audrey Sansbury Talks

Book Guild Publishing
Sussex, England

First published in Great Britain in 2010 by
The Book Guild Ltd
Pavilion View
19 New Road
Brighton, BN1 1UF

Typesetting in Garamond by
Keyboard Services, Luton, Bedfordshire

Printed and bound in Great Britain by
CPI Antony Rowe

A catalogue record for this book is available from
The British Library

ISBN 978 1 84624 416 2

For Christopher and Helen
in memory of our parents
Kenneth and Ethelreda Sansbury
who retained, through everything,
a deep love of Japan.

Contents

CONTENTS

Foreword

This quietly and beautifully written story of an English family caught up in the drama of the two Japans is an important addition to the history of those days. Based on letters and journals, but containing Audrey Talks' own childhood experiences, it is an indictment of the kind of militarism which destroys civilised nations. It is also a wonderful picture of the English abroad in the 1930s and of one sort of social behaviour having to accommodate another. It wasn't enough to learn the language. And there was always the realisation of the Sansbury family – the Reverend Kenneth Sansbury would become Bishop of Singapore and Malaya after the Second World War – that it had to be ambassadorial in the Christian sense and reflecting its mission in whatever it did. They toiled and played, and learnt to love the Japanese, in a period of unparalleled violence, one which stretched from memories of the Great Earthquake to those of the atom bomb. Audrey Talks sets Chiang Kai Shek, Pearl Harbor, the barbarity of Japan's treatment of its prisoners, the clash of cultures etc., all within her family's compass. As an example of how English missionaries lived between the thirties and fifties her book is excellent in its ability to reveal the pleasures and horrors of their task, the liner voyages, the loveliness of Japanese cities before the war, and most of all the spiritual bond which still exists between the Sansburys and the Japanese. It is like an experienced summing-up of all the mid-twentieth century stories about Japan – a kind of 'I was there' statement which makes unusual reading.

Ronald Blythe

Preface

This is the story of my own family's experience of Japan during the years that have been called in Japan *kurai tanima* or 'dark valley', the 'dark valley' that was to lead from Japan's invasion of Manchuria in September 1931 to Japan's attack on Pearl Harbor in December 1941. My parents sailed for Japan within a few months of the invasion of Manchuria; my brother, sister and I were born during those years; and our family left Japan on the last Japanese ship to cross the Pacific before the outbreak of war in 1941.

My parents, and especially my father, had an uncommonly varied experience of Japan. They spent the years 1932–1934 in a Japanese town where there were no other westerners, and so there they experienced 'old' Japan. But that 'old' Japan was already under threat from the course on which Japan's military leaders were set. From 1934–1941 my parents lived in Tokyo, where my father taught at a theological college and was also chaplain at the English church, so there he moved both in Japanese and in foreign circles. From 1938–1941 he was also chaplain to the British Embassy and from that vantage point he followed the development of the war in China, the war in Europe and the disastrous course that was to lead to Pearl Harbor. Later my father became Bishop in Singapore, so my parents returned to Asia to a place with most bitter memories of the Japanese.

For us as children, the move from Japan was traumatic, for we lost our home, our father disappeared into the war, and from that time we lived in a world where Japan was the enemy, when Japan was the only home we knew. So this is a tale of two Japans, of the peaceful Japan that we knew and loved, and of the military Japan, which brought disaster on itself and on the world.

This book is based for the most part on a wealth of unpublished sources: memories, letters, diaries, reports. The most important are the letters my father sent from Japan to his parents in England; there are also the letters he wrote to my mother in the anxious days leading to the outbreak of war in 1939; and the letters and reports he sent to the missionary society in London. Other sources are the letters of Stanley Woodward, the other English lecturer at the college, the letters of Caroline Rose, wife of Larry Rose, the American lecturer at the college, and the diary kept by Larry himself during the grim months of late 1940. The most important published source is Bishop Heaslett's own account of the time he spent in a Japanese prison following his arrest on 8 December 1941, the day of the attack on Pearl Harbor.

Acknowledgements

There are many people whose help has been invaluable in enabling me to write this book. I owe a great debt of gratitude to Ronald Blythe, who has so generously written the foreword; to Anthony Thwaite, who has read the script at different stages and made most helpful comments and suggestions; to Dr Andrew Finch, who has proved a tower of strength through his knowledge of Japan and of computing, and who prepared the maps; and to the late Dean Alan Webster, who was reading the book as work in progress and wrote, 'This should certainly be published. How fascinating the whole book will be.'

Others have generously shared their material with me. Most importantly, David Woodward sent me copies of the letters of his father, Stanley, and Peg Webber (Peggy Rose) let me work on the letters of her mother, Caroline, and the 1940 diary of her father, Larry. My cousin Catherine Lang passed on to me a brown leather handbag of our grandmother's containing letters of my father for 1938–1939; John and David Brackley gave me their father's account of the great Kanto earthquake of 1923; and the family of Bishop Eric Cordingly gave me material relating to their father's time as a prisoner of the Japanese in Singapore and on the Burma–Thailand Railway. To all these I am most grateful.

I should also like to thank Lucy McCann, archivist at the Rhodes House Library in Oxford, and the staff for help in my researches into the records of the Society for the Propagation of the Gospel (SPG) which are housed there.

I am grateful to the following for permission to use copyright material: Lutterworth Press for extracts from *Captive Christians* by Eric Cordingly in *Beyond Hatred*, edited by Guthrie Moir; SCM Press for extracts from *From a Japanese Prison* by Samuel Heaslett; Yale University Press for extracts from *Edmund Blunden, A Biography* by Barry Webb.

Finally, my greatest thanks must go to my husband, David, who has been the companion of all my journeying back to the East, and to my family who have understood.

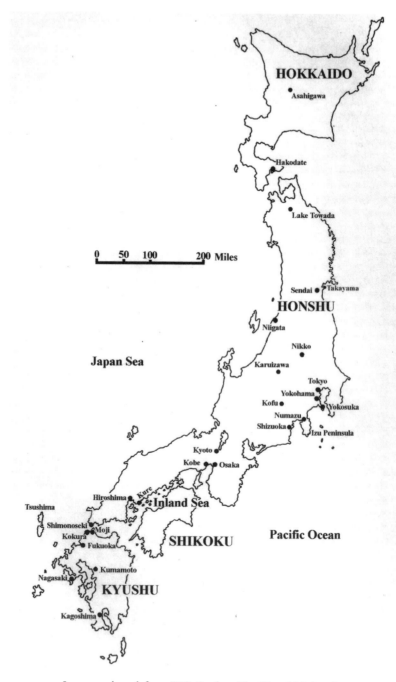

Japan – adapted from WG Beasley, *The Rise of Modern Japan*
(Weidenfeld and Nicolson, London, 1990)

PART I

Travelling Back

1

By Way of Hong Kong

And Japan, I thought, I shall go back to Japan. The idea was new, unexpected. Japan was the world of my childhood. It was nearly fifty years since the door had closed on that world, so abruptly, so absolutely, I had never imagined returning that way, pushing open that door and entering again that lost world.

Now I found myself already on the way. I taught a little, pupils from overseas. I liked the work and thought it appropriate, for I myself had felt an outsider at school, too English in Canada, too Canadian in England, never quite speaking the right language. Lately, more and more of my pupils had come from Hong Kong. They came in and out of the house chattering together in Cantonese and sat round the dining table taking lessons in English. Gradually I felt returning to me, from a great distance, a sense of recognition, of familiarity, a sense of being at home. I knew where that feeling came from. Their oriental faces were like the faces of my childhood.

Now, as I sat near the front of the church, I looked at the Japanese lady helping in the service. I had met her once: English husband, daughter at the high school, western clothes, western hairstyle, but Japanese features. Already I had begun to think: One day I shall go to Hong Kong. But now another thought was added: And when I do I shall go on to Japan. The idea took shape in my mind. When I went to Hong Kong I would visit all three places most important to my family in the East: Singapore – my parents had lived in Singapore in the sixties; Hong Kong – my brother had done his National Service in Hong Kong in the fifties; and Japan, I thought, I shall go back to Japan.

A year passed and a letter came from Hong Kong, from the mother of one of my pupils:

My husband and I tentatively plan to move to the States in the summer of 1991, so between the summer of 1989 and the summer of 1991, I invite you or your children or your friends whom you can trust to stay in our home in case you come to Hong Kong or visit any nearby places in the Far East. There is no need for you to look for accommodation. There are many fascinating places for you to visit and things for you to see.

I read the letter, showed it to my husband, told him I should like to visit Hong Kong. He looked at me in amazement, unable to believe I could seriously be thinking of travelling to the other side of the world. Indeed, I wondered myself if I might be indulging in fantasies. My husband had never travelled outside Europe, and I had not travelled outside Europe since I had sailed with my family from Canada to England in a converted banana boat at the age of nine.

A year later, a second letter came:

How are you? Terribly sorry that I haven't written to you for some time. Life in Hong Kong is full of uncertainties. People in general are full of fear and anxiety. It's possible that we might leave Hong Kong for good in June 1991. So, if possible, please make a trip here. We would be only too happy to share our home with you and it would be an honour to us.

This time I was sure. Again I showed the letter to my husband, again told him I should like to visit Hong Kong. Still he was incredulous, not understanding why I should want to travel so far. I began to explain that I should like to visit those places in the East that had been most important to my family. He looked at me in dismay, wanting no emotional journey to the past. 'No, it won't be emotional,' I could not be sure of this, 'but I should like to go to Singapore, to see where my parents used to live; and to Hong Kong, because I've taught so many pupils from there; and to Japan, because I was born there and have never been back since I was a child.' This sounded reasonable. 'And to San Francisco...'

San Francisco? The pupil whose parents had invited us to Hong Kong was now studying at Berkeley. 'And surely, if we are going as far as Japan, it will be just as easy to carry on round the world as to go back the way we've come.'

Singapore, Hong Kong, Japan, San Francisco. Thirty years before, my parents had made a journey round the world. Air travel was not so common then, and to the whole family their journey had seemed an amazing adventure. I recalled how pleasant my parents had found the greenness of Singapore after the dust and heat of India; how they had looked down from the plane as they flew out of Hong Kong and wondered if they would ever see that breathtaking view of the harbour again. Japan had been the heart of their journey too. And, afterwards, how much they had enjoyed San Francisco.

I sat down to write letters. A reply came first from Hong Kong:

Both my husband and I are very delighted to know that you have finally decided to come and visit us in October, so don't hesitate to plan ahead. October is almost the best month to visit Hong Kong, unless the weather becomes too unpredictable with an unexpected typhoon.

Soon afterwards a letter came from Berkeley:

I'm really glad to hear that you will be coming to Hong Kong and California. Two weeks in Hong Kong, did you say? I'm sure my parents will be very happy. I hope you might be able to visit here at Thanksgiving, as we have four days free for the holiday. You can stay here on campus and I can show you round San Francisco.

My parents received letters from friends in Singapore: 'It will be our pleasure to welcome your daughter and son-in-law to Singapore ... How good it would be if you were able to come with them ... It is a pity that you are not able to travel so far these days ... Singapore has seen many changes even since your last visit...'

My mother received a letter from a Japanese friend staying in Cambridge:

I am happy to hear that Audrey and her husband will be visiting Japan later this year and I shall try to help them as much as I am able. I am sorry that I cannot invite them to stay at my house. Not having had a maid for three or four years and my interests being in other directions than keeping house, the house is not much better than a pigsty. I can arrange accommodation for them, if they would like, in a hostel at the university where visiting professors and scholars can stay. If they would like me to arrange this, please could you ask them to let me know as soon as is possible, for October is such a busy month with annual conferences of literary and other societies. In some respects, September might be a better month for their visit, places of interest being less crowded then. October has better weather, of course, except for typhoons, but places are crowded, it being the time of year for school parties.

So it was settled. I was going back to Japan. But I could not go back knowing nothing of the language. As a child I had spoken Japanese as naturally as English, but when my family left Japan, I forgot it all. I do not know how long we had been in Canada when a small girl came up to me one day in the school playground:

'Did you live in Japan?'

'Yes.'

'Can you speak Japanese?'

'Yes.'

'Say something, then.'

I could not remember a single word but, not wishing to lose face, I declared, 'No, I don't want to!' Then, to lend conviction, I added, 'Japanese has a lot of zeds!'

It was my brother who felt most keenly the loss of the language. He was seven when we left Japan and so knew more than his two younger sisters. He would say to our mother, 'You should have made us speak Japanese when we were in Canada.' And she would protest, 'How could I, when you wouldn't speak Japanese except to a Japanese face?' Later he clung to a story he had heard of an Englishman who spent his childhood years in Japan but then went to England and forgot the language. Returning to Japan as a young man, he went into a crowded restaurant and there, surrounded by the sound of Japanese voices, he found himself speaking again in Japanese. My brother returned to Japan as a young man, but no such miracle happened to him. He was on National Service in Hong Kong and obtained a passage on a troopship to Japan. He went to see our Japanese amah and she, in her joy at seeing him again, talked and talked, while he could only smile and listen. Her presence was familiar, but he could no longer speak to her or understand her words. Now all his memories of Japanese people are in dumb show.

Being younger than my brother, I must have forgotten more quickly. Now I enrolled for a class: 'Japanese for Beginners'. The teacher was a woman with a Japanese name. I thought of the Japanese women of my childhood: middle-aged, hair drawn back in a bun, perhaps even wearing a kimono. The teacher was young and modern. And the members of the class were not aspiring young businessmen, as I half expected. There was a Frenchwoman interested both in speaking the language and writing the characters; a Peruvian girl interested in a quick conversation course for visitors to Japan; an Englishwoman interested in reading instruction leaflets for Japanese braiding. None of the others had been born in Japan or spoken Japanese naturally as a child. I wondered if any Japanese, stored in some deep layer of my memory, might rise again to the surface and help me to learn more quickly than the others. But nothing rose to the surface. I had to start again from the beginning.

It was not only the language I had to learn before going back to Japan. My sister asked: 'What are you hoping to find when you go back there?' I understood what she meant, but I was not deceiving myself, not thinking I would find again the lost world of my childhood. Yet I needed to know more of what that world had been. My mother sometimes spoke now of our life in Japan. I said: 'You've never talked about these things before.' My mother replied: 'What I could not bear was that it made you so unhappy.' Of course, I knew that.

I went into a bookshop where, just inside the door, was a pile of Germaine Greer's book, *Daddy, We Hardly Knew You.* I stared at the title, fascinated. A few years before, I had heard Germaine Greer taking part in a discussion of war poetry on television. She had expressed regret that there was no poetry of the Second World War with the power of the poetry of the First World War. She had said, 'We need such incantations to help us to understand why our fathers were so disorientated.' I remembered this as I bought the book, and went home with a sense of expectation that Germaine Greer would speak for me and for all of our generation whose fathers had gone away to the war and stayed away too long.

But, as I began to read the book, I felt puzzled. This was an account of Germaine Greer's experience, but it bore hardly any relation to my own. It seemed that Germaine Greer hardly knew her father, not only because he had gone to the war, but, more importantly, because he was not what he pretended to be – his background, even his name, not his own. At first I felt a sense of disappointment. I had hoped, in her story, to find something of my own story. But then I seemed to understand. It was no use hoping that someone else would write my story. I must write my own story.

Earlier that year I had read two books that had interested me greatly: Eugenie Fraser's *House by the Dvina*, a young girl's experience of living in Russia in the years before and during the First World War and the Russian Revolution; and Christabel Bielenberg's *The Past is Myself,* a young woman's experience of living in Germany through the years of Hitler's rise to power and the Second World War. Perhaps it had entered my mind that my family had lived in Japan through just such momentous years: the years leading up to Pearl Harbor and Japan's entry into the Second World War.

That was the world of my childhood, the world on which the door in my mind had closed. But how could I write of that world? I was barely five years old when my family left Japan. I celebrated my fifth birthday on the ship that took us to Canada. My memories were only fragments.

2

A Metal Cabin Trunk

How had my family come to be in Japan? I knew my parents had met at a missionary breakfast. Had my mother then hoped to be a missionary too?

The idea of mission always had a great appeal for me. Of course, I grew up in Yorkshire and Northumberland and was brought up on stories of the conversion of the north and the northern saints, St Cuthbert and St Aidan, St Hilda and St Bede. And the idea of travel also had a great appeal for me. Perhaps it was because my father was a sea captain. Although he died when I was very young, I always associated him with voyages and with the sea. But if I could have chosen, I should have gone to India, because of Kipling's stories about India.

If I had not married, though, I should not have gone abroad at all. I should not have felt I could leave Mother and Aunt Flo. At that time, unmarried daughters were expected to put their duty to their families first. When I was a student, a girl in the year above me went home for a year to help when her mother was seriously ill. When your father was a student, his father was seriously ill, but no one suggested that he should go home from university to help. That was the difference.

Of course, we were among the early generations of women undergraduates, and there was a certain feeling that we should make the most of our education and not marry but concentrate on our careers. For at that time, when a girl married, she almost always gave up her own career. In my year, there was a girl who was a brilliant science student. She married a dentist and had children and that was the end of that. Her husband used to say he always felt guilty at having deprived the nation of such a potentially

9

distinguished biochemist. Her brother became President of the BMA and she might have become just as distinguished. If I had not married, I should like to have become an archaeologist. But, instead, I married your father and that has given me all sorts of opportunities to travel and meet people and do things that have interested me.

When your father and I became engaged, we knew we should be going to Japan. Your father had heard the Bishop of Tokyo speak at a missionary rally. He was the first Japanese Bishop of Tokyo, and one of the first bishops in the church overseas not to be English. That is why there is a picture of him, with two other bishops, in a stained-glass window at the central house of the missionary society, because they were the first. But whether your father heard the Bishop speak and then volunteered for service in Japan, or whether the missionary society asked him to go to Japan and then he remembered having heard the Bishop speak, that I'm not sure.

We did not get married straight away. Your father had to finish his theological training. Then he became a curate. At that time, newly ordained clergy were expected to serve two curacies and there was no provision for curates to be married. But as your father was going abroad he served only one curacy. Even so, we were engaged for three and a half years.

We were married in July 1931 and were expecting to sail for Japan in the autumn. When we were asked what we should like for wedding presents, we said that we should like presents that would be easy to pack and take with us, and especially no china or glass. Even so, we were given a good deal of both. Aunt Flo thought it would be nice for me, when I was far from home, to drink my tea from a proper English tea set – 'like Eileen's'. For her wedding, my sister Eileen had been given a very pretty tea set. It was decorated with roses such as grow round cottage doors, all pinks and blues with just a touch of gold. We picked up a cup and read the name of the maker on the bottom – 'Noritake'. The tea set had been made in Japan!

We were due to sail for Japan in October. Your father said his farewells to the parish and had his presentation cheque in his pocket. We were standing among the packing cases in the drawing room, when the vicar knocked at the door. He said, 'What would you say if I told you that you couldn't go?' Your father looked a bit perplexed, then answered, 'Well, I don't know,' and added, in the words of an advertisement of the day, 'Time for an Abdullah, I suppose.' The vicar replied, 'No, no, I'm serious.' England came off the Gold Standard in the autumn of 1931 and the Bishop of Tokyo had sent a telegram saying that for the time being he could not take financial responsibility for any more English personnel. So we had to unpack our cases. Your father was found a temporary curacy in Wimbledon and we were lent a house in the parish to live in. It was seven more months before we sailed for Japan.

One good thing came from the delay. We were travelling to the other side of the world and wanted to see as much as we could on the way. If we had sailed in October, we should have sailed on one of the new P&O liners, either the SS *Corfu* or its sister ship, but when we sailed the following spring, we sailed on one of the last of the P&O's coal-burning liners, the SS *Naldera*. This meant we had to stop at more ports to take on coal. Our voyage took six and a half weeks and we called in at sixteen ports between Port of London and Yokohama. You couldn't make such a voyage now.

My mother paused and added thoughtfully: 'If you would like to know more about our life in Japan, then I think you should speak to Helen. I think she must have a box of letters your father sent home from Japan.' Helen? A box of letters? I telephoned. My sister sounded astonished. 'Letters from Japan? How could we have? We had all the letters from Singapore and kept them for ages, though I'm not sure if we have them now. But we've certainly never had any letters from Japan. How could we have?' Of course. How could they have?

But the idea of those letters did not go away. In the garage was a metal cabin trunk. My mother had said that it contained old papers belonging to my father, that he had meant to go through them one day but had never got round to it. I went out to the garage. There was the trunk lying on the floor, on the lid my father's initials painted in white: C.K.S. I lifted the lid. Inside were piles of pamphlets, folders of notes, packets of newspaper cuttings, envelopes of photographs. Near the top was a small black book. I opened the book and knew at once what it was.

During the war my father had served as a chaplain in the Canadian Air Force. By the time my family reached Canada, it was already late May 1941. Our ship docked at Vancouver and we crossed the continent by train. For the summer my father took a holiday chaplaincy on Centre

Island in Lake Ontario. But he felt badly that he was still a civilian when the war in Europe was now far into its second year. As soon as he could, he settled the family into a house on the outskirts of Toronto and settled us children into school. Then he enlisted as a chaplain in the Canadian Air Force. It was with a sense of real relief that he found himself in uniform at last.

That image of my father in his Air Force uniform was with us for the next four years, for his photograph in its silver frame stood always on the table in the corner of the sitting room. He came home on leave at least once, for it struck me as strange to see that tall figure in pale blue uniform standing in the kitchen. Perhaps that was his last leave before he sailed for England.

Once, while he was in England, we listened to his voice. A service for Canadian airmen stationed in England was being broadcast on Canadian radio, and my father was taking the service. It was during the hot Toronto summer and our family had left the city for a holiday by Otty Lake. My mother arranged for us to hear the service on a neighbour's radio and we walked over the fields to the neighbour's house. But the quality of the sound must have been poor, for later my mother said the experience left her feeling desolate. She knew it was her husband speaking but could hardly recognise his voice.

There were letters, of course. One Christmas my father sent me a letter which must have gone something like this: 'I hope you are having a very happy Christmas. I wonder what you found in your stocking. Was there an apple and an orange and some nuts? And is there a star on the Christmas tree? I hope you enjoy the chicken and the pudding for Christmas dinner.' But instead of writing the words 'stocking', 'apple', 'star', 'tree' and 'pudding', my father had drawn little pictures. He sent many letters to my mother. She kept them for years.

As the war drew towards its end, the troops began to return. A message came to our house that a telegram had arrived for us from England. My mother thought the telegram would say that my father was coming home. We all felt excited. But when the telegram arrived, it said: 'Aunt Flo died fifth funeral ninth.' To the consternation of my mother and the amazement of my brother and sister, I wept inconsolably. Was I weeping for the father I could hardly remember or for the great-aunt I could not remember at all? I scarcely knew myself why I wept.

The day my father returned was altogether unusual. My mother woke us early, before it was light, and we dressed and put on our shoes while still half asleep. Outside, the streets were deserted. A neighbour was watching from her window to wave to us as we passed. At the station we waited in an area away from the trains, where a rope was stretched across to keep back the crowd. Through a tunnel came a stream of men from all the services, of all ranks, in all kinds of uniforms. Some had twigs and leaves in their helmets, and all were laughing and waving. Would I know which one was my father? My brother was eleven – he would know; my sister was seven – she would not know; but I was in the middle – nearly nine now – and I was not sure. Suddenly he was there, round-faced, smiling. We went for breakfast to a restaurant high up in a hotel not far from the station. At home my father put on the radio and a voice announced that the war in Europe was over. The children in the neighbourhood held a victory parade. We carried flags and marched round the block. My father stood outside our house in his uniform and took the salute. He had a box of milk chocolate bars from the ship and gave them to all the children. It was VE Day, 8 May 1945.

Each Sunday our mother gave us sweets. I stored mine in a large glass jar. Now it was time to eat them. I took the jar and sat down in a field and found I didn't want them. We went round the neighbourhood giving away our toys: the outgrown tricycle, the scooter and the sledge, the ice skates and the roller skates. It was time to pack away our life in Canada, we were going to England.

I looked again at the black book. Across the top of each page, in my father's handwriting, was the name of a place: 'Cologne', 'Munster', 'Hamburg', 'daylight on Ruhr'; then the name of a crew: 'Fleming's crew', 'Dunwoodie's crew', 'Blyth's crew'; then a date some time in 1944 or 1945. Below were particulars of each member of the crew. It seemed there were always seven and the entries followed always the same pattern: number, rank and name; position in the crew: 'pilot', 'nav.', 'b/a', what looked like 'wop/ag', 'a/g', 'a/g' and 'f/e'; then there was usually the one word 'missing' and a date; religion and age; 'N.O.K.': father or mother, wife or brother, sometimes a fiancée too, with an address somewhere in Ontario or Alberta, British Columbia or Saskatchewan; lastly the date of a letter sent. There were occasional snapshots, and one photograph of a crew standing beside their plane.

Sometimes more was known about what had happened to a crew. Gibson's crew, on an operation to Dusseldorf, crash-landed near Brussels: four of the crew were killed and buried at Fosses in Belgium, while the other three were recovered. Two of Wilding's crew were killed in a crash on return from an operation to Le Havre, but the rest of the crew baled out safely. The entry for a Flight Officer, entered as 'missing 12–13/6/44', was amended to 'Back in UK Aug 1944'; a note adds: 'reports aircraft shot down by fighters on second run-up to target. Believes only he & B/A got out & that rest crashed with the kite.'

The original entries were written in black ink, additional entries in red: 'killed', 'bld killed', 'died of wounds', 'POW', 'recovered', 'safe'. There were notes of replies received, further letters sent, sometimes interviews with next of kin. Below the names of two members of McIver's crew, both entered as 'Missing Bld killed', was written: 'The above two Belgians who escaped from Belgium & flew under assumed names.'

I looked inside the front cover of the book: 'Casualties at RCAF Station, Linton-on-Ouse, Yorks. April 1944.' At the back was a list of all the operations carried out by 408 and 426 squadrons during the time my father was stationed there. At the end was a note: 'posted to Warrington 10/4/45'.

Inside the cover of the book was a letter:

Dear Padre,

Received your very much appreciated letter today. It was very kind of you indeed, to write me, although I must admit I was almost afraid to open it.

I want to ask a favour of you Padre. I wonder if you could speak to some of the boys in 408 squadron and try to locate the person or persons who saw the incident. You see I was told that two kites were 'shot' down – later I heard there had been a head on crash in mid-air – also I was told that four chutes left the plane and developed. While I was on your station the other day my mind was in too much of a confusion to think of getting more accurate details myself. I quite understand that security must be maintained but perhaps you can help me an awful lot by getting accurate details for me. You will understand that, if I know exactly what happened to the kite he was in, I will be either more hopeful or I will realize that my hopes are in vain. We have always been very practical in our family Padre – possibly through necessity, and consequently I prefer to know the facts straight from the shoulder.

If Vernon was killed I only hope that he did justice to the rest of the crew – that he manned his gun well as I feel sure he did. Kindly write again soon and should any information whatever come in, whether it is good or bad news, please do not hesitate to let me know. I suppose my mother has been informed. If it becomes known that my brother was killed I wonder if I could be the one to let my mother know?

I must close now Padre.

Thanking you again, I remain

I looked for his brother's name in the book. There was the entry: 'missing 2/3/45'. Underneath one word had been added: 'safe'.

I turned back to the trunk, searched down through the piles of files and folders and pamphlets. I found what I was looking for in two large box files, each bearing a label: 'Personal Papers. Found in study after departure for Singapore. January 1961.' As I opened the lids, I caught sight of postcards and envelopes bearing the Japanese stamps familiar to me from my stamp album as a child: 2 sen green, 3 sen pink, 5 sen purple, 6 sen pink, 10 sen blue, each with a chrysanthemum, emblem of Japan, at the top. There were so many letters, so many postcards, that I thought this must be the complete collection. I carried the boxes into the house in triumph.

I began to sort the letters. Most had been taken out of their envelopes and consisted of two or three sheets fastened together with a pin or a paperclip gone rusty with age. The letters began in May 1932, when my parents sailed for Japan. There were letters sent from every port where their ship docked, and letters sent on their arrival in Japan. Once they had settled into their new life, it seemed that my father sent a letter home every week. As I checked the letters through, week by week, I began to feel anxious. There were so many for 1932, so many for 1933 and 1934. In March 1935 the letters came to an end. I turned to my mother in dismay:

'Why do the letters stop?'

'Well, remember we came back to England on furlough.'

'Yes, but that must have been in 1937, because Helen was born while we were on furlough, but the letters stop in 1935.'

'It may be something to do with your grandparents moving. Your grandfather was ill while we were away, and by the time we came home, they had moved away from the house in Streatham and gone to live with your uncle in Bristol.'

Of course, that must be the reason. My father would have gone on writing a letter home every week, but for some reason his parents had no longer kept the letters or the letters had since been mislaid. It was not so surprising.

I went to look again at the contents of the trunk. The files contained my father's notes on theology. The pamphlets contained articles on the church in different parts of the world. There were folders of letters and envelopes of photographs from every stage of my parents' life: Lincoln, Canterbury, Singapore, London. But I was interested only in the early years, the years that were hidden from me. I picked out a few pamphlets on Japan; a folder of cuttings from *The Japan Advertiser*; a file of letters sent from home to my parents in Japan; a packet of studio photographs of the family in Japan. Then I added an envelope labelled 'Canada & RCAF'. Childhood home and childhood father: I lost them both together.

3

Once More in Japan

There was no time to read the letters now, for we would soon set out on our journey. My mother prepared two envelopes of photographs, one for Singapore, the other for Japan. The photographs showed people we might meet or of whom we might be expected to have heard.

One photograph showed a middle-aged man with his two young daughters. The girls were dressed in tunic and trousers in the Chinese style. 'He is Japanese,' said my mother, 'but he has connections with Singapore too. In the war he was an officer in the Japanese army and during the early part of the Occupation he was based in Singapore. He is a Christian and it was largely due to him that St Andrew's Cathedral was kept open for services all through the Occupation. Every Sunday he would be driven to the Cathedral in a staff car and his car would be parked conspicuously outside the Cathedral during the service. He came back to Singapore during the time we were there. Our house had been a club for Japanese officers during the Occupation. When he visited us, he said, "It is very strange to be in this house again." A service was held in recognition of what he had done to keep the Cathedral open, but the service was very small and quiet, for there was still a lot of bitter feeling towards the Japanese when we were in Singapore.'[1]

My mother was speaking of the sixties. Twenty-five years later, the pain was still there. When we arrived in Singapore, we went for lunch with one of my parents' friends. She had retired from work when her granddaughter was born and made her home with her daughter and son-in-law. They had been living in Korea and Japan and had only recently returned to Singapore.

'Did you like Korea?'

'Oh, yes, I liked it very much. I liked the people. They were so friendly and happy. I liked the way of life.'

---

[1] This officer was Lt (later Captain) Andrew Ogawa.

'Wasn't it cold?'

'I liked the cold!'

'And Japan?'

'I didn't like Japan so much. The people are more reserved. They are not happy and outgoing. They seem more tense and shut in on themselves ... And then, we have such bad memories of the Japanese. They treated us so cruelly in the war. In my own family, we lost an uncle and three cousins in one day. And the worst thing is that we never knew what happened to them. That was how it was. People just disappeared and we did not know what had happened. And if people did not do as they wanted, they gave cruel punishments. They made people kneel all day in the hot sun ... But the young people in Japan, they know nothing about it. When we were living in Japan, we became friendly with the people who lived next door. They were quite a well-to-do family. They had a daughter aged about fourteen. She came to our house one day and said that her father had been in Singapore during the war and that he could still remember some words of Malay. So that means that her father was one of the people who were so cruel to us. But she knew nothing about it. She was quite happy telling us about it ... But Japanese people are not the same now as they were in the war. They do not even look the same. They are bigger now and their faces do not look the same.' Suddenly she became confused: 'Oh, are you going to Japan? ... Yes, of course, I remember that your parents used to be there.'

A few years before, there had been a series on television called *Tenko*. It was set in a Japanese prison camp for women on an island near Singapore. My sister had watched the series and said that it helped her to relate to a part of our family's background that she had been too young to experience. My sister was three and a half when the family left Japan. She did not remember Japan, did not remember our father, could speak of herself as a happy Canadian child.

I could not have watched *Tenko*. In my mind there was a division which I knew to be irrational. I could read articles and watch programmes concerning Germany and the war in the West; yet concerning Japan and the war in the East always I played the part of the three wise monkeys, stopping my eyes and my ears and my mouth against sight and sound and word.

Sometimes I was caught unawares. It was about ten years after the end of the war when I went to buy a present in a Regent Street store. I chose a coffee set, white with a small pattern in gold round the rim. The salesgirl looked at the coffee set, then turned to me very politely:

'I have to tell you that the coffee set was made in Japan. Many of our customers will not buy anything Japanese.' The shock came suddenly, like a slap in the face.

At home I have a small photograph, taken in the garden of our house in Tokyo. It shows my father and mother standing side by side, and in front of them my brother, aged perhaps five, very upright to attention, and myself, aged perhaps two, squatting on the ground. My parents' hair is dark, my brother and I are still ash blonde. All are dressed in kimonos. It is a charming photograph: an English family dressed in Japanese clothes. But for me the photograph has a special meaning. The Japanese clothes do not hide the fact that my brother and I are English. But the fair skin and blonde hair do hide how much inside ourselves we felt Japanese. Japan was our home, the Japanese were our own people. But other people did not see the inside. They saw only the fair skin and the blonde hair.

So what was I hoping to find when I went back to Japan?

Before I left England, I received a letter from my mother's friend, now home again in Tokyo:

I am so sorry that I shall not be able to meet you at Tokyo Station, it being such a busy time for me. On Friday I have the annual meeting of the Virginia Woolf Society and on Saturday the annual meeting of the Thomas Hardy Society. Fortunately I shall be free on Sunday and shall be able to spend the day with you. I do not think it will be worthwhile for you to come to my house to pay your respects, as you suggest, as there is nothing at all interesting in this house or this neighbourhood. But, if you like, we can visit the National Museum, where there are many national treasures which will be interesting for you to see.

A few days later a postcard arrived with a picture of pandas chewing bamboo stems. The message read; 'If you like to see pandas while you are in Japan, we shall be able to see them in the zoo, which is quite close to the National Museum in Ueno Park.'

Shortly afterwards another letter arrived:

I am wondering if you would like to visit the place where your family used to live in Ikebukuro? As you will know, the house where you lived is no longer there, having been destroyed by fire bombs in the war. However, one of the houses where western families lived is still there. If you like to do this, we can meet at Ikebukuro Station and go to the chapel at *Rikkyo* for the service which begins at ten o'clock. Then we can go across the road to look at the compound where your house used to be. My sister is still living nearby in Ikebukuro. Her house was also destroyed by fire bombs in the war, but she has built a new house on the same ground and is now living there with one of her sons. Her other two sons have also built houses on her ground. We shall be able to have lunch at the house of one of her sons, my nephew Keizo, who used to be at kindergarten with Christopher. I am not sure if Keizo and his wife are able to speak well in English. I know they are happier in French, having lived three years in Brussels.

I looked at the letter in amazement. When my mother had seen our plans for travelling in Japan, she had said doubtfully: 'You haven't left enough time for Tokyo.' I had wondered what she meant. I knew there were two people whom it was important we should visit in Tokyo: my mother's friend, who had travelled with my family to England when she was a student nearly fifty years before; and my brother's godfather, who had come to know my parents when he was studying in England, before my parents first went out to Japan, nearly sixty years before. But when we had met my parents' friends and spent time with them, why should we linger in Tokyo?

When my brother returned to Japan during his National Service, he went to Ikebukuro, the district of Tokyo where the family had lived. Our house had been destroyed, but he saw where it had been and he walked round the area and saw what else had been destroyed and what still remained. I was impressed that he could remember. I had no picture in my mind of our house or its surroundings. I knew only that our house stood near two other houses and that those houses were occupied by an English family and an American family and that each family had children of about the same age and that all three fathers taught at the theological college.

I had not even thought of returning to Ikebukuro. I thought of Tokyo as a city devastated by bombs during the war and almost entirely rebuilt after the war, a huge, sprawling, modern city. The idea that we could return to Ikebukuro and still see the place where my family had once lived astonished me. I wrote at once to say I should like to go to Ikebukuro more than anything.

When we arrived in Tokyo, we found a note waiting for us: 'I am so sorry but I made a mistake when I said that one of the houses for western staff is still standing. I was walking around the compound a few days ago. All three houses have gone, although I think some of the trees must be the same.'

On the Sunday we met at Ikebukuro Station. As we walked towards *Rikkyo*, my mother's friend said more than once, 'Of course, Ikebukuro was much nicer when your family was living here. There is so much traffic, so many people now, but it was quiet and peaceful then.' We came in sight of the university. I had seen a photograph, yet still felt a sense of surprise: it looked so like an English college set down by mistake in Japan. We went into the chapel. A professor approached and asked us to sign a piece of paper. It seemed to be the custom in Japanese churches for visitors to stand up and be welcomed by the congregation. My husband took the paper and signed for us both, but then I took the paper and signed for myself, my married name first, then née Sansbury. I did not think anyone would remember the name, but still it seemed right to record that one of the family had come back. The chapel was filling rapidly with students. They looked modern in their western clothes, but the main buildings looked much as they did when my parents were here.

As we came out of the chapel, the professor approached once again:

'I am so glad to see you here ... Yes, I have met your parents. How is your father now? ... I was taken to your parents' house when I was in England five years ago. I was attending a conference at the university nearby.' He turned to introduce his wife. 'My wife's grandfather was principal of the theological college when your father was on the staff here.'

'Grandfather? Not father?'

'Oh, no, no, grandfather.'

(That made it seem even longer ago!)

Another lady approached: 'My mother was one of your father's students. (Mother? Were there women at the theological college then?) Your parents will be sure to remember her. I will write down her name for you. She came to see your parents when she was in England, about ten years ago. They will be sure to remember. She has moved down to Kobe now.'

We took photographs, wrote down names. Then we all crossed the road to look at the compound. That was where the theological college had been before the war, though since the bombing it had moved away. The compound was much larger than I had expected. Perhaps it was the word 'compound' that had made me imagine a small, enclosed space. I had a rough sketch plan of how it used to be. At the road end two entrances were marked. They were still there. My husband took a photograph of me standing by one. Inside there had been four houses for Japanese staff on the left, and three houses for western staff on the right. At the far end had been the main college buildings. It was at that end that the bombs had fallen. 'It was a mistake,' we were told. 'The bombs were not meant to fall there.' The main college buildings were destroyed and at least one of the houses for Japanese staff, as well as the house where my family had lived.

When my brother returned, his host had said, 'Your house was here.' But he had replied, 'Oh no, it was there.' For he knew the three houses were not in a row and that ours was set a little apart. Our neighbours' houses were still much as he remembered, though the baseball diamond seemed to have shrunk. Now all the houses had gone. Where our house had stood, tennis was being played, and baseball was still being played on the diamond.

I looked at Keizo across the dining table, fascinated by the thought that he had been at kindergarten with my brother.

'I saw Christopher when he came back after the war.'

(Yes, I had heard.) 'Were you here during the war?'

'I was here for most of the war, but for the last year, when the bombing was bad, I was taken away from here.'

'Were you taken far away?'

'No, about an hour's journey away.'

'We went to Canada.'

'Yes. I came with my aunt to see you on the ship at Yokohama.'

I was startled. It was such a vivid memory. I was standing on the deck of the ship with my family. We were all looking back towards Japan. There they were on the quayside, Furusawa-san, our amah, and Takahashi-san, our cook, two Japanese women in their kimonos, with tears streaming down their faces. To me it was a sacred memory. It told me in the darkness that we were right to love Japan, for to us as children Japan had shown only its most kind and gentle, loving face.

Now I learnt that Keizo and his aunt had been there too, that they too had come to say goodbye. My mother's friend laughed: 'And Furusawa-san cried so much.' Yes, I remembered. I would never forget Furusawa-san's tears.

PART II

The First Two Years 1932–1934

1

By P&O to Japan

It was almost sixty years earlier that my parents first sailed for Japan. They sailed from Tilbury on the SS *Naldera* on 15 April 1932. Their closest family all came to say goodbye. It was a big farewell. It would be five years before they were likely to see each other again, five years before my parents were due back in England on furlough.

The next morning they arrived in Southampton, for while passengers embarked at Tilbury, cargo was loaded at Southampton. The *Naldera* berthed next to the *Empress of Britain* and seemed quite a midget beside her. The *Naldera* was 16,000 tons, the *Empress of Britain* a mighty 42,000 tons. Their time of sailing was much delayed: 'It's the amount of cargo we have to load,' said one of the ship's officers. 'In the old days we should have left it behind and sailed at the scheduled time, but nowadays we cannot afford to miss it.'

Among their fellow passengers were holiday-makers for Gibraltar and Tangier, convalescents for Marseilles, naval wives and fiancées for Malta, government officials for Egypt, Sudan and especially India, businessmen for the Straits, engineers for shipping lines or naval stations in the China Seas. 'Do you realise,' said my father, 'that there are only five of us altogether going to Japan?'

Passengers were invited to see over the engine room. The *Naldera* was one of the few P&O ships still burning coal and through the door separating the engine room from the furnaces they glimpsed an amazing scene. In the flickering light of the open furnace doors, bearded and sweating Lascar firemen were stoking the furnaces and wheeling fresh loads of coal, all the time shouting and calling to each other in their own language. The scene resembled a medieval painting depicting the torments of hell!

That evening they found the Spanish coast coming to meet them on their left and soon the African coast on their right. The ship was now rounding the south-west corner of Spain and making for the straits. Her bows were facing due east and the light of the setting sun behind lit up the great gaunt hills on either side. Blues and greens were the chief colours on the African side, deep blues and gold on the Spanish. But as the sun sank lower the colours changed and re-changed. When the sun finally set behind the Spanish coastline the ship was turning north-east and they saw a wonderful picture of jagged hills against a glorious golden sky. But the rock of Gibraltar now came in sight and it was hard to look anywhere else.

If the impression by daylight was magnificent, by moonlight it was entrancing. When they came up on deck after dinner, they looked out on an enchanted scene. At the foot of the rock and on its lower slopes were the lights of the town; above was the solid black mass of rock, silhouetted against the sky by the full moon shining immediately over it; and between the ship and the shore was the harbour, with the water shimmering in the brilliant moonlight. It seemed quite unreal, like the landscape of a dream.

They began to make plans for Marseilles. Here the ship would stay two nights, for it had both to take on coal and wait for the Indian mail. They hoped to sleep the first night on shore and to go the next day to Avignon. It all depended if they could go so far without breaking the bank. The day before they arrived in Marseilles they received a bill for excess baggage. 'It's £6,' said my father. 'We shall have to draw in our horns.' So they decided to sleep on the ship and to go no further than Arles.

They sailed into Marseilles harbour in the early evening and set off to explore the town. A young American in their group, David Murphy by name, dealt effectively with all would-be guides by announcing: 'Say, I'm Tammas Cook himself, ancestor of the great voyageur!' As they wandered through the streets, Murphy urged them to call in on his home town on their way home: 'Say, it would be just marvellous to see you folks in San Louis; we have the finest zoological gardens in all Amurrica!'

The next day they travelled to Arles. Their train puffed leisurely through the Provençal countryside, through fields green at that time of year and vineyards stretching in every direction. They arrived in Arles in siesta time and made their way through narrow streets, past shuttered shops, to the great Roman amphitheatre, its walls decorated with posters of bullfights. As they looked inside darkened churches and sipped lemonade at pavement cafes, they felt deep in the heart of France.

But that night, when they returned to the ship, they were met by an eerie sight, a glimpse already of the East. The Indian mail had arrived, having been carried across France by train. Darkness had fallen, and by the light of an arc-lamp Lascars were sorting the mails for East Africa, Australia, the Straits and India. They counted the mail bags by the primitive process of one Lascar giving another a stick for each mail bag passed, and then hoisted them in a steel net into the hold. There must have been a great quantity, for the sorting, counting, hoisting went on all through the night and the ship did not sail until dawn.

'The subsequent proceedings interested us no more.' So wrote my father of the Mediterranean crossing, for after Marseilles they were tossed about on choppy seas and both my parents suffered from seasickness. It was only as they were approaching Malta that they began to recover and to look about themselves once again.

They reached Malta in the evening. Through passengers were not allowed to land, so they watched over the side of the ship as passengers were taken ashore in the high-prowed, brightly-painted Maltese boats called *dghaisias*. Numbers on board were now noticeably reduced, especially as regards the younger female element. They were becoming a party of sturdy he-men going to the wilds of Empire with well-attached wives in tow.

The Captain invited my parents to tea on the bridge. He was chuckling over a recent incident, for the P&O had a reputation for superior snobbishness in the East. An oil tanker had signalled in the usual way: 'Who are you?' Being high and mighty they had refused to reply. When the question was repeated three or four times, the answer was sent back proudly: 'Royal Mail Ship, *Naldera*.' Back came a message from the skipper of the tanker: 'What line?'

They arrived in Port Said early in the day in bright sunshine. Hawkers descended on them in droves. One wanted to guide them round the town, another to sell them necklaces, others to load them with flowers or Turkish Delight or rugs. Nothing seemed to shake them off and by the time they arrived at the famous emporium of Simon Arzt they were followed by quite a procession. They were fitted out with solar topees and, decked in this headgear of Empire, set out to explore the town. It was the first eastern town they had seen. They found it rather untidy, rather smelly, and with no sights of great beauty to be seen. Yet it was made fascinating by the men in flowing robes and fezes, veiled women in black selling oranges, women carrying pitchers of water, open shop fronts and the pervasive atmosphere of the bazaar.

Their return to the ship was triumphant. A gentleman selling necklaces, who addressed my father indiscriminately as 'Meester George' or 'Meester Macgreegor' and my mother as 'Mees Melbourne', reduced his price for a charming necklace from 12/6d to 2/-d, a flower-seller was pulled down from 2/6d to 1/3d for a bunch of roses, and a sweet-seller from 2/-d to 6d for some very nice Turkish delight. Even when they returned on board, there were half a dozen small boats beside the ship with hawkers of rugs, sweetmeats and sponges haggling with customers, or potential customers, over the side, while goods were sent up and payment sent down on ropes.

Later that morning they started to pass through the Suez Canal. On the eastern side was endless desert, with the only mark of civilisation at Kantara, where the railway to Palestine began. On the western side a main road and the railway to Cairo ran side by side with the canal for a good many miles. Ships were not allowed to go above eight knots, so that it took till late evening to get through. Once darkness fell the ship turned on a big headlight, which lit up both banks of the canal. It gave an eerie feeling to be moving through the water with little more noise than that of a punt on a river and none of the usual throb of the engine. That night they entered the Red Sea.

They awoke to find themselves out of sight of land with no likelihood of seeing any again until the evening of the following day. The heat became stifling and oppressive, while the wind blew as warm as the air from a gas oven. They wore the fewest and thinnest clothes possible and perspired as they sat. Even the effort of wielding a pen left them wet with perspiration. There was a swimming pool now on board, so swims and cool baths became the order of the day, while two fans working hard and a wind-scoop outside the porthole made bearable the nights.

The arrival in Aden was particularly trying. The ship was taking on coal and they had to dress with the porthole shut. Everything was so hot and sticky and the air so utterly breathless that they felt quite exhausted by the time they left the cabin. But they quickly revived as they were taken ashore, for there was a pleasant breeze blowing across the harbour and occasional splashes of water as the oarsmen missed a stroke.

They walked along the sea-front to the English church, where they found there was a service at a time just convenient. They went inside and revelled in the coolness. The church was well-built to keep out the heat, the windows covered with gauze and not glass, and the chairs comfortable, cool, cane armchairs.

They returned to the quay by taxi and were greeted by the usual struggle for their custom. The motor-boat owners felt they had first claim, while the rowing-boat men shouted alternately that there was still room for them in the present boat or that they would be much more comfortable if they waited for the next. At last they started, in company with their American friend, David Murphy, who made much play of the fact that they were returning in a boat owned by 'non-union' men. The idea of American Trades Unions in relation to these sweating African-Arabian oarsmen was so incongruous that, when he shouted in his best Yankee twang, 'Say, pals, show me your union card, else I swim straight ashore', they all collapsed in mirth.

After breakfast they returned on deck to look at Aden. They had heard that people liked it as a place to live, yet this first viewing made them find that surprising. At the back of the town were three towering peaks, the legendary site of Cain's burial. This was supposed to account for the barrenness of the place. Whatever might be believed about the legend, there was no doubt about the barrenness. There was not a vestige of a tree, not a blade of grass, not a shrub or a flower anywhere; only bleak, barren, dark-brown hills, descending to the harbour with a very disorderly arrangement of bungalows on the lower slopes. The harbour was impressive, it was true, but otherwise the natural unattractiveness of the place, combined with a terrific heat and a rainfall about once in three years, suggested to their minds a thoroughly unpleasant resort.

Now they were in the Indian Ocean and heading north-east. They had three days' sail into Bombay and life on board became very lively, with deck-sports, concerts and parties. The highlight was a fancy-dress dinner and dance. My mother went as a Japanese lady, wearing her kimono and slippers to match and arranging her hair in Japanese fashion with the aid of a pair of black silk socks and a flower. My father went as a Red Indian, with a headdress bought at the barber's shop on board and a bath-towel of vivid colours, borrowed from a young female passenger. She was one of the brides on board and her fiancé was a captain in the Indian ASC. They had not seen each other for more than three years and were due to be married the morning after the ship landed in Bombay. This seemed a risky prospect and the girl was in a state of apprehension. The Captain shook his head: 'Every voyage there's one who loses her nerve, and we have to take her home.' My parents did their best to keep her up to the mark, however, and packed her suitcases while she lay on her bed prostrate with anxiety.

In Bombay my parents were met by friends from England and set off by car for their bungalow on Malabar hill. Their friends pointed to a crowded Indian beach in Back Bay: 'Some of Gandhi's followers made salt here in the troubles a few months ago.' It was two years since Gandhi had led his followers on a great march to the sea to extract salt in defiance of the British Government's monopoly. Gandhi declared the tax on salt to be particularly iniquitous, for salt was an essential of life and so the tax fell hardest on the poorest of the poor. Civil disobedience spread like wildfire and salt was extracted all along the Indian sea coast. When the British Government tried to crack down there were indeed troubles: rioting and shootings and many imprisonments. Now this beach looked in holiday mood again and was as crowded as Brighton beach on an August Bank Holiday.

They returned to the ship to find numbers on board much depleted, the saloon now less than half full. Among those they had lost was their American friend, David Murphy, who had gone on his way 'seeking for beauty throughout the world', and the nervous bride, now reunited with her bridegroom and due to be married in the morning.

They found Colombo more attractive than any place they had visited so far, and thought that if Ceylon as a whole was as delightful as Colombo then it must be a wonderful place to be posted. As their ship entered harbour early in the morning, they were met by a scene of tropical luxuriance, of vivid colours scattered among great masses of green foliage and framed by a sky and a sea of beautiful blues. As they came ashore they found themselves in wide streets of bright, clean buildings among exotic trees with brilliant hanging blossoms, whose lush foliage, more luxuriant than any seen in England, formed a natural shelter from the sun.

They took a side turning and entered the crowded lanes of a native quarter. On either side were open-fronted shops: sweet shops, basket shops, pottery shops and fruit shops with large bunches of green and yellow bananas, bright orange pumpkins and exotic fruits of which they did not know the name. They drove through very slowly and could not have gone faster if they wanted, for the narrow lanes were teeming with people, bullock carts, bicycles and rickshaws.

They left the town and drove on through avenues of coconut palms past native huts to a headland, which commanded a fine view of the bay. There they listened to the waves coming in over the rocks, watched the fishing-boats with square sails coming into the beach and inhaled the 'spicy breezes' of the East. They returned to the ship rather late for lunch.

During the next few days, there was at times a considerable roll on the ship. 'It's not surprising,' said my father, 'seeing that there's no land between us and the Antarctic.' It caused them no trouble, however, as they now had their sea-legs and felt well-established sailors. They were enjoying wonderful sunsets, with the colours changing every few seconds and the sky lit up with gold shading off into dark blue, and clouds of every shape and hue cutting across the rays. But even more wonderful was the sunrise as the ship approached Penang, when the sun rose behind the long line of hills on the mainland of Malaya, dyeing them a deep, rich purple and turning the whole eastern sky at one moment to red, at another to orange and at another to flame.

A friend was waiting on the quayside at Georgetown to greet them. He had been badly down with dengue fever and there had been talk of moving him to a temperate climate, but he had recovered and now looked as well as ever he had in England. He had come to meet them in a rather antique Austin Seven and in this they set off to explore the sights. Georgetown was very attractive to look at and reminded them of Colombo. It too had fine clean streets and glorious trees, so that every open space was like a piece of tropical forest. But the heat was damper and there was more cloud.

The most striking difference between Penang and Colombo was the predominance of Chinese in Penang. Many of the westernised streets had palatial Chinese mansions where the wealthy merchants lived. In the side streets Chinese open shops and houses predominated. Rickshaws all had Chinese runners and taxis Chinese drivers. This Chinese presence gave a cheerful appearance to the town, as their buildings were in bright colours and their signs picturesque. The Chinese seemed to have everything on a bigger scale than the Singhalese in Colombo: their streets were wider, their shops and houses more substantial.

Their next port of call would be Singapore. The Captain was a great friend of the Chairman of the Harbour Board, Mr Trimmer, and every voyage he invited a group of passengers to a swimming party at Mr Trimmer's bungalow. On this occasion he included my parents, so they accepted with pleasure and looked forward to being cool.

They arrived in Singapore harbour early in the evening. As they neared the quay a number of hollowed-out canoes with a Malayan in each came round the ship, waiting for pennies to be dropped. As soon as a penny fell into the water the nearest man dived overboard and in half a second collected the penny and climbed back into his canoe. The expert ones smoked cigars all the time, putting the lighted end in their mouths while diving and turning the cigars round again when back in their boats. They were fine-looking people, very quick and very keen to collect the pennies.

As they came on shore they were taken in a car to Mr Trimmer's house, which stood in a splendid situation, just on the edge of a hill overlooking the harbour. The bungalow itself was the acme of luxury, with every possible comfort for the dweller in the East. They were led down a path in the moonlight and came to a spacious swimming pool lit up by coloured lights. The scene appeared quite unreal and my father remarked: 'I can't help feeling that I'm taking part in the bathing parade of a musical comedy.' They had a refreshing bathe in the warm water and for the first time in the day felt cool.

So far the sea had been like a stagnant lake but the next day there was a change. They awoke to find themselves in a strong sea, which increased as the day wore on. They held up until the early evening, when they retired from those present and lay down for the rest of the evening. Nearly everybody else did the same, so that only thirteen passengers faced the dinner table, of whom several retired hurt before the end of the meal. The reason for this havoc was that they had hit the tail of a typhoon. All they could say was, 'Thank heavens we didn't go through the middle!'

They arrived in Hong Kong feeling rather battered, so they drank some whisky to soothe their insides and watched the scene over the side of the ship. The ship reached the harbour through a narrow channel running between the island and the mainland. It was a fine approach of clear blue sea and sloping green cliffs, with attractive bays at every bend. But the view of Hong Kong itself, the harbour, the town and the towering peak behind, was so magnificent that they decided that of all the fine harbours they had seen on their voyage, Hong Kong must easily take the prize.

They were sailing up the coast of China in a fog, with only occasional glimpses of land. Somewhere to the east must have been Formosa, but that was quite invisible. The weather grew cooler and the atmosphere more humid, so everything they touched felt damp. At night they were woken by the sound of the siren and by day it sounded intermittently. Navigation must have been tricky, for, as well as the fog, there were fishing junks to avoid and steamers entering or leaving the Yangtze.

They came up the Yangtze to the point where it is joined by the Whangpoo and passed Woosung, where the Chinese had built forts overlooking the bay. In January the Japanese had sent forces to the north of Shanghai to protect their interests from the anti-Japanese agitation set off by their invasion of Manchuria. The Chinese resisted for more than a month before having to withdraw from the forts. The Japanese attacked the village of Woosung with incendiary air bombs and smashed up the forts altogether. Now all that was left were the battered, derelict remains.

Shortly afterwards they passed a ship, the *Bombay Maru*, on fire. Two fire-boats were alongside pouring water into the hold, from which clouds of smoke and bursts of flame were arising. Yet everyone seemed unconcerned and the crew semaphored quite cheerfully. Later they were surprised to learn that she was a transport vessel with one hold laden with explosives!

The river below Shanghai reminded them of the Thames below Tower Bridge. There were the same miles of docks and wharves and warehouses and power stations. Shanghai had a tremendous amount of shipping and many of the tramps were the same as those lining the banks of the Thames. But there were three kinds of shipping that would not have been found in the Thames: naval destroyers and cruisers – English, American, French, Italian and Japanese; river boats of the China Navigation Co; and Chinese junks and sampans.

Shanghai did not strike them as an attractive place. It was modern in style and the confined area due to the limits of the International Settlement made it feel crowded and cramped. They decided to stroll up to the Bund and have a look at the shops in the Nanking Road. That seemed the only interesting bit of the town and had been much photographed for the newspapers at the time of the recent troubles. They passed in a few minutes from modern western streets with buildings like miniature skyscrapers to Chinese streets with open shops and pungent smells.

They hired a Ford and went to look at Chapei. Like Woosung, it was a scene of devastation. Houses, shops and offices were all knocked to pieces. When they reached the railway they found Japanese soldiers with fixed bayonets on duty at the level crossing. All Chinese wishing to cross were being searched for firearms. The Japanese would not allow any cars to pass, so their car took some back turnings to arrive at the North Station. Nearby were sandbag emplacements and in front of the station masses of barbed wire with only one small gap for passengers wishing to reach the occasional trains running from the end of one platform. The station itself was badly knocked about. There were bent girders and smashed bits of platform where shells had landed, and everywhere broken glass and marks of rifle bullets. But Chapei was due to be evacuated in the afternoon, so if they had gone the following day they would have found Chinese police instead of Japanese soldiers and sailors, and presumably no searching of Chinese civilians at all.

There were now only seven second-class passengers on board and, as there were even fewer first-class passengers, the second-class passengers were transferred to first-class accommodation. This change proved less agreeable than expected, as the first-class stewards looked down on them as poor relations and they especially missed their young Cockney deck-steward, who had kept them amused with his jokes and good humour.

Two days after leaving Shanghai they awoke to find the ship rapidly approaching the coast of Japan. The coastline was impressive, with rugged mountains and tree-covered hills sloping down to the water's edge. They dressed quickly and went on deck as the ship began to enter the beautiful Straits of Shimonoseki, separating the main island of Honshu from the southern island of Kyushu.

They anchored off the quarantine island and all the crew and passengers had to present themselves, while Japanese medical officers came on board to check their medical credentials. The ship then steamed up to her anchorage between Moji on the Kyushu side and Shimonoseki on the Honshu side. Here they had to parade again, with passports, and face an examination on their origins, purpose in coming to Japan, length of stay and many other questions.

While waiting to go ashore, they watched the coal being carried on to the ship. The Japanese had devised a method reputed to be the fastest in the world. By the use of ropes, they rigged up two wooden stairways from the barges to the bunkers and then formed chains of men on each side of the stairways, who passed up baskets of coal at lightning speed. The baskets were emptied into the bunkers and then thrown back to the barges to be refilled, often by women, and so the process was repeated.

They were greeted from the ship by a lady missionary, Miss Simeon, and accompanied her up to her house. Shimonoseki was a smallish fishing town and seemed to them somewhat untidy, as the modest houses with their brown wooden walls and grey-tiled roofs were huddled together in higgledy-piggledy fashion, and the condition of the roads was appalling.

But the houses, though plain from the outside, were attractive and compact within. Miss Simeon entered hers by sliding sideways a screen of lattice-work and they entered a porch where they changed their shoes for slippers. Outdoor shoes were never to be worn in a Japanese house and having seen the state of the roads they understood why. The slippers were easy to slip the foot into but equally easy to slip the foot out of, so they clambered rather awkwardly up a steep staircase and crossed the *tatami* matting of the sitting room to admire the view from the verandah across the harbour to the hills of Kyushu.

Before lunch they washed by pouring water from a jug into an enamel basin, for there was no water laid on in the town. Indeed the sanitary system seemed as primitive as the roads, and reminded my father of childhood holidays spent in a coastguard cottage on the cliffs in Sussex. Lunch they ate downstairs in western fashion, though the Japanese cook greeted them in eastern fashion by kneeling and bowing with her head to the floor. After lunch they lay on *futon* mattresses on the floor and read newspapers and caught up with news from England.

They then set off for the house of another missionary, Miss Kennion. It was an astonishing walk, up one slope and down another, round corners and through alleyways, until they were completely mystified as to their direction. At last they arrived and were welcomed with tea and bowls of fresh strawberries. Before they left England their doctor had given them only one piece of advice: 'Whatever you do, don't touch the strawberries. Just think how they're grown!'

They sailed in the late evening and for a time watched the lights on either side of the ship. But soon they came into a wider expanse of sea and could see nothing, so they went to bed and resigned themselves to missing one of the sights of the world: the Inland Sea of Japan.

They woke early and looked out on a vague line of hills, a scattering of green islands and scores of fishing boats with their nets outspread. The Captain invited them to join him on the bridge. This proved fascinating, partly from the point of view of the navigating itself and partly on account of the course they had to take through the last strait of the Inland Sea and through the large number of craft lying off the entrance to Kobe harbour.

They berthed in Kobe in the early afternoon, having gone through the same medical and passport inspection a second time. They found Kobe fairly attractive, but noisy (hooters were going all the time), and dirty (chimneys were belching smoke). They enjoyed most their first visit to a Japanese shopping street and to a fox shrine on a slope of the hills overlooking the town and the harbour.

They sailed into Yokohama in brilliant sunshine with the sea as smooth as a lake. They were due to be met by the Bishop of South Tokyo, but he had not yet arrived. Suddenly the ship was swarming with Japanese. As soon as the gangway was fixed they came on board in family parties and explored all over the ship. 'It always happens like this,' said a ship's officer. 'The Japanese have such a thirst for knowledge. Sometimes they bring whole schools up from the country to look over the liners in port.'

Bishop Heaslett arrived at last, full of welcomes and apologies, and whisked them off to his house in a taxi. They took with them just two small suitcases and a hat box, so the next day they returned to collect their heavy baggage for passing through customs. All their luggage came through safely, except for their books, which had to be examined by a special inspector. 'The Japanese,' they were told, 'are very strict about dangerous thought.'

2

The First Shadows Fall

Towards the end of their journey, my father wrote home:

> There seem to have been a good many events happening in the
> big wide world while we have been coming east. Three assassinations
> – the French President, the Japanese Premier and the Japanese at
> Shanghai – riots and shooting in Bombay, a political crisis in Japan
> and the disaster to the French liner, *Georges Philippar*, off Aden
> create quite a record.

On 29 April 1932, in Hongkew Park in Shanghai, a large crowd
of mostly Japanese had gathered for a celebration of the Emperor's
birthday. The national anthem was being sung when a young man darted
forward to place a cylinder in front of the dais where seven of the
Japanese civil and military leaders in Shanghai were standing. The bomb
exploded with such a dull sound that many of the crowd did not at
once realise what had happened and the music continued to play. Then,
as the leaders on the dais were seen to collapse, wounded and bleeding,
soldiers rushed forward, some to assist the injured, others to seize the
culprit.

No Chinese had been admitted to the park, and the perpetrator proved
to be a Korean, Yun Pong-gil. He was a member of a group known as
the Korean Patriotic Association, whose aim was to recover the independence
of Korea by the assassination of Japanese leaders and other acts of terror.
In the previous January another member of the group, Ri Pong Chang,
had thrown a bomb at the Emperor's carriage outside the Sakurada Gate
of the Imperial Palace in Tokyo. That assassination attempt failed, for
the bomb did not hit its target, but Ri Pong Chang was hailed as a
martyr both in Korea and in China.

In Shanghai the bomb placed by Yun Pong-gil did hit its target and with devastating effect. All the seven leaders standing on the dais were wounded, three so seriously that they subsequently died of their injuries. These were General Shirakawa, Commander-in-Chief of the Japanese forces in Shanghai, Mr Murai, Japanese Consul-General in Shanghai, and Mr Kawahashi, leader of the Japanese residents.

Soon after arriving in Japan, my father accompanied Bishop Heaslett to a conference at Hiratsuka, a coastal town to the west of Yokohama. My father appreciated the opportunity to meet the Japanese clergy present, but he did not have enough Japanese language to understand the papers being read, so in the early afternoon he said goodbye and caught the train to Tokyo. For the second half of the journey the route was thronged with people. At every station there were soldiers lining the platform and at every open space between stations great numbers of adults and parties of schoolchildren. At Tokyo station the crowds were very dense and along the road from the station to the Imperial Palace crowds had gathered as on Armistice Day in London, while official cars filled with dignitaries left the station and drove along the route. The reason was that just behind the regular train was a special train bearing the body of General Shirakawa, killed by the bomb in Hongkew Park in Shanghai, and the people had turned out to pay him due honour and respect.

It was little more than two weeks after the assassinations in Shanghai that Prime Minister Inukai was assassinated in Tokyo. On 15 May 1932 a group of nine young Japanese officers from the army and navy worshipped at the Yasukuni Shrine, paying homage to the spirits of the dead soldiers and sailors to whom the shrine is dedicated. They then proceeded to the Prime Minister's official residence and burst in upon the old man in his private apartments. He greeted them with dignity, suggesting they talk before using their weapons, but they gunned him down and made their escape. An attempt to follow this up, by throwing a handful of bombs at banks, party offices and police headquarters, was a fiasco and the young officers gave themselves up.

The assassination of Prime Minister Inukai was the third significant murder in Japan that spring. In February, Mr Inouye, a former finance minister, and in March, Baron Dan, managing director of the huge Mitsui holding company, had been killed by youths from the country. These were members of the Blood Brotherhood, a small association of young, ultra-nationalist fanatics, hostile to politicians and capitalists and embittered by poverty in the countryside.

Rural poverty at this time was deep and widespread. The 1929 collapse of the American stock market and consequent slump in world trade had

had a devastating effect in Japan. Between 1929 and 1931 exports plummeted. This was calamitous for small businesses and banks. Farmers suffered even more. Good rice harvests at home, combined with imports of rice from Japan's colonies, caused the market to be glutted. Demand for raw silk thread dried up. By contrast the largest firms, such as Mitsui, prospered, for they controlled a wide range of interests and enjoyed a privileged relationship with government. Their success at a time of general hardship aroused bitter resentment and contributed to political instability.

The troubles in the countryside were exacerbated by the small scale of Japanese farming. As my father wrote, the appearance of farmland in Japan was not at all like that of farmland in England:

> The impression is much more that of a patchwork quilt. For the land is not worked by big farmers, but is divided up into small strips like allotments, each of which is worked by a peasant farmer. Hence the patchwork effect, because one man may be growing barley, one may have already reaped his barley and be sowing rice, and another may be growing something different again. Another difference between the land here and in England is that every inch here is intensively cultivated. Grass is poor, so that there are very few cattle and consequently all the land is arable. What will happen in the future is difficult to say, but Japanese farmers are very badly hit at the present time and many of them are in a condition of desperate poverty.

Against this background of general hardship, particular tragic cases stood out. In the town where my parents were living, a married woman, whose husband was a councillor, drowned herself in the sea. The reason for this was obscure: 'It may have been bad treatment on the part of her husband or it may just have been the unending struggle of bringing up a family of four – the youngest deaf and dumb – on a pittance, her husband's shop being, like so many in the present depression, next door to a failure.' A few weeks later the husband took the youngest child and drowned both the child and himself in a nearby pond.

The assassination of Prime Minister Inukai was the first political murder to be carried out by officers in uniform. Early reports gave out that the Prime Minister had been shot by 'men wearing officers' uniforms', as there was a reluctance to believe that genuine officers could be involved in such an incident. In fact, there was much political agitation in the army and the young officers were hoping to create an opportunity for the army to seize power from the politicians and capitalists and establish military rule. They saw this in terms of a 'second restoration', in which power would be returned to the Emperor, who would thereupon entrust it to faithful soldiers and patriots.

The murder of Prime Minister Inukai precipitated a political crisis in Japan. It brought to an end cabinets composed of party politicians, for the army would no longer supply a Minister of War to a government headed by a party leader. Prime Minister Inukai's successor was thus a non-party man, Admiral Saito. He was himself restrained and cautious, but the most powerful man in the cabinet was General Araki, the Minister of War. He was one of the leaders of the 'Imperial Way School', a dominant faction in the Japanese army and one committed to a programme of expansion on the continent of Asia.

These developments created a tense situation in Tokyo. In the month of August 1932 my parents were in Karuizawa, a mountain resort popular with westerners anxious to escape the stifling summer heat. Among those they met were Mr and Mrs Hind, missionaries from Kyushu, who had stayed on in Japan after retirement. Mr Hind went up to Tokyo on the day on which the Emperor opened an emergency session of the Diet and said that he had never seen such a police presence there before. Apparently, after the murder of the late Premier and other officials, the authorities were prepared for anything and frightened of a *coup d'état*. One of the high officials who was spending his holiday in Karuizawa said he was glad to be there, because in Tokyo he always had to wear a bullet-proof waistcoat. My father said of the authorities:

> They are frightened of violence, not only from Communists but also from so-called Fascists – violent extreme-right military organisations. The recent murders were carried out by members of these societies and so strong is the power of the military that not one of them can be properly punished by the police. There is a big struggle going on between the military and the civil forces and at the moment the former are definitely the stronger and the real rulers of the country.

These events within Japan did nothing to reassure an international community already dismayed by Japan's actions in Manchuria and Shanghai. Japan had a treaty right to maintain troops in Manchuria to protect the Japanese-owned South Manchurian Railway. In the previous year, on 18 September 1931, the general in charge of these troops claimed that Chinese soldiers had attempted to blow up a stretch of track and on this pretext sent his troops to attack their army in Mukden, and from there to spread out and occupy more and more of the country. Army leaders in Tokyo were party to this plan but the government knew nothing of it. They were therefore put in an impossible position, as they tried to reassure the outside world that this expansion was temporary, while the army ignored all such assurances and continued to move forward and overcome all resistance.

The situation became more alarming to the international community when Japanese and Chinese forces began fighting in Shanghai in January 1932. This was a development of the situation in Manchuria, for the Japanese in Shanghai were anxious to follow up the successes of their army in Manchuria, while the Chinese were motivated by a desire to resist Japanese aggression. Japan took care to consult with other nations to ensure the protection of their nationals in the International Settlement, but world opinion was shocked by the heavy bombing by Japanese naval airplanes of Chinese positions in the crowded district of Chapei.

On 1 March 1932, the puppet state of Manchukuo was set up with Henry Pu Yi, the last of the Chinese emperors, as its titular head. Japan tried to persuade the world that Manchukuo was set up in accordance with the wishes of the local population and that, although brought into being with the help of the Japanese army in Manchuria, it was genuinely an independent state. Japan hoped, in particular, that the Lytton Commission, sent to the Far East on behalf of the League of Nations, would accept the legitimacy of the state of Manchukuo. But inevitably the Lytton Report, although diplomatically phrased, condemned Japan's military action in Manchuria and refused to accept the legitimacy of the puppet regime.

In October 1932, following the presentation of the Lytton Report in Geneva, my father wrote home:

I expect papers at home, as here, are full of the Lytton Report. Japan does not like it at all but, so far as I have read it, it seems to me eminently sane and balanced.

Later he added:

At the moment Japan, as judged by the newspapers, is rather calmer, hoping for better things at Geneva than she did at the time the Lytton Report was published. That report seemed to me eminently

41

fair and impartial, and because of that it has not pleased Japan or certain circles in China. Japan, in fact, was furious, partly because of the offence to her pride but partly also because she has, I think, thought of the League of Nations as an instrument for settling European problems only. It is here that she has dropped her worst brick, because she hasn't realised that the West is not going to allow pre-war methods in a post-League of Nations world.

My father was not entirely without sympathy for Japan's situation, however, and added:

I think the West ought to have had more sympathy with her situation in Manchuria, which stands to her rather as Egypt does to us. Just as we couldn't stand hordes of bandits roaming round the Suez Canal, so Japan cannot stand interference with the South Manchuria Railway. Something has obviously got to be done in that utterly lawless and bandit-ridden country and Japan is really about the only nation who can do anything to restore order. If only she had appealed frankly to the League instead of acting off her own bat, I think she would have won full sympathy and support for her claims.

The League Council accepted the Lytton Report by a unanimous vote and in March 1933 Japan withdrew from the League of Nations.

And so, even as my parents began their new life in Japan, the first shadows were falling, shadows of military aggression abroad and murderous conspiracy at home, shadows that would lengthen and darken until they would drive our family out of the country nine years later.

3

Numazu

But, for the first two years, my parents lived far from the centre of political or military activity. My father was to be a lecturer at the *Shingakuin*, the theological college in Tokyo for the training of Japanese priests of the *Nippon Sei Ko Kai* (the Anglican or Episcopal church in Japan). But neither of my parents knew any Japanese when they arrived in Japan, so first they must spend two years in studying the language.

A missionary, Miss Edlin, was returning shortly to England and her house in Numazu would thus become available. Bishop Heaslett proposed that my parents should move into Miss Edlin's house and have a tutor in Numazu to teach them Japanese. When they went to Karuizawa, to escape the heat of the summer, their tutor should accompany them. After their return to Numazu, my father should go up to Tokyo twice a month to take services at the English church of St Andrew's.

So, within a few days of their arrival, they set out for their new home in Numazu, a small coastal town in the north-west corner of the Izu Peninsula. It was a town where there were no other westerners, so there they were to absorb Japanese language and culture by a process of total immersion. At least that was the idea, though later they thought they might have learnt the language more effectively if they had studied at a language school in Tokyo.

My parents used to say that the Japan they went out to in 1932 was 'old Japan', closer to Japan when it first opened its doors to foreigners than to modern Japan. In Numazu they experienced kimonos, rickshaws, wooden houses, elaborate ceremonial about everyday matters, constant reminders of a picturesque history and a highly developed civilization totally different from anything western.

Soon after their arrival a shared memory brought home to them how close the picturesque past was: the Canadian widow of an early missionary told how she was often left alone with the Japanese servants while her husband travelled round his district. On one occasion their house was burgled. After that their landlord told the servants to let him know when Mr Baldwin was away, and each time he came quietly and sat all night in the entrance of the house, wearing his two samurai swords – there were no more burglars. Long before the 1930s the wearing of two swords was forbidden, but in and around Numazu the dress seen in old prints was still usual both in the fields and in the streets.

My parents lived in a wooden house with a view of Mount Fuji from their beds. They had a Japanese bath, a wooden tub with a charcoal-burning stove built into it, where they could relax in the very hot water, after having washed and rinsed before stepping in. They had electric light, to which my mother had not been accustomed in English villages, but they cooked on two or three charcoal braziers, the charcoal being kept alive overnight in a large pot of ash.

Their servant, Matsuno-san, had learnt a little English through working in the house for Miss Edlin. She helped my parents in learning Japanese, for she told them household words in Japanese and smiled with pleasure whenever they were able to produce any of these words in conversation. She cooked western food of a plain variety, but was eager to learn, so my mother hoped to introduce her to some of her 'Mrs Beeton made economical' ideas.

Foreigners were a curiosity in Numazu. There had been one or two resident missionaries but they had been normal, brown-eyed people. After studying my mother for a time, a group of children asked their teacher: 'Can Mrs Sansbury really see? She doesn't bump into things like blind people, but how can she see with doll's eyes?'

Western ways were beginning to appear. My father had noticed at the clergy conference at Hiratsuka that the older men found sitting on a chair difficult, while the younger men found sitting on the floor difficult. At the lunch, which was served on the floor, the older men sat comfortably on their heels, while several of the younger men sat tailor-fashion, with their legs crossed in front of them, or with their legs to the side, as English people might at a picnic. On train journeys too, while younger passengers sat with their feet on the floor, older passengers sat with their legs tucked under them on the seats.

Women wore kimonos, bright colours for the young, sober for the married, sombre for the old. But when a bazaar was to be held at the church, my mother was asked to help make foreign-style dresses for sale, for it was thought very dashing, very up-to-date to wear western dress.

My parents' teacher, Yorimichi Imai, announced: 'I shall now teach you one daily manner.' So each day he would describe to them one Japanese custom and the conversation used in that context. He also began to teach them the characters. My father described the scale of the task ahead: 'There are about fifty sounds in Japanese and each sound has two characters to represent it – what are called *katakana* and *hiragana*. This means that we have to master one hundred Japanese characters. Only when we have done that do we begin to learn the far more difficult Chinese characters, so you can see we have a pretty stiff task ahead of us!'

A pattern for each day was provided by the street vendors: 'Although it is calculated that there is a shop for every five people in Japan, there are as many hawkers here as in England, if not more.' The first to appear was the baker, who shouted *pan* in a nasal voice 'like a Communist decrying the universe'. The next were not hawkers, but advertising people. But instead of carrying sandwich-boards and looking down-trodden, they were dressed in fantastic costumes and beat a big drum in a regular rhythm – tum, tum, tum, tum, tum titty tum tum. In the early afternoon peace descended, but about tea-time began a perfect cacophony of horns. These were blown by sellers of bean-curds and other delicacies, who went about on bicycles with large boxes containing their wares hung perilously on the back-carrier. Their last visitor was a Chinese selling a sort of hot macaroni, who came round about nine o'clock, and who was much patronised for a late supper by those Japanese not already in bed. He pushed his wares round in a barrow, rather like those of Italian ice-cream merchants in England, and announced his arrival on a kind of bagpipes, on which he played a very attractive little tune.

My parents arrived in June, at the start of the rainy season, for everything in Japan, even the weather, was regulated to begin and end on fixed days. There had not, in fact, been much rain as yet, but the weather was becoming increasingly sultry, which made any effort, mental or physical, exhausting. As the heat was very damp, possessions began to go mildewy, and books and clothes had to be watched to see they were not going green. The damp heat brought out the insects and especially the mosquitoes. My parents slept under a mosquito net, but the mosquitoes got at them somehow and they were both considerably bitten. Then the rains came and on one day combined with a mild typhoon. The wind blew furiously, whirling the rain round in great gusts and eddies. The wooden shutters outside the windows on the south side had to be pushed together and the house became filled with a steamy heat. It was a relief when the day came to set off for Karuizawa.

They returned in September, the month of the autumn festival of the local Shinto shrine. The whole town looked in festival mood, for all the streets were decorated with bunting and every house had a lantern hanging outside the gate. In the evening a procession passed through the streets, with high wooden carts, all draped in bright colours and lit by lanterns. These were pulled by twenty or thirty boys and girls and young men in gaily coloured costumes. On the carts bands were playing music which sounded strange and monotonous to western ears, while some carts had what seemed to be a religious emblem in the shape of a box in the centre. On the last of the three nights, the procession grew increasingly high-spirited. Geisha sat on one or two of the carts and many of the men following had drunk a good deal of *sake*. The procession continued to weave its way round the town till one o'clock in the morning.

At home my parents were faced with a minor domestic disturbance. Matsuno-san had about ten sisters ('too much sister' as she put it) and one of them had been in Kobe trying to train as a nurse. But she was slow-witted and short-sighted and was not capable even for housework. So Matsuno-san had to take her back to the northern island of Hokkaido, where their home was, to try and fix her up with some occupation. Matsuno-san would be away for the month of October, but fortunately a former servant of a missionary from Shizuoka was able to take her place. Which was how Furasawa-san first came into our lives.

When Matsuno-san returned at the end of her month's leave, she was laden with presents, as was the usual Japanese custom, but perhaps even more so than usual, as my parents had helped with the expensive fares to Hokkaido. In the middle of her luggage was a sack of potatoes and among her various parcels were a bag of apples, a box of eggs and a bottle of grape juice. She was always saying how good everything was in Hokkaido, and now they were able to prove it, as the gifts she brought back were delicious and especially some jelly that she concocted using the grape juice.

November was the season of the rice harvest, for there were two main harvest seasons in Japan. When my parents had travelled to Numazu in early June, the barley, wheat and millet were being gathered and the fields then soaked with water ready for the rice sowing. Now the farmers were cutting the ears of rice and taking them away and hanging up the straw to dry on poles, supported by forked sticks. The work was interesting to watch, but it must have been tedious to perform, as every bit was carried out by hand. My father set out for a bicycle ride in the country.

He found it strange that almost no one but 'oldest inhabitants' and children were to be seen in the village streets and was astonished by how hard the agricultural people worked, both men and women. 'From early morning till dark they are in the fields, doing all sorts of back-breaking jobs and then they come home either carrying loads that an English workman would be aghast at or pulling small carts that look as though they needed at least a horse.'

This was the time when chrysanthemums were at their best. My father bought one for my mother, which had small petals and which was trained in the trailing style beloved of the Japanese, for it was a plant with a double stem, one stem going straight up, the other drooping over and hanging down about twelve or eighteen inches. My parents visited a chrysanthemum show, where the exhibits came in every conceivable shape and colour, many looking as unlike English ideas of chrysanthemums as possible. They ranged from little red daisy-like flowers to enormous blooms that had to be supported on wire stands. There were also fantastically-shaped plants, made to look like boats, aeroplanes and even a fish in a bucket!

Early in December, my parents witnessed a ceremony taking place on the open ground to one side of their house. It meant, unfortunately, that the open space would soon be built upon, for the ceremony was the traditional Shinto one for the blessing of the site and the buildings to be erected on it. Before the ceremony, the workmen put in the ground four bamboos in a square, joining them to each other with ropes, from which they hung the paper symbols that represented offerings. On the north side of the square a narrow wooden table was erected, to serve as a makeshift altar, and on this were placed offerings of cakes and wine and vegetables. The priest made an impressive figure in a long, light-blue robe, with a short, green gauze robe over the top, and a black hat that looked like a cross between a mitre and a tam-o'-shanter. The ceremony consisted of prayers chanted before the altar, alternated with sprinkling of food offerings to the four points of the compass. While this was going on, the workmen stood reverently in a row on the west side of the square. When it was finished, the priest gave each of them a spray of the bamboo boughs, which they placed on the altar in turn, afterwards clapping their hands as a symbol of prayer, then bowing and returning to their place.

At this time of year, there was an occasional cold, wet day, when my parents would shut all the windows and huddle round the oil stove. But, for the most part, only the nights were cold, the days being warm and sunny. There was a sprinkling of snow on the hills and Fuji itself was completely white. But in the middle of the day they could slide back the panels on the verandahs and bask in the sunshine. The latitude of that part of Japan was similar to that of the Riviera and the winters were not severe.

My parents spent Christmas in Tokyo but returned to Numazu in time for New Year. The tradespeople called round with their seasonal gifts: a box of oranges from the washerman, sugar from the carpenter, bread from the baker and bulbs in a bowl from the gardener, while Matsuno-san's mother sent a chicken from Hokkaido. Numazu was in festival mood, for the streets were decorated and the people were out and about in their best kimonos or in frock coats. Along the front of shops, or between the trees beside the roads, were hung lines with short pieces of bamboo hanging on them, and in front of people's houses were small bamboo trees or sometimes three bamboo stems cut diagonally at the top. Hanging on doors or gates were rings of rope with green foliage at the top and an orange tied in the middle as an offering to bring good luck. The children played battledore and shuttlecock and were dressed in brilliantly coloured kimonos. Everyone called on their neighbours to leave a card and congratulate them on the season, and every house had a table placed in the porch, where cards could be left, each table spread with a piece of silk brocade.

My mother attended the New Year's party for the women's group at the church. First they had a feast of rice, decorated with ginger and seaweed, and all kinds of shredded vegetables. Afterwards they played childish games. My mother made two mistakes in speaking Japanese: once she refused some tasty-looking pickle that she meant to accept, and once she introduced herself in honorific terms instead of humble ones, a mistake that brought the house down. She took comfort in the news in the next day's paper that Prime Minister Saito had dropped a tremendous brick at court at the New Year's Day ceremonies. He had read a speech of thanks for the 'gracious message from the throne' before the Emperor had had a chance to deliver the 'gracious message from the throne'!

Early in February, the catechist at the church, Masamichi Imai, was due to leave Numazu, so a farewell meeting took place in his honour. My father found the speeches more sentimental than his English background had prepared him for. 'We had to listen to a succession of speeches, one or two accompanied by handkerchiefs and sniffs, in which fond mothers told how their children hung on the words of the good Imai-

48

san and how desolate they would be when their wonderful friend was gone.' He hoped that the Japanese did not take this all at face value 'or Masamichi will be departing with a very swollen head!'

If my father found the farewell speeches for Masamichi Imai sentimental, he found his final send-off at the station impressive:

> In some ways I think the Japanese do the farewell business better than we do. Instead of everybody's crowding round the door of the carriage till the last minute, racking their brains for something to say, each person on arriving on the platform says a few words to the person who is leaving and then drops back about three or four yards from the train. When all have said goodbye and dropped back into the crowd, the person leaving gets into the train and stands by the door at the end of the carriage. There may still be a minute before the train goes, but he just stands there silently and the people say nothing either. Then, as the train starts, everybody bows very low and says '*Go-kigen-yo*' which means roughly 'May you fare well'. It is certainly impressive and makes an English person, used to much less formal goodbyes, feel that it must be at least a member of the Royal Family, who is being seen off with such respect and ceremony.

March 3 was the day of the Girls' Doll Festival, a very festive day for all girls in Japan. The custom in any household where there were girls was to have a display of dolls representing the Emperor and Empress and all the officials of the court. A setting of several tiers was made and covered with red cloth. Then the dolls were arranged in order, with the Emperor and Empress on the top tier and the officials graded according to rank on the lower tiers. All the toy shops were filled with these dolls and there were many varieties to suit both rich and poor. The more expensive ones were exquisitely made, with elaborate costumes that were a replica of the old court dress.

A girl who came to church, and who was more or less dumb, made a set of these dolls for Matsuno-san, who was very kind to her. The girl was very clever with her hands and the dolls were beautifully made and dressed. Matsuno-san's room was not big enough for such a display, and so the scene was set up on my mother's desk in the dining room and there it remained for the festival week.

Shortly afterwards came a Buddhist festival. There were no outward signs in the form of processions or decorations, but it was believed that at this time the spirits of the departed returned to earth and that, in consequence, it was an inauspicious time for anyone to die. The spirits of the dead returning to the earth were not likely to be pleased with spirits coming from the earth, and in cruder superstitions it was thought that they would express their displeasure by giving them a crack on the head with a mallet! In consequence, anyone who died during the festival was buried with his head encased in a metal pot to protect it from such desecration.

Buddhists buried their dead after cremation with a strip of paper stamped with the face of seven coins, worth about a tenth of a farthing each. This represented the earlier practice of putting actual coins in the coffin, the idea being that after crossing the river between this life and the next the dead must pay a fee on the far bank of the river before they could enter the next world. This is, of course, very like the Greek idea of paying Charon for ferrying the dead across the River Styx. When this was being discussed after the morning service at Numazu, one man quipped that he hoped that there was no moratorium at the bank across the river as there was at the banks in America after the Wall Street Crash!

At the end of March came the day appointed for my parents' annual spring-clean. This was a matter of police regulation and a week in advance they received notice that the Dowager Empress was coming to stay at the Imperial villa on the shore near Numazu and that the spring-clean must be completed before her arrival. So, on the morning stipulated, a young assistant from the greengrocer's arrived with another young man punctually at 7.30 am. My mother was unwell, so the timing was unfortunate. However, they started by turning out the spare room, so, once that was put straight, she was able to move in there and leave the rest of the house in their hands. Everything was put outside, either on the roof or in the garden. The straw *tatami* mats that covered all the floors were taken up and put out too. The young men then proceeded to beat everything with hand-mops, made up of strips of cloth tied on the ends of wooden sticks. My father was not altogether impressed: 'This is the Japanese idea of cleaning; you flick everything, raise an infernal dust and then let it settle down again in a different order! The floors of passages are washed, but that is all that receives cleansing with water. However, it satisfies the Japanese, who refer to the day as the "honourable cleaning", so who are we to complain?'

April was the month for cherry blossom viewing. My father wrote home:

The Japanese regard the cherry blossom as a symbol of their national character. The fleeting life of the blossom, the unfavourable weather in which often it flowers, the way in which the blossom soon falls to the ground, broken to fragments, are all symbolic – they speak to the Japanese of the shortness of life, the adversities of life and the resolution and courage with which the end of life must be faced.

The Shinto shrine and the Buddhist temple in Numazu were surrounded by a mass of cherry blossom, but, as well as these set pieces, there were innumerable cherry trees in the countryside, so views of cherry blossom were to be had on every side. At the shrines there were cherry blossom festivals. These could become occasions for excessive drinking of *sake*, so it was best to visit the temple grounds in the early evening, when the effect of the cherry blossom lit up by rows of hanging lanterns was extraordinarily beautiful.

Matsuno-san asked for a day off. In Japan there was no unemployment insurance, but the family was a real corporate entity, responsible for family members who were out of work. Matsuno-san was expected, therefore, to help sundry of her sisters, the majority of whom seemed to be poverty-stricken. She was, however, getting annoyed with a married sister in Yokohama, who had been asking for a lot of help. She felt this was unfair and that the husband's family, who were not poor, ought to turn to and give a hand. So she set off at six in the morning, full of indignation and fervour. She was to have returned the same evening, but missed her train and had to stay with her sister. That, doubtless, spoiled her resolute stand and the fact that she had to borrow an under-kimono from her sister, because Yokohama was distinctly cooler than Numazu, must also have spoiled her dignity. At any rate, she returned very subdued and gave my parents no confidences, so they feared she had given way.

My parents were given a fortnight's leave from lessons, as their teacher, Yorimichi Imai, was about to be married. In fact, Yorimichi was no longer called Imai. His bride came from a family in which there were no sons, and so, in accordance with Japanese custom, Yorimichi had already been adopted into the bride's family and taken their name of Muramatsu. After the marriage the bridal couple would be going away, not on honeymoon in a western sense, but to visit the husband's relations, which was the Japanese equivalent.

The weather was becoming warmer and there was much more sunshine.

All the blossoms were over, but to compensate there was real green grass. By the end of autumn the grass had all been burnt up by the sun, and through the winter it had remained yellow and bedraggled. Now in the garden the lawn was green once more and the roses and azaleas were in flower.

May was the month of the Boys' Festival and throughout the town, at all the houses where there were boys, cloth carp were blowing in the breeze from flagpoles. The cloth carp were open at both ends, so that the wind could blow through them and fill them out. The carp was a symbol of courage and perseverance, for the carp is a fish that swims against the stream. Around the town, boys were flying kites, on which the faces of heroes of old legends or historical stories were painted. In the houses were special corners with a succession of shelves covered with red cloth. These were like the tiers of shelves for the Girls' Festival, but instead of having the Emperor and Empress and court figures on them, they had banners and scenes of the old stories of heroes and warriors.

At the beginning of June, a car drew up at the house, bearing exalted guests. These guests had been to pay their respects to the Dowager Empress and come straight from the Imperial villa. Matsuno-san was terribly flustered, but at length succeeded in producing tea in the best silver tea service. When the guests left they presented my parents with a box of delicious strawberries, which had been given to them by the Dowager Empress and grown in one of the Imperial gardens. My parents in turn gave some of the strawberries to Matsuno-san, who was thrilled. Imperial strawberries were something she had never expected to see, far less handle or eat. But Matsuno-san was not a selfish person and so, as each of the favoured tradespeople came for their orders, a single strawberry was solemnly presented. The milkman was greatly impressed. He wrapped up his strawberry and took it home carefully, so that each of his children might have a small bite.

In church life there was an upset. A girl committed suicide in a love pact with a fellow Christian from a church in Tokyo, because her parents were arranging a Buddhist marriage for her with someone else. Nearly all marriages in Japan were arranged by the families and at best the couple could protest against the particular arrangement. The story was given wide publicity in newspapers and magazines and there was even the possibility of a film, though that was stopped for fear other couples might follow their example. The story had a great appeal to the Japanese, for whom suicide in heroic or romantic circumstances had a particular fascination.

The weekly meeting of the church congregation was being held at a house on the outskirts of Numazu, where the father of the family seemed to have come out of old Japan with his venerable, Buddha-like face and white hair. The meeting began with much fumbling of a hymn book and an order of proceedings drawn up by his daughters and at last he announced a hymn. Then he continued: 'Last year we had the weekly meeting here and I spoke. Afterwards my family told me I spoke for too long. Tonight I shall talk for ten minutes only.' With that he placed an enormous turnip on the table. What his harangue was all about my father did not fully understand, but its main point seemed to be: 'A journey costs money and the further you go the more you must pay. Heaven is a very long way off, so you will need much money for the fare.' However, it took more than ten minutes, for, when the appointed time was up, he looked at his watch again, said that he was going on some more and called for tea to quench his thirst. After his harangue he called on rows of people to talk, until everyone thought they would be there for the night. At last he brought the meeting to an apparent end and everybody sat back with a sigh of relief, eagerly looking forward to some tea, for it was a frightfully hot evening and all the windows were shut. Then he suddenly called for another hymn and they waded through eight verses, each accompanied by a four line chorus, by which time many of those present were rocking with mirth.

This old man had become a Christian in an unusual way. His wife and family were Christians but he resisted: 'Why should I go to church and do all this standing and kneeling business?' Then the Prince of Wales, the future Edward VIII, paid a visit to Japan. He was due to arrive in Holy Week, but a somewhat agnostically-minded British Ambassador planned a full programme for him with no opportunity of going to church either on Good Friday or on Easter Day. A few days before the Prince's arrival, a cable came from him saying that he would be going to church on both days. The Ambassador had, therefore, to climb down and alter his programme. This made a great impression on the Japanese and when this elderly man read in the paper that the Prince of Wales had attended the services at St Andrew's Church in Tokyo, he said to himself: 'Well, if the Prince of Wales can stand up and kneel down in church, I can also,' and so he became a Christian. As my father commented: 'He is the first convert to Christianity made by the Prince of Wales of whom I have concrete evidence!'

The shops were selling lanterns in readiness for the *O Bon* Festival, when it was believed that the spirits of the dead returned to their families for three nights. On the first night the families put out lanterns and little fires to guide the spirits back to their former homes. On the second night they offered special food before their household shrines for the departed. On the third night they put the food into little boats and sent them sailing down the rivers. My parents had missed the ceremony the previous year, but they had heard it was very beautiful to see all the little lighted boats going down the river. They knew too that the ceremony meant a great deal to the Japanese, as so much of their religion was concerned with the departed, and at the time of the festival they felt a real closeness to them.

This year my parents would miss the festival again, for the heat was becoming stifling and oppressive. It was time to leave Numazu once more and to set off for Karuizawa.

4

'This Beautiful Land'

Numazu, a grey town by the sea, is set in some of the loveliest scenery of this beautiful land. It stands at the head of a bay that has been compared to the Bay of Naples for beauty. To the south rises the great mountainous peninsula of Izu, the home of some of the oldest folk-tales of Japan; to the east, running up from this peninsula, lies the Hakone mountain ridge; far to the west another range of snow-covered mountains is visible on clear days; while to the north, towering above the ruins of an infinitely older volcano, stands Mount Fuji, perhaps the most perfectly shaped mountain in the world.

So my father described my parents' new home. Numazu itself was burnt out in 1926 and had been rebuilt with wider and straighter roads. These roads, with the exception of one or two main roads, had a rough, pebbly surface, which was disastrous to shoes and uncomfortable for motoring. My parents both acquired bicycles. My father went to the Town Office in Numazu to pay the bicycle tax and was surprised to discover how expensive the tax was. Apparently Numazu was very much in debt since the fire of 1926 and was using the bicycle tax as a means to become solvent again.

Fire remained an ever-present hazard. One evening my father was writing letters when he heard the sound of shouting nearby. Matsuno-san rushed to look out and then came racing along the passage crying in panic: '*Kaji! Kaji!*' (Fire! Fire!). My father dashed upstairs and saw a house about 50 yards away blazing fiercely. This might not have been too worrying in England, but in Japan, where every house was made of wood, it was a different matter. Twice in the previous twenty years Numazu had been more than half gutted and had there been any wind that night they would very likely have been burnt out. As it was, sparks

55

Central Japan – adapted from WG Beasley, *The Rise of Modern Japan*
(Weidenfeld and Nicolson, London, 1990)

were flying, and my father hastily got out the available suitcases and packed valuables and clothes as fast as he could. In the middle of the commotion, the vegetable man came up with an enormous pail of water, prepared to drench the outside wall, if necessary. Fortunately it wasn't. The Fire Brigade soon got the blaze in hand and within an hour it was out. Result: one chicken farm gutted and hundreds of chickens roasted alive. The chickens provided a feast the following day for Koreans living in the town. Afterwards tradespeople and friends called round to express sympathy for the anxious time and congratulations on escape. The silkworm place opposite quickly had a table outside and all enquirers were regaled with tea.

Numazu was the centre for the silk industry of the region. My father was travelling to Kofu, north of Fuji, when he broke his journey to visit a village where there was a solitary Christian. She had previously lived in Tokyo, but had married a man whose home was in the country. He was a maker of *han*, the signet stamps used in Japan on all official papers, and sometimes travelled as far as Manchuria and Formosa. So why did they live in a village buried in the country? The answer was that the husband's father lived there and the family system demanded that they live with the father and look after him. Perhaps also there was an economic reason, for the district was one of the silk districts of Japan and every farmhouse kept silkworms. The family had a substantial farmhouse, with a large kitchen containing a great brick oven. In the centre of the house was a semi-dark room with bamboo shelves on either side. The shelves were about a yard deep and accommodated sixty trays – each about three feet by a foot and a half – full of silkworms. At the time of the visit, the silkworms were fairly young and had to be fed six times a day with mulberry leaves, so a great many leaves were used and the people were kept pretty busy.

Numazu was also a bustling fishing town. From the time of their arrival, my parents delighted in the pine trees along the shore and in the views of Numazu Bay and the magnificent headland opposite. Now they set off in a fishing boat for a village called Ko on the opposite side of the bay. They got away to time and chug-chugged down the river towards the sea. They passed the picturesque old fishing port of Numazu, where there was much activity concerning a whale being chopped up on the quayside. Soon they left the town and passed between tree-lined banks as far as a small fishing village at the mouth of the river and so they entered the sea.

The boat sailed past a tree-covered promontory and then cut across to the headland opposite with its long line of rugged hills stretching down to the sea. All along were little bays, each with a fishing village on the slope behind. These villages were quite tiny, just a handful of houses on the slope and a small quay at the water's edge. They landed their cargo of two crates of vegetables at the first village and then wound their way through fishing nets to the next village and so on to Ko. On the way they passed a series of watchtowers, built sometimes on boats, sometimes on cliffs and sometimes in trees, and all looking very rickety and unsafe. They were used to spot the movements of shoals, with the watchman blowing a horn when he saw a shoal to let the fishermen know. On their return trip, as the boat came into each little harbour, the boy who did all the odd jobs blew a blast with a shell. It sounded like a peculiarly soft and harmonious trumpet. Their cargo back was three buckets of a very large fish, which were landed at the fish market ready for auction.

When my parents set out by boat for a second time, the boat did not cut across the bay to the opposite headland, but kept close by the shore right to the bend of the bay. The villages they visited were almost enclosed by land, so it was difficult from the seashore at Numazu even to guess they were there. The first bay they reached was the most attractive, for it was almost a perfect semi-circle with houses round the shore and tree-covered hills rising steeply behind them. In the middle of the bay were large numbers of fishing nets and near the shore crowds of boys, mostly nude, were sunbathing and sea bathing. There the boat landed about twenty planks of timber and then went on to the next and larger bay. Here they landed fourteen trays of sprats. As the village was very small and as there were already a dozen trays of sprats on the quayside, they were much intrigued as to what they were for. Even the proverbial Japanese love of fish might wear a bit thin on so many sprats, so they guessed that some, at any rate, must be used as bait.

My parents were invited by Bishop Heaslett to accompany him on an expedition to Hakone. The first part of the journey was quite unadventurous, over the flat land to the next town of Mishima and so on to the foothills of Hakone. Then the bus began to climb. The surface of the road was abominable, but the building of it was a wonderful piece of engineering. It wound by twists and turns and hair-pin bends up and up through villages and past farmhouses to a height of about 3000 feet. At last it reached the top of the pass and then dropped a couple of hundred feet to the village of Hakone on the edge of the lake.

They left the bus and set off to the top of a hill. It was a stiff climb but the view from the top was magnificent. To the south lay the way they had come: flat countryside, broken by hills, ending in the beautiful bay of Numazu. From that height they could appreciate how perfect was the semi-circle of the bay, with a great headland on one side and rolling hills stretching into the far distance on the other. To the east lay the wild, mountainous country of the Izu Peninsula and further to the east a fine sea view of the bay which stretched from the Izu Peninsula to Kamakura about forty miles away. But that was not all, for in the other direction was the most glorious lake and mountain scenery imaginable. In the centre was Lake Hakone, wonderfully blue in colour, stretching away for about three miles and forming bays with the slopes of the hills among which it lies. For Lake Hakone is volcanic in origin and lies in some prehistoric fissure between the colossal hills around it. Mountains and hills stretched in every direction, ridge after ridge appearing as far as the eye could see. And dominating them all was Mount Fuji. They had not seen Fuji on the way up, as she was hidden in clouds, but as they stood on the hilltop she appeared and capped the whole glorious scene.

In October the *Naldera* was back in Japan and my father was struggling to make contact with Captain Harrison. Two days before the ship was due at Kobe, my father wrote to Captain Harrison there, inviting him to come and stay for a couple of days and explore the Izu Peninsula. But before the Captain could receive that letter, he had wired from Shimonoseki, asking my parents to dine and stay on board at Yokohama. My father wired back that he would not be in Tokyo that weekend and that he had already written to him. The Captain then wired from Yokohama, saying that he had not received the letter and asking my parents to do a three days' walking tour near Nikko, beginning on the following day. Again my father wired back to decline, for it was not long since they had returned from Karuizawa and they could not go gallivanting off again. Instead he repeated their invitation to him to stay at Numazu. A final wire came from the Captain to say he would be arriving that morning and so they sallied forth to the station to meet him just before lunch.

They returned from the station by taxi, as Captain Harrison's suitcase was very heavy, surprisingly so for a visit of two or three days. When they reached the house all was explained, for the suitcase was laden with provisions for the household store, brought in case my parents were unable to obtain foreign foods in Numazu.

My mother had already decided that she would not join the walking party, for Matsuno-san did not like being left too often alone in the house at night. So Captain Harrison discussed with my father what they should do and they settled in favour of the Fuji lakes rather than the Izu Peninsula.

So in the afternoon the walkers caught a train and then a bus to Lake Kawaguchi, where they stayed at a lakeside inn built on a small headland of lava. The following morning they started along a pathway that ran right along the shore. It was splendid walking in the sunshine, with the deep blue of the lake contrasting vividly with the bright green of the hillsides. Soon a youth overtook them with a contraption on his back used by the peasants for carrying heavy loads. He obviously wanted to take their haversacks, so they gave them to him gladly, though he seemed rather small to carry such a load.

Towards the end of the lake, they climbed a couple of hundred feet, went through a tunnel built through the pass and came out on the other side by Lake Saiko. That again was a lovely lake, though when first seen it looked very small, as its shape was rather like a bent figure of eight. At the end of this lake they said goodbye to their carrier, put their haversacks on a bus going to the next lake, Shoji, and then started to walk. There was a matter of five miles between these two lakes and the road wound its way through trees almost all the way. It was beautifully shady, which was very welcome, as the sun was very hot, and it provided a pleasant contrast of scenery from the lakes. They reached Lake Shoji in about an hour and a half, collected their haversacks and caught a motorboat to the Shoji Hotel, where they planned to stay the night. The hotel was in a superb situation, on a promontory on the north side of the lake, and commanded a fine view of Mount Fuji. As the motor boat drew near the quay, two smiling maids came running down through the trees to greet them and to carry their haversacks up to the hotel.

The next day they set out to walk the best part of twenty miles to Tokiwa on the Fuji River. They walked first to Lake Motoso, but from there on they had more or less to guess their way, as they had no sufficiently detailed maps to guide them. They hoped first to find a path round the south side of the lake, but after going some way the path faded out and they found themselves faced with the alternative of going back or scrambling on over rocks. They chose the latter course and reached the end of the lake pretty tired. Nor did the outlook seem good, for there were no obvious signs of habitation at that end of the lake and in front of them was a line of hills 1,500 to 2,000 feet high.

Fortunately, they came across a small cottage, where they were given instructions about which path to take, and so they began to climb the ridge. About 500 feet up they came to a woodman's hut, where they asked again about the route, and where they found, after much palaver and waving of maps, that they had come the wrong way. About half way up they should have turned off to the right and the woodman accompanied them down to show them just where the turning was. So at last they were on the right path and for most of an hour they climbed up and up to the top of the ridge. Then they began the long descent on the other side to the valley of the Fuji River, which took them a good three hours' hard walking. The scenery was grand, which buoyed up their spirits after the misadventures of the morning, but by the time they reached the railway, they were pretty well exhausted. They drank some tea, caught a train and, with a change at Fuji Station, did the last lap home, having circled Fuji in just over 48 hours.

My father received an invitation to join a party of students from the theological college who were visiting two hot springs in the Izu peninsula. The trip was being arranged by Dr Shaw, a lecturer at the college, for he knew that this was an outing that every Japanese loved. They set off first to a hot spring called Nagaoka, which had a first-rate Japanese inn. There they were received in great state and escorted to the two rooms set apart for their use. They changed into the cotton kimonos known as *yukata*, drank tea, and went down to the *onsen* or hot springs for a bath. There were two baths, one quite large with warm water and one quite small and very hot. Quite what qualities there were in the water my father was not sure, but the baths were certainly relaxing.

They then set off for Ito, their destination for the night. It was an adventurous drive, as they had to cross the range of mountains that runs down the middle of the Izu Peninsula and so they had to twist and turn up the side of the mountains to get over the pass. Unfortunately there was a steady drizzle all the time, for in fine weather the views would surely have been spectacular.

At Ito they again changed into *yukata*, drank tea, bathed and had a meal. The inn here had a charming fish pond with a covered balcony on one side and a rock garden on the other. A surprising fact about the fish was that the new ones each year were trained to come for their food by a new note on a whistle. Thus, by producing different notes, it was possible to collect the fish of different ages, for the fish knew the distinction between the notes perfectly and never answered to the wrong note.

In the evening they all went out for a stroll in their *yukata* and *geta* (the Japanese wooden sandals). My father found this an amusing experience and felt quite Japanese walking about in the national dress. Then it was time for bed, but the night proved all too short: 'The Japanese are early risers, I know, but when the maid starts hovering about at 5 am, ready to pack your bedding away in the cupboard, I think it is a bit thick! Dr Shaw got up, but I slept for another hour, thereby trying the maid's patience considerably!'

At the time of their departure all the staff lined up to say goodbye, as was the custom: 'At least they do if you have tipped them well. Dr Shaw says you can judge by the send-off they give you if they are satisfied with your tips! At Ito we had no less than six maids, all in very attractive blue kimonos, who bowed profusely as our bus started off. The last we saw of them was the tops of their heads, so horizontally do they bend!'

In January my father was passing through Yokohama just as the *Naldera* was tying up. He had read the announcement of her coming in the papers and had written to Captain Harrison inviting him to visit them again if he could spare a day or so. A letter came accepting their invitation and the following day Captain Harrison arrived himself.

Over lunch they planned a jaunt in the Izu Peninsula, so in the early afternoon they all three set off and followed a road that came into the broad valley that runs a good distance down the peninsula. It was quite a flat walk, but very attractive, as the afternoon sun lit up the hills that surrounded them on almost every side. An electric railway ran down the farther side of the valley and they made for one of the stations and caught a train to Shuzenji, the terminus of the line.

Shuzenji was a hot spring resort with many Japanese visitors. There were about a dozen inns, many of them of enormous size, and for the rest there was little to the town but shops – except for one thing. By an odd freak of nature a hot spring bubbled up between rocks in the middle of the river. Around these rocks an extremely inadequate fence had been built and in the hot spring the populace bathed *en masse* and in the nude. As my father commented: 'The average English seaside borough councillor would have apoplexy if he saw the scene, but here it is all taken so much as a matter of course that nobody turns a hair!'

They reached their inn and, after settling in and changing into *yukata*, the first thing to do, of course, was to visit the bath. This inn had a magnificent hot-spring bath, or rather four. In the main building, built into a sort of grotto, were two baths big enough to hold three or four people easily, while in two adjoining rooms were smaller baths big enough for one person. My mother and Captain Harrison went into the separate baths, while my father shared one of the big baths with a Japanese gentleman from Yokohama, with whom he had quite a long conversation.

After the bath came a feast. There was a delicious soup, containing egg, beans and bamboo shoots; raw fish with soy sauce and horseradish to dip it into; smoked fish and, as if that were not enough, half a dozen fried oysters; then there was a dish of vegetables, including several Shuzenji specialities, some tiny shellfish and, to act as a digestive, a kind of radish known as *daikon* cut into slices. After the meal a little desultory conversation brought them to an early bedtime. Captain Harrison caused a mild sensation by demanding six *futon* mattresses to sleep on. He was piled up on a sort of bier, much to the amusement of the maids.

When Bishop Heaslett first wrote to my parents about their coming to live in Numazu, he had said that they would 'never lack for a view', as they would always have Mount Fuji to look at. This proved to be not strictly accurate, for more often than not Fuji was hidden by clouds. My father suggested that perhaps this was a good thing, for they did not become so accustomed to seeing the mountain as to make them indifferent to its moods: 'When Fuji appears we stop and look at it, and twice at least this week the mountain has made us stop and look. Once we did so in the evening, just as the sun was setting, when Fuji appeared in that sandy-coloured light that one associates with "sunsets in the desert"; and the other time was in the morning when, just for a few minutes, the clouds broke and we saw the top of the mountain sprinkled with its first fall of snow, glistening in the sunlight. It is no wonder that to the Japanese Fuji-san is the most sacred mountain, symbolic of the life of the nation.'

My father arranged to climb Mount Fuji with Fred Woodd, a friend from theological college days, who had now arrived in Japan and was based in Osaka. They planned to make their climb in early July, before the summer exodus for Karuizawa, so they took the train from Numazu to Gotemba and then caught the bus to Yoshida, for they wanted to be in a good position to start the climb the following morning before the sun got too hot.

When they boarded the bus at Gotemba they saw three girls in their late teens wearing kimonos. A few minutes before the bus started, another girl, slightly older, came to the bus and spoke to them and they all got out. Then, just as the bus was starting, the three girls jumped in again and, though the fourth one ran towards the bus, the others told the driver to go on and not wait. On the way to Yoshida the road climbed over a pass, which was really a low ridge running off from Fuji. Just as they began descending, a car came up behind them and with much honking passed the bus and stopped dead ahead. The bus had to stop and they then saw that inside the car was the older girl who had been left behind and a woman who was a good deal older. The woman got out, went to the bus and ordered the girls to get out. They refused and urged the driver to go on, which he did at last, just having room to get past the car. On they went to Yoshida, the car close behind them. When they stopped, the girls got out of the bus, but the woman got out of the car more quickly and before they had run ten yards she had grabbed the flowing kimono sleeves of two of the girls and pulled them up short. The third girl ran down a lane, but the older girl, who had come in the car, chased her and soon had her caught too.

It was an intriguing spectacle; it seemed that the three girls were from a school party at Gotemba who had played truant and were out for a spree. The older girl was a young teacher and the woman who was in charge of the party was the head teacher. My father was struck by how, in the end, the girls caved in so easily: 'In England three girls who had come a fifty-minute bus ride would have made a fight for it, I think. But as soon as the teacher got hold of their kimono sleeves they submitted and all the fight had gone out of them. It was a striking example of moral force and of the respect for a *sensei* (a teacher) inherent in this nation.'

The two walkers set out just before 8 a.m. for their climb. Between Yoshida and the mountain the ground was not very steep, so it was best to cover this by car in order to reach the real climbing part quickly. While they were waiting for the car, the man who had sold them the tickets came to them and said, 'Beautiful Japanese girl go with you.' My father commented: 'Knowing the propensity of this nation for mixing religious things like pilgrimages with less desirable elements, I wondered what on earth we were to be let in for!' When the time came to start, a nice-looking girl got in the car, accompanied by a small boy aged about five. They felt that the boy was a fairly safe insurance for respectability, but they could not make out who or what the girl was. It seemed impossible that she could be taking this infant to the top and yet she persisted in asking them to walk with her. When they reached the third station the mystery was solved. She was the daughter of the keepers of that hut, anxious for a little company on the way back to her summer home. All entirely respectable, but made to sound doubtful by the ticket man's English!

On the way up Fuji there were huts at regular intervals, the mountain being divided into ten stations. It was all very civilised and there was a perfectly good path the whole way up. It was not really mountaineering at all, but rather 'a long walk up a steep hill'. The whole path was one long series of zigzags with a steep gradient which made the going very hard. Large numbers were climbing, including a whole party from Osaka who were doing pilgrimages and sightseeing together. At first the path climbed through trees; then the tree line was left behind and shrubs and low bushes remained; then they too were left behind and ash from the lava, looking like nothing so much as clinker, was the only thing left. They reached the eighth station, at just over 10,000 feet, about 3.45 p.m. and there they stayed for the night. They had intended to do so in any case, as the accommodation at the hut there was very good, but they could not have gone any further. Their heads were beginning to ache and their stomachs to feel somewhat squiffy, common discomforts, apparently, brought on partly by the strain of climbing so steeply and partly by the comparatively quick change of altitude.

So they turned into the rather grandly named Fuji San Hotel, which was a substantial hut with two rooms and about eight bunks arranged as in a ship, and went straight to sleep for nearly three hours. One of the hut attendants then woke them to ask about supper and they were very glad of hot food to warm them, for 10,000 feet was definitely cool at night. Again they slept well and then at 3.45 a.m. they got up, had some breakfast and went outside to watch the sunrise. It was a beautiful sight to see the sun come up, red and gold, over the clouds below them. It was interesting too to see how people greeted it. Some took photographs, some smoked stolidly, some prayed fervently.

They then climbed the last 2000 feet or so to the top. The first impression was that they had arrived in a village. The path was lined with huts, where picture postcards were sold, walking sticks were stamped, food was served and papers given to pilgrims were blessed by a priest. There was also another 'hotel', where twenty or thirty people could sleep side by side on the mat floor. Only when they had passed these huts could they realise what an amazing place the top was:

It is over a mile round and consists of a series of knobs surrounding a vast crater over 500 feet deep. It is most awe-inspiring and weird and one is glad that the huts are built of lava stones mostly, so that they do not disturb the wildness to any great extent. The view from the top is wonderful – ranges of mountains appearing in all directions and yet all below you. It is like 'sitting on top of the world'!

5

Earthquakes and Typhoons

When my parents arrived in Japan, the country was still recovering from one of the worst natural disasters ever recorded: the great Kanto earthquake of 1 September 1923. The earthquake itself, and the huge fires and tidal waves that followed it, devastated the two cities of Tokyo and Yokohama, and killed 143,000 people.

Accounts of the disaster caused shock around the world. One such account was given by Major (later Air Commodore) Brackley, known as 'Brackles', and was based on hastily scribbled notes. In 1921 Brackles had gone out to Japan with the British Civil Aviation Mission to teach the Japanese navy how to fly. On 1 September 1923 Brackles made his way from the naval base at Yokosuka near Yokohama to a meeting of the Navy Department in Tokyo:

Up at 7 a.m., caught 8 train for Tokyo ... Talked to Ohzeki at Kaigunsho for some time and learnt latest news – when, at noon – Earthquake! Rushed out only just in time, plaster all over us. Terrible scenes all round, fires starting and people rushing everywhere. Buildings crashed to ground. Stayed short while with Ohzeki then worked way to Imperial. What a sight! Fires everywhere! Met two Americans and decided to walk to Yokohama; terrible scenes all along route, dead bodies, houses down, fires. As we approached Yokohama – even worse; thousands of people all along route, earthquake shocks every few minutes. Worked our way as far as Kanagantu Station by 8 p.m. but fires too fierce – had to retreat. Oil tanks exploded – narrow squeak; ran for our lives. Whole of Yokohama burning fiercely; worked back amid tangled ruins to hill – begrimed and done up – at 11 p.m. Stayed on hill till dawn. What a dawn! Worked way through dead bodies to docks – still burning and oil burning in the water. It is now Sunday. – Trapped on dock with oil fire coming towards us. Tried to make bridge with steel rails – too short, they only fell in oil. Rushed back to next wharf – burning furiously. Hailed sampan to take us off – no good. Rushed to next pier and tried to make the *Australia* – pier broken, could not get on bridge. After anxious time, got small sampan to steam launch (Japanese) – engine broke down and we drifted dangerously near fire; taken off by French *Andre Le Bon* dinghy to end of wharf. Rushed through burning go-down to American ship *Steel Navigator* jammed against *Australia*; climbed over to *Australia*, exhausted. Met many friends and heard horrible news. Yokosuka burnt out, Yokohama and Tokyo ditto. Casualties enormous.[2]

Brackles sailed for Canada and then on to England, where he was besieged by journalists eager for his first-hand account of the earthquake. He did not return to Japan, for the earthquake brought an end to the work of the British Civil Aviation Mission. Then the political landscape changed and the work of the Mission became an embarrassment. Many years later his son would shake his head ruefully and say that his father's best pupils led the attack on Pearl Harbor.

When my parents arrived in Japan, nine years after the earthquake, they were impressed by the extent to which the devastation had been made good. Here and there were temporary wooden buildings, but for the most part Tokyo and Yokohama had been rebuilt with fine wide roads and good buildings. It seemed a wonderful example of a city's power of recovery. Sometimes my father felt that opportunities had been missed: 'The Ginza, the main shopping street of Tokyo, is of considerable length, perhaps as long as Oxford Street or Regent Street, but its architecture is for the most part poor. It seems a pity that after the earthquake no effort was made to bring about some coordinated plan for the buildings, such as we have in Regent Street and shall have soon in the Strand. Each building is independent and big and little shops jostle each other in the same higgledy-piggledy way that they did in the old days in the Strand.' Sometimes he felt too that distinctively Japanese character had been lost: 'In all the rebuilding western models have been copied and in many parts of Tokyo there is not very much except the people walking about to show that it is Japan!' The earthquake remained

---

[2] *Brackles, Memoirs of a Pioneer of Civil Aviation*, compiled by Frida H Brackley (W & J Mackay & Co Ltd., Chatham, 1952), p. 212.

a vivid memory and sooner or later people who had lived through it spoke of their experience: 'I was in a tram and of course they shake so much that at first I didn't notice, but then I saw all the houses along the roadside falling like a house of cards.'

My parents attended a dinner party at the residence of the British Consul and his wife in 1935:

Conversation turned to the subject which takes the place of the War here – the Great Earthquake of 1923. Just as at home we talk of events and so on as having taken place before or after 'the War', so here people date things as having happened before or after 'the Earthquake'. It really did mark a turning-point in the life of the community out here. Many people went home after it and never came back. Others were uprooted because they lost everything. In Yokohama, where the whole place was laid flat and burned, the community had to start again from scratch, and the same was true in a lesser degree of Tokyo. Although it happened twelve years ago, it still provides a conversational topic of unceasing interest and one hears from person after person of hairbreadth escapes, hours of separation from relatives, the loss of all possessions and the organising of relief work.

My father sought to reassure his parents by adding,

Such an earthquake only happens about once a century and by no means always in so thickly populated an area as Tokyo and Yokohama. In any case, there cannot again be such fires. In the rebuilding of the cities, broad streets have been made, while in Tokyo extra anti-fire lanes have been built at strategic points. The roads at these points are about half as wide again as Kingsway, so that it is possible to confine fires to a limited area. So you needn't worry about us!

This reassurance was much needed, for letters from home included many enquiries as to the occurrence of earthquakes. My father kept trying to allay his parents' fears: 'Earthquakes, so far, have been a wash-out. There was a very slight one at Numazu one evening, when Ethelreda and I were alone, but as she was writing and I was reading and we never noticed anything, we could not regard it as troublesome!' Or again, 'We had our first earthquake here the other night. The windows rattled and the house shook a bit. Ethelreda was awake and felt it as something considerably less than the one in England a year or so ago. I slept through it and felt absolutely nothing!'

As my father's parents continued to be anxious, my mother added her support:

Kenneth is quite honest about earthquakes. The books may say that there are so many a week, but most of them are only registered on the instruments and are not noticed by ordinary people. Besides which, all Japan is not prone to earthquakes, and Numazu happens to be off their beat. There were four quakes in Tokyo a few weeks ago, not one of which was felt outside the city. And none did any damage.

Still my father's mother was not persuaded and so, in a letter dated 10 November 1932, my father wrote:

Mother seems very doubtful about the truth of my remarks about earthquakes and so herewith I beg to state that on Tuesday evening last, the 8th inst., at or about 9.30 p.m., I experienced my first earthquake. I was reading a book, when suddenly I felt the house rock from side to side for about five seconds. The rocking was very mild and at first I thought some lorry must be passing, but there was nothing outside and so I suspected an earthquake, which afterwards I found out it was. Ethelreda was reading in bed and experienced nothing.

A few months later, on 5 March 1933, my father reported quite a fair-sized earthquake:

At least, it was nothing very much here, but it was enough to wake us up and to bring Matsuno-san rushing up to our room. She is very nervous of earthquakes and indeed of anything out of the ordinary. It lasted very nearly two minutes, but it was of the non-dangerous variety – that is to say, the shaking was from side to side. The dangerous ones go up and down and then from side to side and it is the change of shake which does the damage.

That earthquake was felt in all parts of Japan, and up in the north-east, in the neighbourhood of Sendai, it caused great destruction. Reports of the damage appeared in the English newspapers and caused great alarm in my father's home. Once again, he sought to reassure:

You do seem to have had a fright about us, poor dears, but please do remember that Japan, though small on the map, is considerably bigger than Great Britain. The area affected by the earthquake and tidal wave was comparatively small, although in that area the damage was terrible, whole villages being submerged. But, to get your ideas right, imagine that we read in the papers that several villages on the coast of Cumberland had been affected by a tidal wave. We shouldn't worry very much about you in London, because 300 miles is a good way off. And that is just about the distance we are from the distressed area. He added, by way of advice: 'Please get a map of Japan and have it at hand. It will be of value when future earthquakes occur!'

A year later, on 6 July 1934, my father wrote: 'No, Mother, we did not feel the particular earthquakes you mention! Both Naples and the Atlantic are thousands of miles from here and you would have felt them long before we should have done!'

In fact, it was typhoons rather than earthquakes that created drama in my parents' lives during their first years in Japan. On 17 November 1932 my father wrote of a typhoon 'about which the most exaggerated reports seem to have reached England'. Sunday was a cold, cheerless day and Monday dawned even worse. Unceasing rain and a moderate wind continued throughout the day, so my parents wrapped themselves up in rugs and sat as closely over a charcoal brazier as the fumes would allow and tried to work. About teatime the wind began to increase in force. It was coming from the north, so they kept the wooden shutters on that side of the house closed all day. But about 6.30 p.m. they began to close the shutters on the other side of the house. They were in the middle of sliding the shutters along, when Furasawa-san called them to the bath-house. There they found that one of the doors, which was very thin and unsubstantial, had been blown off the groove along which it should slide. My father was leaning with his shoulder to force it against the wind into its groove, when their Japanese teacher, Yorimichi Imai, came racing through the rain into the kitchen. At the same moment my father broke a pane of glass by leaning in the wrong place and they decided that the gap must be barricaded. A dash to the outhouse produced the right piece of wood and for the next ten minutes they were hammering this into position and barricading it with the bath-lid, the ironing board and their Alpine walking sticks. At last the job was done, but at that moment Furasawa-san called them again, for the kitchen doors, equally fragile, were bending and the same process of barricading had to be undertaken. They then set about closing the shutters on the south side: downstairs was easy, but upstairs was more difficult. One of the shutters blew out of its groove and had to be retrieved from the garden; then another was caught by the wind and had also to be retrieved. They were obviously in the path of a strong typhoon and just had to hope that it would not be so powerful as to wreck the house. They decided that whatever happened food was necessary. The electric light had failed but Furasawa-san managed to prepare a meal by the light of one small candle. So they ate their supper, with the house creaking and the wind whistling through the roof upstairs, as though all the tiles were being hurled off. The typhoon was at its height from about 7.30 to 11.30 p.m. and made it impossible to go to bed upstairs. The noise was terrific and the rooms were shaking, so they brought their bedding downstairs. They did not undress, as they thought they might have to run out if the house were damaged, but by 1.30 a.m. it became clear that the worst of the storm was over.

About 7 a.m. they arose to see what damage had been done, but before they were dressed the carpenter who had built the house arrived and he called the necessary tradesmen to make repairs. The bath-house door had to be put back, two panes of glass had to be replaced and the bamboo fence round the garden had to be re-erected, as it had collapsed utterly. The roof also needed some attention, but of serious damage there was none.

After breakfast my father sallied forth with Yorimichi Imai to see what damage had been done in the town. A bus garage had collapsed and a three-storey Japanese inn had had its top floor wrecked, but for the most part it was only a matter of flattened fences and more or less decimated roofs, for the houses had protected each other. In spite of this, a frantic cable reached Bishop Heaslett from the missionary society, asking if my parents were injured and if Numazu church was burnt down!

A few days later my father met Captain Kennedy, the Reuters agent, who explained how this panic had started. At 10.00 p.m. on the evening of the storm, he had been rung from his office to be told that a report had come through that there were many casualties in Numazu and that 600 houses in the town had been burnt or flattened. He cabled this report to England, where it appeared in the papers. The following morning Captain Kennedy received a correction of the telephone message: 'It was feared that there were many casualties and that six hundred houses in a town near Numazu had been burnt or flattened.' That town was Suzukawa, a small town in a very exposed position, about two stations down the line.

On 23 March 1934 my father reported another typhoon. Tuesday had passed as usual, but with the temperature rather high and stuffy. It became so hot in the night that my parents woke up and found the wind was rising. Everything pointed to a typhoon and by Wednesday morning they had it in full blast, with blinding wind and rain. They had shut the upstairs shutters in the middle of the night, but in the morning they had to shut both sides of the house and both floors. The typhoon reached its height at lunchtime and then, just before they settled down to their meal, they had an earthquake. So the house not only rocked sideways with the force of the wind it also went up and down from the earth. Fortunately, it was a fairly mild shock and lasted only a few seconds.

The wind lessened about teatime, but in the evening it got up again and by 12.30 a.m. it was blowing great guns once more. The roof was rattling, the house was shaking and then they had another earthquake. It was nothing very much but, added to the wind and the darkness, it was the last straw. Again my parents decided to sleep on the ground floor. It was the first time they had done that since the typhoon of November 1932 and though this typhoon was not so bad it was quite as much as they wanted. Part of their fence gave way but that was their only damage. In the town no houses were down, but fences and even a stone wall were blown over and tiles from roofs were everywhere.

The one place seriously affected was Hakodate, the port up in the northern island of Hokkaido:

The town is, apparently, in a hollow into which the wind gets and within which it goes whirling round. In the middle of this great gale a fire started and with wooden houses there was, of course, no chance. Today's paper says that two-thirds of the town has been burnt, 1000 lives lost and 2000 people more missing. This is the third or fourth time that the town has been gutted in living memory. So you can see that, whatever else may be said about Japan, it is not the country which allows you to vegetate!

On 21 September 1934, after my parents' move to Tokyo, they experienced another typhoon:

Of typhoons we have had quite a packetful, though nothing to be compared to other districts, especially Osaka. Today's typhoon seems to have blown in from the China Sea over the island of Shikoku and to have hit the mainland fair and square just in the Kobe-Osaka area. What the extent of the damage down there is we don't yet know, but this evening's papers announce the blowing down of over a hundred schools. They are, of course, the first to go, because in nearly every case they are built of wood and have large windows. Once let the typhoon break a few windows and get into the building and it is as good as finished. One of the schools that is wrecked is the Poole Girls' School and reports say that ten girls have been killed and over a hundred teachers and pupils hurt. Another school is reported to have had 200 boys killed. In this school, apparently, when the structure seemed to be dangerous, the boys upstairs were told to go downstairs and then get out, but before they had time to get out the building caved in and numbers were trapped.

In Tokyo, by contrast, there was little damage beyond broken tiles and uprooted fences. The only damage that my parents suffered was the breaking of a wooden shutter, which crashed from upstairs into a tree in the garden, the collapse of two trees transplanted in April and not yet sufficiently rooted in their new positions, the breaking of the bamboo garden fence at one place and the tearing off from the main gates of the iron rings that held the wooden cross-beam:

So used is the Japanese nation to such happenings that the gardener was along by midday to see what would need doing. Tomorrow his men will be here, the trees will be put upright again, the fence repaired and the gate bolt put right and no one by the day after tomorrow will know that anything has been amiss!

6

Karuizawa

My parents took a house in Karuizawa for the summer. My father had duties in Tokyo over the weekend, so my mother and Matsuno-san set off in advance. They arrived to find rows of tradespeople on the doorstep, all vying for their custom. Some had presents for Matsuno-san, some offered her percentages on purchases and all were very insistent. But Matsuno-san had a way with tradespeople and very quickly chose the ones to be favoured, while others were sent off to telephone for their luggage from the station or to carry out various errands.

My father arrived at length, very glad to be in the cool air of Karuizawa, and reporting that the heat and humidity of summer had turned Tokyo into a vast Turkish bath, in which no exertion was needed to make one's clothes wring with perspiration.

Karuizawa, by contrast, was a mountain resort, situated on a plateau about five miles long and two miles wide. It was bounded on all sides by steep, knobbly hills and cut in two by the railway, which crossed it from east to west. The main street, where all the shops were, was in the northern half of the plateau. There were houses to either side of the street, but the majority of foreign visitors stayed in houses on the slopes of the hill that formed the northern boundary of the plateau. Those that were highest had fine views over the resort and the hills around, but the one that my parents had taken was lower down and surrounded by trees, for the whole hillside was thickly wooded.

Karuizawa was bustling with English-speaking, and especially American, visitors. The tourist shops were all eager for their custom and competed to come up with the most arresting slogans: 'Buy our gents' socks – strong as bulldog'; 'Come to our sale now – the early bird catches the warm' [*sic*]; 'Unique of service – happy present'. (This last apparently meant: 'Our shop will be of special service to you – we have many things suitable for presents'.)

The shops were hard to resist. There were four bookshops, whose displays were most tantalising for people living far from foreign bookshops. There were woodwork shops, with special Karuizawa designs and staining. There were shops selling fascinating Japanese prints, a superb china shop, tempting lacquer shops, and last, but by no means least in my mother's eyes, shops selling beautiful Japanese silks. For Karuizawa was a place which positively invited one to spend money and where economy was very, very hard.

With so many visitors in Karuizawa, coming from all parts of Japan, the few weeks of the summer season were crowded with social activity. There were lunch parties and dinner parties, tea parties and garden parties. There were also *sukiyaki* parties, at which guests arranged themselves round large charcoal braziers. Deep frying pans were placed on the hot charcoal and into the frying pans was put meat, chicken, mushrooms, bean-curd, onions and noodles, all ingredients that could cook quickly in a mixture of soy sauce, *sake* and sugar. Guests helped themselves with their chopsticks to anything in the pan that took their fancy and ate it, dipped in whipped-up egg, with the rice. As the supply of food lessened, more was put into the frying pan, until the entire company was so replete that they could face nothing more.

There was a golf course and a tennis club, and several of the houses had tennis courts, so invitations began to arrive for tea and tennis parties. My parents were fortunate to have been lent tennis racquets for the summer, for they had not thought to bring tennis racquets to Japan. But there was also first-class tennis to be watched, for the Karuizawa tournament attracted the best Japanese players as well as many foreigners and several of the Japanese Davis Cup team were taking part.

Bridge and chess were both popular, so dinners might be followed by rounds of auction bridge, while rainy afternoons might be spent in hard-fought games of chess. My father signed up for a chess tournament, a double tournament, in fact, being both knock-out and round-robin. He had not played chess for some time, but was learning to avoid foolish mistakes, while the chairman of the chess club showed him 'a very strong queen's pawn opening', so his game began to improve.

Concerts were held every week during the season. One particularly grand concert was given by professional musicians in aid of the local hospital. The hospital belonged to the Karuizawa community and so there was a crowded hall. The concert was very fine and given by only five people. First, there was the Princess of Leuchtenberg Beauharnais, who played twice herself and also accompanied the singers. Of these there were two, a very fat baritone with a Teutonic head and a superb voice, and a tenor with not nearly so impressive an appearance but a very dramatic style of singing. The other two performers were a violinist and a cellist, who played unaccompanied. This concert was one of the 'swell' performances of the Karuizawa season and everyone turned out in their best clothes. Flowers in abundance decorated the platform and bouquets of enormous size were given to all the performers, to the men as well as to the Princess.

Although the Princess and her husband had such grand-sounding titles, they were in fact a tragic pair. She was a direct descendent of the Empress Josephine and so was a member of the old Russian nobility. They had had to flee the country at the time of the Revolution and now had no nationality and no passports, so they were only allowed anywhere on sufferance. It was due to their great skill as musicians that they were allowed to stay on in Tokyo.

They were not the first people of Russian background whom my parents had met since coming to Japan. Within a few days of their arrival, they had paid a visit on Mr Mercer, the chaplain at the English church in Tokyo. Staying at the house was 'a most amusing person', a Russian monk from the great monastery of Mount Athos. He was ostensibly travelling round the world to collect money for a branch house in Korea, but Mr Mercer suspected that he was in reality an agent of the White Russians. He had only become a monk since the War, having been in the Tsarist diplomatic service. Apparently he had been in Japan many years before, in the role of a military attaché, and had received some minor decoration, which was afterwards lost in the Revolution. In order to put himself in favour with the Japanese, who were very nervous about Russians, he had asked for a replica of this decoration to be given him. So, in the afternoon, along came Viscount Matsudaira, 'one of the real nibs of Japan', to hand the decoration over. As my father commented: 'It is not every day that one has the chance of seeing a Japanese nobleman presenting a Russian monk with a decoration!'

Karuizawa was famous for its mountain scenery and for the opportunities it provided for walking. There were walks in all directions and so many side routes and cross paths that even those who had been coming to Karuizawa for years kept discovering new possibilities. Many excursions afforded views of Mount Asama, an active volcano to the west of Karuizawa. My father hastened to assure his parents that it was not dangerous at all: 'The only visible or audible signs of it are clouds of smoke in the sky when it has given a puff, ashy dust which descends occasionally on tables and chairs on the veranda, and a noise like rolling thunder. The latter is difficult to pick out, because we have thunder very frequently in the evenings.'

My parents joined a party setting off to climb Mount Asama. They began by taking a train to a place called Komoro, about fifty minutes west along the line. From here they planned to take a car, but at first the taxi people were very doubtful. They thought that the road was probably washed away, telephoned one or two people to find out, and generally hummed and hawed. At last, after about an hour's delay, the expedition started out along a road that was certainly bad. Great potholes and ruts, mud and stones, sharp bends and narrow stretches made the going exciting, bumpy and difficult. However, the driver succeeded in getting them over the low ground and bringing them very near to the mountain, so they were duly grateful and said he might return, when, just short of their destination, he stuck firmly in the mud and despite three tries failed to get through.

The place where they got out was in a very lovely wood and so they were glad to walk and have a chance to enjoy it. After about an hour they reached the first mountain hut and stopped for lunch. They were just finishing when the rain came down in torrents, so instead of getting away by 1.45 p.m. they could not leave till 2.30 p.m. This was a bit late for climbing to the top of the mountain and descending the other side to Karuizawa by nightfall, but they thought that if all went well they could just do it. So they set off at a good pace to the next hut and reached there about 4.00 p.m.

The rain had begun to spatter a little, but while they were drinking tea it poured down in a deluge, so again they were held up. That put an end to all chance of climbing to the top and getting home that night, so they held a consultation. Should they try and go back the way they had come or stay the night and go on the next morning? A little above their hut was a police hut with a telephone, so when the rain lessened they all agreed to send a message back to Karuizawa and stay for the night. The police were very good about it: not only did the one on the mountain phone down, but a policeman in Karuizawa called round at their three houses to report that the climbers were quite safe but held up by rain. The hut was able to give them rice and soup to supplement their own provisions and they had a good meal. Mattresses and blankets were then brought out, but alack! these were not so innocent as they seemed and soon they were all being bitten. But there was nothing to be done and they slept for two or three hours at least.

At 2.00 a.m. they got up, had some more rice and soup for breakfast, and at 3.00 a.m. they started for the summit with a full moon shining to light the way. The place from which they started was an extinct crater. On either side were great rocky precipices and crags stretching up perhaps a thousand feet and looking most eerie in the moonlight. Gradually the path wound out of the old crater, crossed a fairly level piece of ground, climbed above the tree line and finally zig-zagged up the final slope through lava slag and ash to the edge of the active crater. This last part of the walk was very beautiful, as the sun was beginning to rise and the colours in the sky kept changing.

When they came to the summit they were faced with an awe-inspiring sight. The crater must have been 100 or 200 yards in diameter, was almost perfectly circular and in most places absolutely sheer. They could not see far across or down, because all the time a dense mass of sulphur steam, like a thick mist, was rising, but far below they could hear the lava boiling, as if in an enormous cauldron. This was a favourite place for suicides and seven men had jumped in only three weeks before. After walking half way round the edge, the party struck the path leading down in the Karuizawa direction. The descent was easy, as they ran and scrambled through the ash at a great pace.

Another expedition brought their party zig-zagging up a wooded slope to a point from where there was a wide view over the plain towards Karuizawa, with its surrounding hills dominated by Mount Asama. It was a perfect view of Mount Asama, for they could see its whole stretch, but the one thing my father really wanted was to see it 'blow off', as that would show the mountain at its most impressive. However, nothing was to be expected that day. Only a thin smoke issued from the volcano and their hope of seeing anything really awe-inspiring passed.

Three years later, a friend, Stanley Woodward, described just such an awe-inspiring sight as my father had been hoping to see. He was with a party setting out on a walking expedition to Mount Asama. They were approaching the hut on the lower slopes of the mountain, when the volcano 'blew off' with the loudest report they had experienced that season. It was nine o'clock in the morning, the weather was beautifully clear and so they had an excellent view of the whole performance. A black column of smoke and ash roared thousands of feet into the air over their heads and clouded them from the sun. They were near enough to see great rocks like houses go plunging down the higher slopes, raising a trail of dust and ash behind them. The ash shot up so high in the air that it passed over them before any fell and they had no shower on them. Their walk back through the woods was not pleasant, however, as they had to make their way through the dust and ash from the mountain.

On their return they heard how loudly the clap of the explosion had been heard in Karuizawa, how a spectacular cone of black smoke had risen high into the sky and how three showers of ash and dust and cinders had fallen on the resort during the course of the day.

A party set off on a gentler expedition in cars to see the lava beds on the northern slopes of Mount Asama. The lava beds were the result of a great eruption of Asama in 1780. The molten lava had come pouring down the northern slopes, overwhelming one or two villages and stretching for two miles or so from the mountain. In time the lava solidified, but was broken by pressure underneath, so what remained was a solid wall, about forty feet high and many feet wide, of rock-like material, broken into all sorts of strange and fantastic shapes. On the skyline they picked out 'Queen Victoria', a 'lion', a 'monk' and several other figures. One or two of the party clambered over the lava and managed to reach 'Queen Victoria'. When they returned the whole party had lunch under trees overlooking the lava beds. It was a desolate scene and yet in many places vegetation was growing through the lava. Some lava eruptions of much earlier date were quite grown over and so it seemed likely that in time the 1780 ones would also be covered in green.

My parents set off for a three-day trip. They started by train, changed to another train, proceeded by bus and completed their journey by cable car up to Lake Haruna. The inn at which they were staying was by the lake and from their window they looked straight across to the mountain opposite, known as Haruna Fuji for its resemblance to the sacred mountain of Japan.

They were fortunate in the night they were staying at Haruna, for it was the time of the *O Bon* festival, when the dead were thought to revisit their former haunts on earth for three nights. The cemeteries were decorated, candles were lit in the stone lanterns and incense was burned to welcome them back, while offerings of food were set out on small stands to sustain them. On this last day of the festival, a beautiful ceremony took place. From dusk onward, little square boxes of wood and coloured paper, inscribed with the names of the departed, were sent floating across the lake, each little box-boat being lit with candles. While the hundreds of little boats drifted across the lake, there was dancing on the shore and fireworks in front of Haruna Fuji.

The following morning my parents left Haruna, crossed a pass which overlooked the lake and caught a bus to Kusatsu, their destination for the night. It was a lovely drive through one of the most beautiful gorges they had seen. Again and again the road crossed the river and each time they caught a glimpse of the steep slopes covered with bushes and the blue water tumbling over the rocks and shingle on the riverbed.

Kusatsu was a famous hot-spring resort with sulphur springs bubbling up everywhere and clouds of steam rising even from the gutters. The water was reputed to have curative properties and many people suffering from skin complaints came to visit the baths. The sulphur was thought of as a cure for leprosy and so, from time immemorial, there had been a leper colony in Kusatsu, which had cast something of a blight over the town. In the past the lepers were allowed to wander freely in the town, but in more recent years they had been confined to what was known as the lower village. This was divided from the rest of the town by two great posts on the roadside, marking the limits of the leper colony.

In the leper village, Miss Cornwall Legh, an Englishwoman working in the American Mission, had set up St Barnabas' Mission to the Lepers a good many years before. Now there were homes of all kinds, schools, a dispensary and a most lovely church. The effect on the life of the lepers could be surmised from the fact that when the Mission started there were six or seven suicides a week. People who found they had the disease tended to draw every penny they possessed, blow it all in a burst of riotous living and then commit suicide. Now there were not more than two or three suicides a year.

My father took a service for the lepers and found it a moving experience to do so. Afterwards my parents looked over the village and visited houses and schools. They were impressed by the naturalness of the village, for it was a real village with its own life. There were shops kept by lepers, which were patronised by the leper community. Leper families lived in cottages, and those who had the disease only mildly gave treatment in the dispensary to those who were far advanced. My parents were surprised to learn that leprosy was not nearly so contagious as was commonly supposed in the West. It seemed that it was only through such things as open cuts that leprosy could get into the blood and there were a number of wives living in cottages, whose husbands had leprosy, but who were themselves quite immune. In fact, it seemed that it was positively difficult to develop the disease unless there was a hereditary tendency in the family.

On the way back to their hotel, my parents stopped at the public bath in the centre of the town and watched the amusing ceremony that took place four times a day. At this bath the water was specially hot and probably no foreigner could have got in. Even the Japanese, whose baths were usually very hot, found it difficult. The bath consisted of a series of troughs parallel to each other, with just enough floor space for people to stand in a line facing each trough. In hot-spring baths no distinction was made between men and women and everybody went in the water naked together. The difference of sex was taken for granted and nobody took any notice of the matter.

At the beginning of the ceremony people lined up in rows in front of each trough, wrapped round with a towel and nothing else. Each person took a plank, put one end in the water and held the other. Then, rhythmically, everyone working together, they turned the planks, first on to one edge and then on to the other. The water was churned up and cooled by it and the bathers got heated and more ready to go in. This rhythmic working of the planks went on for about ten minutes and then the bath attendant clapped two pieces of wood as a signal for people to get in. Gradually they lowered themselves into the water until only their heads were showing. They stayed like that for three minutes. At the end of each minute the attendant intoned something, like a Buddhist priest, and all the bathers made a response. My father imagined what the words might be: 'Attendant: "One minute has passed and only two minutes more rema-a-ain." Bathers: "Thank heavens for tha-a-at."' Anything more like Dante's Inferno my parents found it hard to imagine on earth!

On their return to Karuizawa, they found the pace of life was slowing down, for the holiday season was coming to an end. Schoolteachers had already gone, others were drifting away, and within a week or two the place would be nearly empty. So it was time to pack up and return to Numazu. They had seen beautiful places, met old friends and made new ones, and felt that, wherever they went in Japan, they would always find someone they knew. But now they were ready to return, to be among their own things again and especially to have their own books around them, for their reading matter was running low.

They were all the more ready to depart as there had been a good deal of rain during these last days in Karuizawa. The two snags about Karuizawa were always thunder and rain. Both were attracted by the hills around and scarcely a day passed without at least a mild thunderstorm. The normal experience was to wake up to a lovely day and have fine weather till about three o'clock. Then it would begin to get dull, and about four or five the thunder would start. By seven it was frequently pouring. But in recent days the rain had scarcely stopped, so they felt very ready to leave the hills and return to the warmer plains.

In the summer of 1936 there were great celebrations in Karuizawa to mark the jubilee of its foundation as a summer resort. In the summer of 1886, Archdeacon Shaw was travelling through the hills with his family in search of a cool place to stay. On 8 August they arrived in Karuizawa, liked it, and stayed for the rest of the summer. Others followed their example and Karuizawa's popularity as a mountain resort was established.

Fifty years to the day later, on Saturday 8 August 1936, the jubilee celebrations were held and were very splendid, although somewhat marred by thunder showers. In the morning there were speeches from many notables, including Prince Asaka and a former Mayor of Tokyo and a number of foreigners. During the bright intervals of the afternoon there was an exhibition display of tennis by Japanese Davis Cup players. In the evening there was a grand dinner, followed by a lantern procession and fireworks. Crowds of people came for the festivities, three special commemorative postcards were issued, and Archdeacon Shaw's memorial stone was decorated in his honour as founder of the resort.

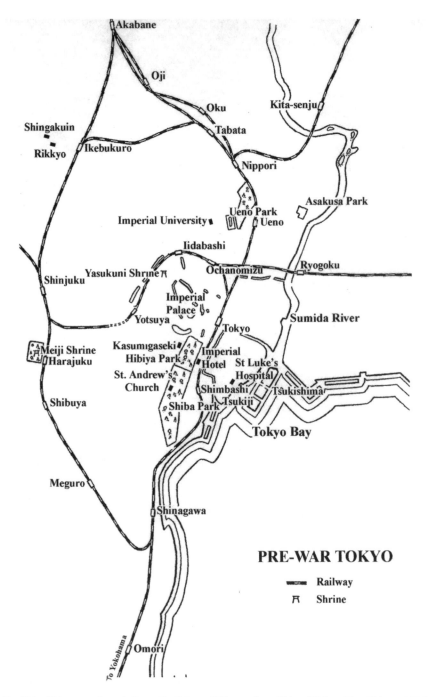

Pre-War Tokyo – adapted from G Caiger, *Tell me about Tokyo* (Hokuseido, Tokyo, 1939)

7

In Tokyo and Yokohama

Twice a month my father caught the train from Numazu to Tokyo to take the services for the English-speaking congregation at St Andrew's Church in Shiba. This was a congregation whose history went back to the very early days of nineteenth-century foreign settlement in Japan. For over 200 years before that, Japan was a closed country and Christianity was banned as an illegal religion. When my father accompanied Bishop Heaslett to a clergy conference, shortly after his arrival in Japan, he was shown one of the antiquities belonging to the house – a seventeenth-century anti-Christian noticeboard, threatening anyone who professed Christianity with death.

Following the arrival of Commodore Perry with his 'black ships' in 1853, Japan was constrained to open its ports to American vessels and then to vessels of other western powers. In 1858 these powers obtained by treaty the right for their nationals to exercise their religion and to build churches in Japan. In 1873 the Edict condemning Christianity as an 'evil sect' was removed from the public noticeboards, and from that time it was accepted that Japanese as well as foreigners could practise Christianity without fear of persecution.

In that year of 1873 the first two Anglican missionaries, the Revd (later Archdeacon) AC Shaw and the Revd WB Wright, arrived in Tokyo and settled in a Buddhist temple named Yosenji in Shiba. Here they cultivated friendly relations with the Buddhist priests and settled down to study Japanese. They began to hold regular services for the English community in a large room in the temple, but this room soon proved inadequate and plans were put forward for the building of a church. The first English service took place in St Andrew's Church in 1879 and so the connection of the English congregation with the church and the site on the hill in Shiba began.

This brick church served the English congregation for fifteen years but in 1894 an earthquake damaged the building so badly that it had to be demolished. Almost immediately work was begun on a new church, which was erected within a few months. This building, 'larger than, but not nearly so sightly as its predecessor',[3] was built of wood as a temporary church and was intended to last for fifteen years. However, this 'temporary' church, hastily built after one big earthquake, survived the shock of the far worse disaster of 1923, for Shiba was one of the areas of Tokyo that escaped the worst of the destruction. So it was this 'temporary' church that was still in use when my parents arrived in Japan in 1932 and which continued to be used by the English community until the outbreak of war.

For the previous five years, the Revd FE Mercer had served as chaplain at St Andrew's Church and he and his wife had lived in a house in the compound. Now his term of service expired and he and his wife returned to England. It was then that Bishop Heaslett asked my father to take the services on two Sundays each month and to arrange for other clergy to take the services on the alternate Sundays. So began the pattern by which my father went up to Tokyo on two weekends each month and my mother accompanied him on at least one of those weekends.

This was a congenial arrangement. There were, after all, no other English people in Numazu and my parents were spending almost all their time in studying a difficult language. As my father said, 'It is going to be a long time before one is any real use in this land of involved sentences and complicated thought forms!' So he was glad to be given responsibility for a congregation where a lack of Japanese was no barrier.

The people who attended St Andrew's formed an interesting group. For the most part they were professional people and many had a wide experience of working and travelling in other countries. And although they were all English speaking, they were not all members of the British Commonwealth, but included, at one time or another, citizens of Japan, America, Holland, Denmark and former citizens of Russia.

Congregations on a normal Sunday were not large – perhaps a dozen for the early service and forty for the main service – for on Sundays many English did as the Japanese did and went out for picnics or games, while missionaries usually attended Japanese services. For this reason it was proposed that St Andrew's Church should amalgamate with Holy Trinity Church, which was the American Episcopal church. This would make for one large congregation rather than two small ones. With

---

[3] S Bickersteth, *Life and Letters of Edward Bickersteth Bishop of South Tokyo* (London, 1905), p. 302.

business competition from Japanese firms, the English-speaking population in Tokyo was diminishing, so it seemed the sensible thing to do.

Yet there were difficulties. Holy Trinity undoubtedly had a more solid building, a finer organ and superior amenities, yet the congregation of St Andrew's owned the property and site in Shiba in perpetuity, while the American congregation was not legal owner of Holy Trinity. Furthermore the association of St Andrew's Church with the English community in Tokyo went back nearly forty years and people were reluctant to give up its traditions. It was here that services had been held at times of national mourning or rejoicing, here that members of the royal family had attended services on visits to Japan and here that members of the English community had come together for weddings, christenings and funerals. Then diplomatic questions arose: would the British or American Ambassador take precedence in a combined church? So the question of amalgamation remained unresolved and each congregation continued in its own church until the outbreak of war.

The first special service for which my father was responsible was the Armistice Commemoration Service, held on the Sunday before Armistice Day, in 1932. For this service there was a grand turnout: the British Ambassador and the Canadian Minister, who read the lessons, all the officials from the British Embassy and the Canadian Legation, including the Army, Navy and Air Force attachés, and a large section of British Tokyo residents. My father wrote out his sermon, which was mainly about peace, in order to have the language and ideas quite clear and in order to avoid pitfalls in talking on a somewhat delicate subject before such a distinguished assembly.

At this time the chairmanship of the Church Council was held in alternate years by the British Ambassador and the Minister of the Canadian Legation. My parents called at the Embassy to leave their visiting cards and were distinctly impressed:

The Embassy is a magnificent series of buildings built on one compound. It consists of houses for the Ambassador and the attachés and other officials, grouped round a central building where the offices are. The buildings are in the classical style, with the Royal Arms over the portico of the main building. They are built of vivid stone that almost shines in the sun and they have an appearance of real distinction. We felt distinctly proud of being British!

The Canadian Legation was newly established and the Minister was the first to hold that position. On the day of the Armistice Day service, my parents were invited to the Legation for tea and found it to be an agreeable, though not large, building. The following year, however, the Legation moved to new and grander premises, with two handsome buildings, the Chancellery on one side and the Minister's house on the other. But it was at the earlier, more modest, Legation that my parents spent their first Christmas in Tokyo.

It was not only leading members of the international community who were prominent in the church life of Tokyo: there were also leading members of Japanese society. Among these were two families with whom my parents already had a connection before they set out for Japan. These were the Sekiyas and the Watanabes. Mr Sekiya was Vice-Chamberlain of the Imperial Household and his wife was an influential and strong-minded woman leader in the *Nippon Sei Ko Kai* (the Episcopal church in Japan). It was Paul, the eldest of their four sons, whom my parents already knew well. He was studying at theological college in Cambridge and stayed with my parents on a number of occasions while my father was a curate at the parish church in Wimbledon. Paul was due to return to Japan at the end of the year and would be ordained in the following year. While in Wimbledon my parents also came to know one of the two sons of Viscount and Viscountess Watanabe, for he was staying as a paying guest at the vicarage and came to see them a good deal, so that they became great friends.

My parents were invited to dinner at the Sekiyas' house, a most attractive post-quake house, half-foreign and half-Japanese in style, situated in an avenue set aside for the residences of ministers of the Imperial Household. They were ushered into a very up-to-date drawing room and soon Mr and Mrs Sekiya came in, both wearing Japanese dress. It was the first time they had met Mr Sekiya and they were both charmed by him. They imagined him to be typical of the higher-class of Japanese, very kind and courtly, speaking English well and displaying all the old Japanese courtesy and charm. Viscount and Viscountess Watanabe and their two sons were also guests at dinner. It was the first time that my parents had met the Viscount, for he, like Mr Sekiya, had been occupied with official duties during the summer and so neither had been in Karuizawa with their families.

The evening was a delight:

Our dinner was most aristocratic and as becomes an aristocratic dinner it was a dream! The cooking – all foreign – would have delighted a Parisian chef and when at the end we had iced melon brought straight back from California by the returning Ambassador from the States we felt indeed that our cup of gastronomic happiness was full! But, as if that were not enough, Mrs Sekiya sent to us at the hotel next day a large basket of fruit including the unheard-of luxury at this time of year – oranges. She really is a gem of a woman!

My father wrote of Mr Sekiya:

He is not a confessed Christian. His position as Vice-Chamberlain of the Imperial Household would make an open profession very difficult, especially as the Emperor is regarded in a religious light, and so, although he fully approves his family's allegiance and uses his influence to help the Church, he 'follows secretly'.

This was not enough to keep him out of trouble, however, and later in that autumn of 1932 both he and his chief, the Minister of the Imperial Household, had to resign:

There was some bother, apparently, though no one seems to know what happened, but the real reason appears to be that Dr Ikki and Mr Sekiya are too liberal, too friendly with foreigners, and that does not fit in with the prevailing mood. The country is full of an excessive nationalism, partly fostered as a counter-move to 'dangerous thought' and partly the result of the Manchuria business. Japan finds herself isolated from world opinion and naturally there is a strong nationalist reaction. That does not mean that the Japanese are treating foreigners badly. There is no trace of anything but friendliness and courtesy to individuals, even if they are Chinese, but those in authority want the Emperor's advisers to be hundred per cent pro-Japanese, without any admixture of foreign sympathies.

On their visits to Tokyo, my parents usually stayed in the Sanno Hotel. This was conveniently situated for St Andrew's Church, being just a ten-minute tram ride away. It was also very comfortable, for it was brand new with all the latest amenities. The bedrooms were fitted up in western style and most had their own bathrooms; on the ground floor was a good-sized dining room, a tea-room and a lounge; while in the basement was one of the finest skating rinks in Tokyo.

Although the hotel had its own dining room, my parents sometimes preferred to go out to a restaurant. On their first visit they chose the Olympic restaurant, where all the food was served in foreign style. The place was crowded with Japanese, for a tremendous change was taking place in Japanese eating habits. In the old days, it was considered by Japanese to be rather improper to eat in public: eating was something to be got over quickly and unostentatiously. Now crowds of Japanese were flocking to foreign restaurants and eating foreign meals regularly. There was one thing, however, that many Japanese had yet to learn about foreign food and that is that it is far more sustaining than Japanese food. When they ate Japanese food, with quantities of rice, they felt 'blown out' at the end of the meal, though that feeling quickly passed, for rice digests easily. But they did not feel satisfied unless they had the 'blown out' feeling and so, when they ate foreign food, they ate tremendous amounts, not realising the difference in nutriment between the two kinds of food.

So, at the Olympic, every helping was served on a dish, as no plate could hold a single portion. Two people at an adjacent table had a whole lobster each with piles of accompaniments, while half chickens and haunches of beef were taken to people at other tables. My mother received most of a salmon and my father about five slices of pork. As my father commented: 'I began to understand what those really hearty meals of our eighteenth-century ancestors must have been like!'

My parents were sitting at a table near the telephone and during lunch someone, English apparently, called up the manager and gave an order for sausage rolls. The manager was considerably puzzled as to what sausage rolls were, until he had a sudden inspiration: 'Ah, I see! It is the cream horn with sausage pushed in but without the cream!' After taking the order, he noticed my parents sitting close by and approached them as culinary experts. In a magnificent voice he enquired, 'Do you know the sausage roll?' to which they meekly replied that they did. My father proceeded to give a demonstration of the shape by rolling up the menu and my mother explained the pastry, so they hoped the result would be satisfactory.

It was not only foreign restaurants that were attractive to the Japanese. Certain entertainments also had a great appeal. Thus, a visit by Hagenbecks Circus caused much excitement:

It is the first time such a grand affair has come to Japan and the people of Tokyo are thrilled. There are small circuses here, but they

90

are not very good and the animals are miserably looked after. It is one of the weaknesses of this nation – they have almost no idea how to treat animals and the way they handle horses is incredible – even to a townsman like me, whose knowledge of animals is nil.

If western entertainments, such as the circus, attracted the Japanese, so equally westerners were fascinated by traditional Japanese theatre. My parents attended a performance at the *Kabuki-za* theatre in Tokyo. The first play presented was historical, the story of a quarrel between two retainers of the great military commander, Hideyoshi. The second was a posture play, which depended for its effect on the posturing of the actors to the accompaniment of music. The third was a classical play, in which a widow represses her tears and persuades her two sons to accompany their lord, the great commander Yoshitsune, to the battle front. The fourth play had an altogether more topical relevance, for it was presented in honour of Tokyo, which had just enlarged its boundaries and now declared itself 'the second greatest city of the world'. The whole evening was fascinating:

> The production is superb, the costumes and lighting blending exquisitely, so that the scene seems like a Japanese print come to life. The acting is wonderful, especially when one remembers that all the actors are men, and the grace of their movements and the power of expressing emotions is absolutely perfect.

On the morning of 9 November 1932, my parents rose early and put on their finest clothes, which meant for my father a frock coat and top hat. Their appearance at Numazu station at 7.15 a.m. caused a sensation and the stationmaster enquired if they were on their way to an Imperial Garden Party: nothing less could account for such splendour! On this occasion, however, their destination was not Tokyo but Yokohama, for this was the day of Stanley Woodward's wedding and his bride, Gwen, had just arrived in Yokohama, having sailed from England via Canada. This wedding had a special significance for my parents, for Stanley, like my father, was to become a lecturer at the theological college in Tokyo. This meant not only that my father and Stanley would be colleagues, but that the two families would be close neighbours in the college compound.

Stanley had been teaching temporarily at the college while a regular member of the faculty was on furlough. Now he had returned, and Stanley and Gwen were to start their married life in Fukuoka in Kyushu before Stanley took up a regular appointment in due course. Their situation was, therefore, in some ways similar to that of my parents, for they too were setting up their first Japanese home in a place where westerners were few and far between. In other ways, however, there was a great difference, for Stanley was second generation in Japan. His father had been a missionary in Japan for almost twenty years before the Great War and so Stanley had childhood memories both of the country and of the language.

Like my parents, Stanley and Gwen moved into the house of missionaries who were away on furlough and like my parents they inherited the maid who was already working in the house. The maid was, however, completely mystified by their ways. She had only been with their predecessors, Canon and Mrs Hutchinson, for about six months and before that she had never met any foreigners at all. So she naturally thought that all foreigners lived exactly as the Hutchinsons did. The fact that Stanley and Gwen did not live exactly as the Hutchinsons did threw her completely off her bearings and so she kept coming to ask about everything. To add to the confusion Stanley and Gwen had a much greater variety of implements and especially cutlery and bowls than the Hutchinsons had, so she was mystified as to fish implements, ordinary long and short implements, servers, carvers, fruit knives, soup bowls, soup plates, finger bowls, etc. However, she was entering into the situation with great zest and seemed to think that some of Stanley and Gwen's possessions had points of advantage over the Hutchinsons'. Particularly she was pleased that they had single beds instead of a double bed and she rolled on the bedroom floor to demonstrate to Gwen how difficult it had been to clean under the Hutchinsons' double bed.

Gwen spoke no Japanese before coming to Japan, but Stanley reported that she was making excellent progress:

> She is very anxious not to give me any domestic translating to do, so I mostly leave her to wrestle with the maid and only appear when quite necessary. The two of them are coming to a wonderful understanding of each other, achieved with a minimum of words. Gwen has just ordered the meals for tomorrow and given her full instructions about wash-day without appealing to me once. I've heard a considerable amount of laughter in the process though.

By the summer of 1933 my mother was expecting a baby and found herself in the highest fashion in the land. The Empress herself was expecting a baby and the whole nation was hoping for a son and heir. One veteran missionary asserted that it would be a son, whatever happened. He expressed the opinion that the daughters of noble families who became ladies in waiting at the Palace formed an unofficial harem and that probably several of them would have babies about the same time as the Empress, so as to make sure of a son. Another chipped in with a description of the death and funeral of the last Emperor's mother, who was a concubine and not the Empress, who had died previously: 'It was very funny reading the papers and seeing how they all avoided referring to her as the Emperor's mother. You see, they couldn't very well say that she was his mother. We had buried his "mother", the Empress, with great pomp years before!'

'But,' chimed in other voices, 'if that is the case, why does the Emperor already have four daughters?' Perhaps times had changed, perhaps the earlier customs were distasteful to the present Emperor, for, when the birth of the Crown Prince was announced, my father reported that the published news showed pretty clearly that this was indeed the Empress's child: 'In fact, it seems to be the first case of a legitimate Crown Prince since the feudal period!

> The country is, of course, wild with excitement. After so many disappointments the birth of an heir to the throne would in any case have been a cause of great jubilation; but in the circumstances of today, when Japan has been left in an isolated position internationally, when Communism and various social problems have been prominent internally, the birth of a son is almost like a special act of Heaven's favour. It has given new hope to a people getting perhaps a little dispirited and will certainly react on national life in many ways.

The scenes in Tokyo were tremendous. Crowds of people flocked to the Imperial Palace to bow in reverence before the main gateways and to shout '*banzai!*' Torchlight processions made their way to the Palace in the evening, while early in the morning continuous cheering and singing echoed from the barracks nearby. All over Japan schoolchildren paraded before the shrines to offer reverence to the new Crown Prince. On the official Naming Day, Tokyo was decorated with flags, bunting and Chinese lanterns, while in the evening searchlights played across the city, aeroplanes with illuminated wings circled overhead and fireworks soared up from the palace grounds.

An interesting sidelight on Japanese thinking was revealed by this event:

The Emperor's younger brothers, Prince Chichibu and Prince Takamatsu, have been married for several years, but neither has any children. For them to have a son before the Emperor would be very discourteous, almost disloyal. As it is not yet possible to choose the sex of your infant, there is only one thing to do and that is not have any children until the Emperor has a son, and that is what has happened!

The Empress gave birth on 23 December, while my mother was not expecting to give birth until 25 January, a full month later. My parents were once again invited to spend Christmas at the Canadian Legation, now in its splendid new buildings, but they declined the invitation, feeling that it might prove unwise for my mother to undertake such a visit so close to her confinement. Instead a friend, Emily Foss, came to stay for two weeks over the Christmas period. Emily was teaching at the Nihon Women's University in Tokyo, but sometimes came to visit my parents for a change of scene and a breath of sea air. So while my father was in Tokyo, taking part in the Christmas services, my mother and Emily were enjoying a peaceful time in Numazu and preparing a Christmas celebration ready for his return.

Plans for January had been carefully made. In Karuizawa my parents had met Miss Henty, who ran a settlement near St Luke's Hospital, where my mother was due to give birth. She had kindly suggested that my mother could stay at the settlement for as long as she liked before she went into hospital. My father went out to visit the settlement in Tsukishima and was pleased with all he saw:

> Tsukishima means 'moon island' and is a part of Tokyo that is cut off from the mainland by a river that forks and goes into the sea in two directions. Being near the sea it is wonderfully fresh and cool and its south windows look straight out over waste ground to Tokyo Bay. It will be a lovely place for Ethelreda in January.

So all was settled. My father was to be in Kobe for a clergy retreat for the first few days of January, while my mother and Emily would stay in Numazu. On 5 January my father was to return home and on 6 January all three would go up to Tokyo and my father would take my mother on to Tsukishima, where she would stay until it was time to go into hospital.

All started as planned. My father returned from his retreat and found my mother well and with her bags packed, ready to go. But at about 4.20 a.m. my mother woke my father to say that the first symptom had come. My father set off on his bicycle to fetch a doctor: 'I chose the clever young doctor who is a member of the church here and who has recently become a father himself.' He made a preliminary examination and then called in a second doctor, who specialised in that field. This was part of the medical custom of Japan, where GPs were unknown and every doctor was more or less of a specialist. The second doctor arrived and made an examination about 6.30 am. The possibility was raised of catching an early-morning express to Tokyo, but he was not very keen on the idea, 'not unnaturally, I think, because the inevitable motion of a three-hour journey might have produced a parallel to the "born on the Flying Scotsman" incidents of which reports sometimes appear in the papers.'

So, after discussion about going to Tokyo and then about going to the doctor's private hospital (a possibility that my mother disliked), they agreed she should stay in Numazu. No sooner had they reached this decision than a telegram arrived from Dr Bowles at St Luke's, urging them to come to Tokyo. The midwife and the nurse were strongly against it. Things had gone too far, they said, pains were coming every twenty minutes and a long journey to Tokyo was most unwise. So a decision was made to stay and a telegram sent to that effect. But as time went on it became clear that talk of twenty-minute pains was all nonsense. The more time passed the more desirable St Luke's appeared, so a final conference took place, in which the objections of the Japanese were worn down, and at last it was agreed they should set out for Tokyo. The midwife kindly insisted on accompanying them, (even though train travel made her sick!), and they reached the station at 2.15 p.m. just as the Fuji express came in.

Providentially the American Ambassador and his wife were on board. They had a private compartment, which they kindly gave up, so that my mother was able to lie at full length. The first part of the journey was bearable, even though every second seemed a minute and the stations seemed never to come. But the second half of the journey turned into a nightmare, and when at last they arrived at St Luke's, and my father and Emily handed my mother into the safe keeping of Dr Bowles, they both heaved huge sighs of relief. They had taken a great chance and they had won.

At 7.15 p.m. a nurse came to congratulate my father on the birth of a strong, healthy baby boy. My mother was sleeping, for she was given

8

The Shadows Lengthen

It was on 15 May 1932 that a group of young officers from the army and navy assassinated Prime Minister Inukai, let off bombs at banks, party offices and police headquarters, and precipitated the constitutional crisis that led to the formation of a non-party, military-dominated government under Admiral Saito.

A year later the trials began. All the proceedings were public, the newspapers printed pages of coverage every day and the Japanese people followed the unfolding story with fascination. The prisoners were allowed full freedom of speech, the court was filled with sympathetic spectators, letters (many written in blood) appealed for clemency, while the procurator dwelt on the patriotism of the accused. In this heady atmosphere the young officers proclaimed their ideas of revolution: to overthrow financiers and politicians who acted against the spirit of the Empire; to bring about direct Imperial rule and harmony between ruler and ruled; to spread the Imperial Way through Asia and then the world. Blood must be shed in the cause of national reformation.

If these proceedings fascinated the Japanese, to my father they appeared preposterous:

For the last three months we have had in the papers accounts of proceedings that to a westerner seem fit to belong only to Alice's Wonderland or to the Japan of the *Mikado*. The defendants have made fiery speeches, denounced the political and educational and social systems of the country, and generally called for a radical alteration in everything. Some have jeered at the judge, who, as a result, went humbly to the cell of the chief defendant and asked how he could conduct the case better(!) and generally they have acted in a way which in England would have a) caused their evidence to be put out of court on the ground of complete irrelevance and

b) landed them in for extra punishment for contempt of court. No doubt they went round murdering people from the highest motives of patriotism and as a result they have become national heroes and petitions have poured in for light sentences to be passed on them. We now hear that if the Empress has a son they are all to be let off! It is a wonderful country!

Several of the young officers claimed that they had been driven to join the plot by the London naval treaty of 1930. This treaty curtailed expansion of the Japanese navy and permitted the United States to achieve a superior ratio in heavy cruisers, theoretically 10:6 by the year 1936. This ratio was agreed against the wishes of the Japanese naval general staff, which considered the ratio 10:7 to be the lowest limit that would allow Japan to maintain her position in the western Pacific. Feeling in the navy ran so high that the minister, Admiral Takarabe, was forced to resign. Six weeks after the signing of the treaty Prime Minister Hamaguchi, a party politician, was shot and wounded by a young fanatic. Five months later he resigned, a sick man. The time was fast approaching when it would no longer be feasible for a party politician to be appointed prime minister.

The ringleader of the young officers declared that the Japanese delegates to the London Naval Conference, Baron Wakatsuki and Admiral Takarabe, were influenced by financiers and therefore they failed. The political parties were the tools of financiers, the navy was asleep and Japan had lost through lack of united force. Another said that they had been told that the ratios allotted were calculated on the defensive needs of the countries concerned, but that was a lie and the ratios were forced on Japan by the United States. Another said that the American Naval Academy at Annapolis used a textbook which said that the Japanese were a race which would yield to pressure and that the London naval treaty showed that to be true. The time had come to start a revolution, to restore direct Imperial rule, and it was in that cause that blood had been shed.

The London naval treaty of 1930 aroused primarily anti-American feeling in Japan, but in 1933 the announcement of the abrogation of the 1904 Indo–Japanese trade treaty aroused anti-British feeling. The abrogation of this treaty would remove Japan's protected trading status and was linked to the announcement that duty on foreign cotton goods would be raised from 50% to 75% while duty on cotton goods from Britain would be levied at 25%. Japanese industrialists blamed Lancashire industrialists and the British government over this tariff discrimination and initiated boycotts on Indian raw cotton. By the time a new trade agreement was formally agreed in 1934 concessions had been made by both sides, but the response to the initial announcement was one of hostility and anger.

My father wrote:

Feeling which before was rather anti-American seems to be becoming anti-British and the abrogation is regarded as a sort of 'punishment' inflicted by Britain because she disapproves of Manchuria! Though that is absurd, I think it is very doubtful whether these new trade barriers will do any good ultimately. They seem merely to produce retaliatory methods which deprive the original barrier of any value.

Stanley Woodward put the matter more strongly:

Great Britain is very unpopular now owing to the Indian Cotton tariff, which has struck a terrible blow at about one-third of Japan's export trade. The Japanese are being taught that the tariff is due to sheer spite and greed by England, which is represented as a rich and prosperous oppressor of the oriental Indians and the enemy of Japan. They don't realise that it is the Indian government which has put on these tariffs, and that in this matter the Indians themselves have almost complete fiscal autonomy. So it is a case not of occidental versus oriental, but of oriental versus oriental. But the Japanese know nothing of trade competition in India and the Indian tariffs are a very severe blow to them.

Meanwhile in China Japanese expansion continued. From September 1931 Japanese forces advanced through Manchuria until, within a few months, they controlled the whole region. In March 1932 the puppet state of Manchukuo was set up, with Henry Pu Yi, the last of the Chinese emperors, as its titular head. The Japanese then advanced over the northern province of Jehol and in 1933 annexed that province to Manchuria. They established themselves upon the line of the Great Wall and threatened to advance beyond it: Peking and Tientsin were both in danger of invasion. The Japanese stopped short of Peking only when a truce was arranged. Under the terms of this truce Chinese troops were barred from those areas of northern China occupied by the Japanese army.

Thousands of Chinese soldiers and civilians were killed by the modern, ruthless Japanese army and reports of Japanese brutality appeared in the British press. My father contrasted these reports with other aspects of the Japanese character: 'Though their conduct in Manchuria and Jehol may not suggest it, the Japanese are extremely sentimental, almost their favourite adjective being one whose meaning ranges from "pathetic" to "poor little" (darling or what not).'

In 1933 the fact of fighting in Jehol was as yet making no noticeable difference in conditions within Japan:

> Where Japan is likely to feel it in the end is in the economic sphere: the perpetual expenditure in Manchuria, the fighting further and further away from the base, the continual drain on resources, must in the end bring serious economic trouble. People are very near the bare subsistence level and if prices rise and food becomes expensive, there is sure to be trouble. But so far the effect on the cost of living is negligible and so the present policy prevails.

Two young Japanese students visited Stanley Woodward and spoke of Japan's foreign policy. As Stanley wrote:

> They seemed to think that anyone who stood openly for peace or peaceful methods in Japan in time of war would be in danger not only of imprisonment but also of lynching by the common people. I think it is true. Japanese public opinion is absolutely spoon-fed by the military now, and it is getting more and more narrowly jingoist as they are given an increasingly distorted and unchallenged view of the facts. They are all being worked up on the cry of Asia for the Asiatics and Japan the champion of Asia against the greedy West. It is rather ludicrous of Japan to pose as the saviour and leader of the Orient, considering her present reputation in China, but the Japanese show little imagination and are terribly ignorant about the things they dogmatise on.

It was not only in Asia that there were ominous developments. On 30 January 1933 Hitler took office as Chancellor of Germany. Moves were made immediately against the German Communist Party culminating, on the evening of 27 February, in the burning of the Reichstag building. Brownshirts and Blackshirts were called out and 4,000 arrests made overnight. Thus the way was prepared for the forthcoming elections and the defeat of the Communists, the strongest opponents of the National

Socialist Party. On 21 March, in the Garrison Church at Potsdam, Hitler opened the first Reichstag of the Third Reich. Three days later the majority in the Reichstag, overbearing all opposition, confirmed complete emergency powers to Chancellor Hitler for four years.

Six days later my father wrote home:

Certainly at the moment things seem pretty gloomy in the world, with Germany as the blackest spot. Hitler is a thorough menace, not only to his own people, but to the peace of Europe. It seems to me that trouble is more likely to develop for the world from that quarter than from the Far East. Jehol may develop into a Sino–Japanese war on a big scale, but I don't think the trouble would spread further than the mainland of China, whereas, if sparks begin flying in Germany, the whole of Europe will be involved in trouble.

In November 1933 he wrote again:

You ask about our views on Germany. As far as I am concerned, I am violently anti-Hitlerite. The Nazis seem to be the embodiment of Prussian brutality, their treatment of 'non-Aryans' barbarous and their views about the superiority of the Aryan race fantastic. I think they want peace at the moment because they are not ready for war and only for that reason, and I think they are probably rearming and preparing for a scrap as soon as they are in a position to launch one.

I fully recognise that the cause of Nazi popularity in Germany is the treatment meted out to her by the Allies since the War. The War Guilt clause in the Treaty of Versailles, the enforced disarmament of Germany and the occupation of the Ruhr, left Germany with a sense of inferiority and depression, which has only been removed by the Nazis. They have given a tonic to the whole German people and enabled them to feel they are a first-class nation again who cannot be bullied.

The whole thing is a tragic example of the vicious circle caused by suspicion and jealousy and hatred. Germany is beaten in the War and a generation of peacelovers headed by Stresemann comes into power. If only France can break away from her attitude of suspicion and respond to the peace feeling of Germany. But France has been invaded three times in a century and she is not having any. 'If you want peace, prepare for war' is her motto all the time and she keeps the biggest armaments in Europe. Meanwhile we try to keep in with both sides and adopt the attitude of 'My dear Germany, we should love to meet your wishes, only France, you know...'. And so back comes the war-spirit to Germany and probably there will be hell's own war between the two nations. It is a pathetic exhibition of the bankruptcy of the world's statesmanship – everyone learning nothing and forgetting nothing, going on in the same old nationalist, party spirit and never daring to make one decent venture for the cause of peace.

And so, as the time came for my parents to leave Numazu and start their new life in Tokyo, the shadows were lengthening and deepening both in the East and in the West.

PART III

Seven Years in Tokyo 1934–1941

1

Ikebukuro

In March 1934 my parents moved to Tokyo with their new baby, Christopher. After two years of language study, my father was ready to take up his appointment as a lecturer at the *Shingakuin* (the Central Theological College), which was associated with *Rikkyo* (St Paul's University) in Ikebukuro. The founder of this prestigious university was Bishop Channing Moore Williams, one of the first two American Episcopal missionaries to come to Japan after the country was constrained to open its ports following the arrival of Commodore Perry and his 'black ships' in 1853.

The Revd Channing Moore Williams and the Revd John Liggins landed at Nagasaki in 1859. Both had worked in the American Episcopal Mission in China and the Revd John Liggins had suffered violence there at the hands of a Chinese mob. The injuries he received, combined with malarial poisoning, soon caused his retirement, but Dr Ernest Schmid was sent out in his place and received a licence from the Japanese Government to practise medicine.

The first ten years of missionary work, from 1859 to 1869, have sometimes been called 'the decade of terror'. The Shogun's government became steadily weaker and finally collapsed; the powerful feudal lords were increasingly restless; there was suspicion and hostility towards Christianity; and everywhere there was anti-foreignism, which made it dangerous for westerners to venture outside the settlements. The two missionaries, therefore, remained in the treaty port of Nagasaki. They were suspected and spied on and hampered at every turn, while the Civil War in America meant that they did not receive the backing from home that they could normally have relied on. Against these difficulties they continued with their work and in 1866 the Revd Channing Moore Williams was consecrated bishop and given the oversight of American Episcopal mission work in both Japan and China.

In 1873, shortly after the noticeboards proscribing Christianity were taken down, Bishop Williams moved to Tokyo. He settled in Tsukiji, then the foreign enclave, and in his home set up a chapel and a schoolroom. His school began with five students and three missionary teachers but by the end of the year there were fifty-five students, most living in a dormitory that the school had rented. This was a promising start, but in 1876 disaster struck, for the buildings were destroyed by fire. For two years the school remained closed. Then it began again in a rented building and some of the students returned. A decision was taken to build a proper school. Funds were raised and a three-storey brick building rose from the Tsukiji mud-flats and was crowned with a sixty-foot spire and a golden cross. The people of Tokyo were impressed and enrolment increased by leaps and bounds, as young men flocked to the school in search of western learning.

In 1894 disaster struck again, when an earthquake – the same that destroyed St Andrew's Church in Shiba – destroyed the fine new building. For the next few years the school carried on in temporary accommodation, until in 1909 it was decided to turn the school into a full university. Twenty-three acres of land were purchased in the suburb of Ikebukuro and in 1919 the school moved into handsome new buildings. Three years later it received recognition as a university with the same standing as the government universities and became one of the *Roku Daigaku* (the Big Six universities of Tokyo).

My father had his first view of the buildings of *Rikkyo* when on an introductory visit to the *Shingakuin* in the summer of 1932. They were impressive, built in the style of an Oxford or Cambridge college, though freely adapted. Facing the road was a court with buildings on three sides and an immense gateway resembling Trinity Gate in Cambridge leading through to a second court. It all looked very un-Japanese. The Shingakuin was almost directly opposite Rikkyo but its buildings were very different, for while the university was built of red brick, the college buildings were of wood and more modest in style.

To Christopher, as a small boy, the contrast between the two sets of buildings appeared even greater than it was, for he saw *Rikkyo* as being up in the sky. Returning to Tokyo as a young man he understood why. Looking across at *Rikkyo* from the compound of the *Shingakuin* he could see a low grey building in the foreground and realised that as a child he had seen *Rikkyo* as, quite literally, floating on clouds.

In the compound there were four houses for Japanese staff on one side and two houses for western staff on the other. On my father's first visit he went to see Stanley Woodward, who was teaching temporarily in the college and occupying the house that was further from the road, while the regular member of staff, the Revd Moule, was on furlough in England with his wife.

My father took my mother for her first visit to the *Shingakuin* in the spring of 1933. They were shown the house nearer to the road but also the site of a new house, which was to be built just beyond the Moules' house, on the other side of a tennis court. It was not yet decided which house they would be given, but they hoped for the new house, for the one nearer the road was rather old and had become noisier since the road had been widened.

In the event it was an American lecturer and his wife, Lawrence (Larry) and Caroline Rose, who moved into the house next to the road. They arrived in April 1934 from Montana, where Larry had served as pastor in the parish of Deer Lodge. Larry wrote of Deer Lodge that it

> afforded several years' experience of an extraordinarily varied and happy sort – boom times when it seemed that material values were all absorbing; then depression years when banks and businesses folded, people suffered, and youngsters in town went into the hills for the summer to pan gold, scales making their appearance on store counters once again.[4]

Before those years in Montana, Larry had been a tutor at the General Theological Seminary in New York. The *Shingakuin* was associated with *Rikkyo* and both had been founded by the American Episcopal Mission, yet there had been no American lecturer at the *Shingakuin* for twelve years. Larry was persuaded to go to Japan and to apply his experience of teaching theology in a very different environment. Caroline later wrote of that experience:

> For seven years we worked on language study and the effort of adjusting to a culture in many ways the opposite of our own: tools like a saw or a plane, even a breadknife, work by pulling instead of pushing. Reading is up and down instead of back and forth. Although he [Larry] lectured in English, he required his students to answer questions in Japanese. He could not read these answers

[4] JE Lindsley, *He Was The Dean: a memoir of Lawrence Rose Dean of the General Theological Seminary 1947–1966* (Cincinnati OH), p. 19.

himself, but he could correct them when they were read to him. He wanted to make sure the students were assimilating theology in their own language and not parroting back their notes. He and his co-workers always made it a practice of leaving faculty meetings arm-in-arm even if they had taken opposite sides in a hot debate, to demonstrate that brotherly love need not be affected by difference of opinion. Japanese traditions of loyalty did not include this understanding. We picked up what we could of manners and courtesies (always return something of half the value of a gift received, even a wedding present). Flower arrangement and tea ceremony we tried to learn by osmosis.[5]

My parents moved in the spring of 1934 and were delighted with their new house –

... by far the best we have seen of a reasonable size in Japan or indeed in England! The rooms are light and airy and spacious and our new furniture fits beautifully. There is a lovely enclosed veranda on the ground floor and another upstairs, both facing south and flooded with sunlight. The *pièce de resistance* is the bathroom, where we have a bath enclosed (in the latest style) in a square tiled frame and a shower bath! Such are the rigours of the mission field!

My father's parents were at the time struggling to sell their house in south London and to find a house elsewhere where they could live on very modest means. It was in this context that my father explained how comparatively cheap the cost of living was in Japan:

When you reflect that the whole house cost 7,000 yen, which at the present rate of exchange is £400 or so, you can realise how cheaply things can be done in this land. I am not certain that the proper place for you to retire to isn't Japan! You could live like fighting cocks on a very small English pension here!

My father was later to reflect on the move from Numazu to Tokyo:

It is rather amusing how Ethelreda and I feel about the country now. Having been born and brought up in a town, I appreciate

---

[5] Ibid, p. 22.

the country very much now and quite miss the mountains and fields of Numazu. Ethelreda, on the other hand, having been bred in the depths of the country, is developing quite a metropolitan feeling and is not at all sorry to have exchanged the comparative quiet of Numazu for the noise and bustle of Tokyo.

It was two years later, in 1936, that Stanley Woodward took up his appointment at the college. Stanley and Gwen had recently arrived back in Japan from furlough and stayed first in the suburb of Suginami:

Here we are safely in old Japan once more, in a suburb of Tokyo, in the midst of a maze of narrow winding lanes, with the tofu sellers sounding their unmusical little horns on every side. It is hard yet to realise that we are here – we have stepped out of a European environment so suddenly.

Six months later they moved to Ikebukuro and so from that time on there were three young western families living in the college compound.
The *Shingakuin* was officially the theological department of *Rikkyo*, yet in practice the *Shingakuin* was a separate college, with a Japanese Principal and a staff of three Japanese and three western lecturers. It was not, however, like theological colleges in England or America, for at the *Shingakuin* the students were all undergraduates. My father believed that this should be changed:

I feel the theological college should be made postgraduate. It would mean a longer course, but it would mean less overwork. At present the students have about 26 hours of lectures a week and in addition go all over Tokyo and sometimes further afield on Sundays to help with the services. Is it any wonder that one or two break down every year and that more than one has had to go to a sanatorium, suffering from TB – that dreaded complaint that attacks so many in Japan?

My father found his first term as a lecturer at the college very busy. He had nine hours' lecturing a week and had to provide fairly detailed outlines of his lectures for the students, to help them over the difficulty of hearing the lectures in English. Three hours of lectures were on Greek: 'Picture me an Englishman this morning helping Japanese lads to translate from Greek into their own tongue! It is a bit hard!' But he had other commitments as well as his work at the college: on Sundays he went to Shiba to take the English services at St Andrew's Church; once a month he made the three and a half hour journey to give oversight to a new Japanese church in Kofu; and always there was language study.

That first summer in Ikebukuro, my parents went again to Karuizawa with Christopher, now seven months old. Stanley and Gwen Woodward arrived a little later, having come up from Fukuoka with their new baby, David. Towards the end of August, David's Christening was held in Christ Church, Karuizawa. Gwen was somewhat anxious, as David had recently taken to howling for about two hours each afternoon. However, he seemed to enjoy the taxi ride down to the church and, though wide awake, was beautifully quiet all through the ceremony, thus winning loud praises and admiration from all present.

In September my parents returned with Christopher to Ikebukuro. In Karuizawa my father had taken to wearing a thick suit, but in Tokyo he felt hot even when wearing only a tennis shirt and shorts. The round of lectures and lecture preparation started up once again, even though the weather – hot, damp and typhoonish – was anything but helpful to brain work.

This second term proved just as busy as the first and after seven weeks without a break my parents went on a day's excursion to view the maples at Nikko. The journey in the cable-car up to Lake Chusenji was very beautiful, for the mountainsides were a mass of autumn colours: brilliant reds and golds and russet browns. At the top they walked to the Kegon waterfall. It was an impressive sight, for the water came tumbling over a rocky course and then dropped suddenly about 500 feet in a perfect foam-flecked curve into a hollow crater-shaped bowl worn into the rock through the centuries. From this bowl rose clouds of steam and mist and they could almost imagine they were inside a volcano and watching the vapour rising around them. They descended by car and so had a different view of the maples and other trees: 'I cannot attempt to convey the loveliness of the hillsides. The colours are something we do not have and would find difficult even to imagine in England.'

For New Year my father joined a party of students on a skiing trip in the Japanese Alps. The last part of the journey was by horse sleigh up a river valley with great pine slopes on either side, all covered with snow. The branches twinkled in the sunshine, turning it into a fairyland scene. The first day my father spent on the nursery slopes, testing out his legs, for it was eight years since he had skied in Switzerland and he was afraid that the little skill he had acquired there might have deserted him. The second day the party moved on to longer and more difficult slopes, known as 'Davos'. This was a glorious day, for the sun was shining brilliantly and the air was crisp and bracing. The third day was not so good, for the party got lost on a mountain in a snowstorm and it was a relief when they hit the right path again and found their way back to the hut before darkness fell.

On my father's return to Ikebukuro he found Marie Bath, a friend from Karuizawa, installed for the night. Marie was working at the leper settlement at Kusatsu. There she was keeping a goat and chickens as part of a plan to provide a future for the healthy children of leper parents, for they were not accepted in society. The idea was to employ them in supplying milk, eggs and vegetables to the leper village and to develop industries among them which would enable them to become self-supporting. Marie's goat and chickens were the first acquisition towards the carrying out of this scheme.

Each letter home included news of Christopher's progress. At a year he was crawling round on hands and knees. He also liked to walk holding on to things, while if held by the hands he would do a sort of goose-step round the room, emphasising the fact that he understood the principle of walking, that it depends on moving first one foot and then the other. He was producing a few consonants, like 'ga' and 'ma' and 'ba', but not yet attaching any name to a thing. Yet he seemed to understand that talking in some mysterious way meant something to adults and felt that he could not be left out. If he was put for a rest in his cot on the veranda and anyone came up the garden path, he would rise in his cot and greet them with a resounding yell. His amah, Furasawa-san, always bowed to him politely when she went home for the night. One evening, to her intense joy, he responded and produced a beautiful Japanese bow. It was a deep, solemn bow from the waist and he was perhaps a little hurt and certainly surprised by the mirth and excitement caused by his action.

*   *   *

But here the letters break off and there is no further news of Christopher's progress – at least for the time being. The last letter in the two box files from the metal cabin trunk is dated 31 March 1935.

2

State Occasions

At the time of my parents' move to Ikebukuro in 1934, the life of a great
Japanese leader was drawing to a close. Admiral Togo was the hero of the
Battle of Tsushima during the Russo–Japanese War of 1904–5. Before that
battle, Japan had won two notable successes on land, in the siege of Port
Arthur and in the Battle of Mukden. Now they were to win a great victory
at sea. In May 1905 a Russian fleet of some forty ships appeared in Far
Eastern waters heading for Vladivostock. Admiral Togo judged rightly that
its course would be through the straits between Japan and Korea, and there
the two fleets engaged in battle to the east of the islands of Tsushima. In
this decisive encounter the Russian fleet was destroyed and Japan stepped
into the rank of a first-class world power.

My father wrote of the feelings Admiral Togo inspired in the Japanese
people:

> He arouses in the national estimation the sort of feeling that Nelson
> inspires among British people. His life has been marked by great
> simplicity and quiet devotion to duty and these are qualities which
> appeal especially to the Japanese, whose natural feelings are really
> antithetic to the sort of American boost and push that are so evident
> here.

As the Admiral neared his death, an incident occurred to throw light
on British press methods. My parents were attending a dinner party and
among the guests was Captain Kennedy, the Reuters correspondent. Just
before 10 p.m. Captain Kennedy rose to go, as he had to see if Admiral
Togo's death was yet announced. Apparently there was great rivalry
between Reuters and United Press to get news home first and Captain
Kennedy had received a cable from London: 'Watch Togo – essential
unbeaten death'!

The State funeral was held on 7 June and my father joined a crowd of British people watching proceedings from the Embassy. The procession was very impressive, though there was little to remind viewers of old Japan, except five Shinto priests carrying a long banner with Admiral Togo's name and decorations inscribed on it. For the rest, it might have been taking place in London or Paris. There were bands playing Chopin's 'Funeral March', large detachments of soldiers and sailors, members of the Cabinet and other officials in cocked hats and gold braid, and also detachments from the American, French, British and Italian warships which had come to Yokohama especially for the purpose. After it was all over, an old friend, Miss Ballard, turned to my father and said in her usual emphatic way, 'A very enjoyable funeral'!

The following year, 1935, was the year of King George V's Silver Jubilee and a special service was to be held in Tokyo. My father asked his parents if they could send the proposed form of service to be used in London: 'We are probably going to have a rather big service here on May 6 – diplomats in gold braid and whatnot – and we are anxious to follow the order of service being used in St Paul's if we can.'

A problem arose over the size of St Andrew's Church. The Ambassador felt that at least twenty prominent Japanese should be asked and at least the head of each diplomatic mission. As there were about thirty embassies and legations in Tokyo, this brought the number of outside officials who must be asked to about fifty. Add to that the staffs of the British Embassy and the Canadian Legation and it meant that over a hundred seats would have to be reserved for a start. The church could hold at a pinch 200 people but not more, so that there would not be much room available for the general community. The question arose as to whether it was worth trying to squeeze everyone into the English St Andrew's Church or whether it would be better to borrow the other St Andrew's Church, the one used by the Japanese-speaking congregation, which was in the same compound and very much larger. My father showed the Ambassador round the Japanese church and at a conference between the British Ambassador, the Canadian Minister and Bishop Heaslett it was agreed that the Japanese St Andrew's would be the best place. The Canadian Minister's consent was given grudgingly, however, and afterwards he was seen busily counting up seats in the English St Andrew's to see if it could not be made to hold everyone.

For his part my father was having to spend time in calming down the Canadian Minister, who felt that the Ambassador was going ahead with plans without consulting him:

My father as a chaplain
in the Royal Canadian
Air Force (RCAF)
(see p. 12)

St. Andrew's Church,
Shiba, Tokyo

Far left: My parents,
Christopher and me in
kimonos (see p. 19)

Left: Our amahs,
Christopher and me
(Furasawa-san on left)

Below: A reunion at the
Shingakuin (Central
Theological College),
Ikebukuro, Tokyo

Right: *Rikkyo* (St Paul's
University), Ikebukuro,
Tokyo

Left: *Shingakuin* student

Below: On SS *Hikawa Maru* (my father standing centre row third from right, my mother front row at left holding Helen, Christopher and me on ground at front) (see p. 132)

Right: My parents in the Japanese Alps (see p. 110-111)

Below: Christopher (on left), John Caiger (centre), David Woodward (at right) (see p. 133)

Left: Church with Japanese flags

Below: The kindergarten – the *Jiyu Gakuen* (me at the back, Christopher out in front and David Woodward towards the right) (see p. 165)

Three western staff and families at *Shingakuin* (back row: my father holding Helen, Stanley Woodward, Larry Rose; middle row: my mother, Gwen Woodward holding John, Caroline Rose; front row: Christopher, Peggy Rose, David Woodward, me, Peter Woodward)

Peggy Rose (on right) and me as bridesmaids at the wedding of my godmother Kay Stockdale to Hamish Sutcliff (see p. 166)

Shingakuin staff, signed by
Japanese members of staff
and presented to my father
in farewell, autumn 1940

Bishop Heaslett (see esp.
chapter 'From a Japanese
Prison' p.179 ff)

The situation as between the Embassy and the Legation is not without its humorous side. The Embassy is very jealous of sharing its diplomatic position with this upstart Legation, while the Legation feels it has every bit as much right as the Embassy to represent the King and British interests. The position is bound to be a little difficult at the present time, for separate diplomatic representation for the Dominions has only been recognised (I think I am right in saying) since the passing of the Statute of Westminster in 1926 and these first few years are bound to be experimental. Yet there is no doubt that the Canadian Minister and his wife take far more interest in the general activities of the British community here than our own somewhat exclusive Embassy.

Two or three weeks later my father accompanied Bishop Heaslett to the Canadian Legation for a St Andrew's Church council meeting. They made various plans in regard to the Jubilee service, which was definitely to take place in the Japanese church, and my father was pleased to note that the Minister seemed to have got things smoothed out with the British Ambassador: 'At any rate, all was lovely in the garden and peace seemed to be reigning supreme!'

King George V lived on for barely three weeks after the end of his Jubilee year and died on 20 January 1936. Stanley and Gwen Woodward had only just returned from furlough in England and Stanley wrote home: 'The death of King George has been a great shock and sadness to us all out here, though in many ways his end was very merciful. He was spared to enjoy all the happiness and rejoicings of the Jubilee and though he has had poor health for some time past, yet the end came quickly and mercifully.'

Stanley and Gwen had heard news of the King's illness on the Sunday, when Emily Foss came to lunch after the morning service at St Andrew's. On the Tuesday morning Stanley's secretary was leaving at about eleven o'clock, when he turned back with a *gogai*, or special edition, which gave the final bulletin that the King was quietly sinking to his end. Half an hour later, a newsboy brought another *gogai*, saying that the King had passed away. He died at 11.55 p.m. on Monday evening by British time – 8.55 a.m. on Tuesday morning by Japanese time. Stanley and Gwen heard the news two and a half hours later and so probably before their parents in England, who would almost certainly have been asleep, unless they had stayed up specially to hear the news at midnight on the wireless.

Stanley wrote home:

> We put out our flags of mourning at once, and one of our neighbours
> was kind enough to put theirs out in sympathy. The Japanese Court
> has ordered three weeks' mourning as a token of sympathy. The
> news occupies quite a prominent place in the paper, but the
> demonstrations of sympathy are not nearly so great as they would
> have been in former years. The international tension and the national
> feeling here is against it.

On the day of the funeral in England, a memorial service was held
in the English St Andrew's Church, at which the Emperor was represented
by his brother, Prince Takamatsu. Once again a problem arose over the
small size of the church and so attendance was by invitation only and
was confined to diplomats and national representatives. The memorial
service for the British community had been held on the previous Sunday,
again at St Andrew's, but even then not everyone who wished to attend
could get in. Bishop Heaslett had wanted to have a larger building
somewhere else, say Holy Trinity, the American church, which they
would have lent for the occasion, but the Ambassador would not hear
of it.

In the following December, the news of Edward VIII's abdication
burst into the public domain. My father wrote to the missionary society
in London:

> What a time we have been through! It has been rather grim out
> here, partly because we have been seeing for weeks the American
> papers and knew all about the scandal long before it 'broke' in
> England and partly because one inevitably thinks of it from the
> Japanese point of view. How incredible it must seem to those
> brought up in the samurai tradition, with their strict sense of honour
> and duty!

In Tokyo there were still many who remembered the four-week visit
made to Japan by Edward as Prince of Wales in the spring of 1922.
This followed a three-week visit by Crown Prince Hirohito to England
in the spring of 1921, part of a tour of Europe which was the first
such journey ever made by an heir apparent to the Japanese throne. The
Prince of Wales had received an enthusiastic welcome at Yokohama and
then proceeded to Tokyo, where the Emperor conferred on him the rank

of General in the Japanese Army, a return compliment for the same rank in the British Army conferred on Crown Prince Hirohito by George V in the previous year.

Edward had made a favourable impression on the Japanese during that visit of 1922. Now his abdication was beyond their comprehension. Stanley wrote home:

> We have discussed the national crisis very much among ourselves, but only twice have I said anything about it to Japanese people and then only in reply to questions from Japanese clergy whom I know well. The ordinary Japanese people have been very much puzzled by the whole thing. At first the Japanese papers spread the view that the objection to the King's marriage was because Mrs Simpson was a commoner and an American. The clergy questioned me on that point. I explained the true situation, and they were impressed by the influence of the Church and the strong feeling in England against a divorcée. The average non-Christian Japanese are merely horrified or contemptuous that a man could put 'love' before country in such a way. Our monarchy has suffered a great loss of prestige. This situation has shown so definitely that the monarchy is subject to the people and the Japanese compare it unfavourably with their 'heaven-descended' Imperial Line, which is subject to nobody – in theory.

Further humiliation was heaped on the British by the manner in which the crisis was reported in the press. The Japanese press was exercising admirable restraint but the American press was very outspoken. One evening in the New Year Larry and Caroline had been entertaining friends. They were still clearing away the cocoa cups and putting away the card table, when they heard the strains of 'Should auld acquaintance be forgot' from outside the window. It was my parents returning from an evening engagement. They came into the house to borrow the copy of *Time* magazine which contained the account of Edward's abdication and stayed talking until nearly midnight. As Caroline commented, 'They are still very touchy about the tone of the reports in American newspapers but are avid for every word they can get concerning the crisis.'

The Coronation of George VI on 12 May 1937 marked the beginning of a new era and a renewed respect for the British monarchy. Prince and Princess Chichibu travelled to London for the occasion and the

Japanese were very much impressed by the ceremony and tradition of the service in Westminster Abbey. Detailed accounts filled the newspapers, portraits of the King and Queen and the two Princesses were displayed in the larger stores and restaurants, and the fishing boats entering and leaving Tokyo's Sumida River flew small, paper Union Jacks.

Caroline wrote of the festivities:

The excitement of the Coronation has dominated the week. Larry loaned out his robes for the service and his tails for the ball. Our neighbours went off in the afternoon for the garden party at the British Embassy. The broadcasts in the evening were most disappointing, since all that could be received here was a jumbled description of the procession in Japanese from the Japanese Embassy in London. Only the embassies here in Tokyo are allowed short wave sets and so only they were able to tune in to the service from Westminster Abbey itself.

Stanley also expressed disappointment with the reception from London:

We listened in to a commentary on the wireless, broadcast to Japan from just outside the Abbey, but it was only for half an hour and all in Japanese, done by a member of the Japanese Embassy in London. The atmospherics were bad and we could only catch a word or two here and there.

An official service of celebration was held at the Japanese St Andrew's Church, for once again the English St Andrew's Church was too small. The service was attended by Prince and Princess Takamatsu, the Prime Minister and most of the Japanese Cabinet, as well as most of the Diplomatic Corps, representing all nations – even the Italian[6] – all in braid and ceremonial uniform. The church was decorated with British flags and with flowers, carpets were spread on the floor, a choir of residents sang and three bishops officiated – Bishop Heaslett, Bishop Matsui and Bishop Reifsnider – British, Japanese and American. It was Bishop Heaslett, of course, who played the chief part and Stanley Woodward was acting as his chaplain 'and had to dance around him, both in church and when welcoming or speeding the grandees, so I had an excellent view of everything that went on. The service was simple and dignified and went through very well. The Ambassador was well pleased and he is somewhat particular.'

Ten days later Stanley reported: 'The Coronation pictures have already arrived at the cinemas here. They were brought back by the *kamikaze* aeroplane which has just returned and we shall go to see them tomorrow.'[7]

---

[6] Relations between Great Britain and Italy had been strained since Italy's invasion of Abyssinia in 1935.

[7] In this context the word '*kamikaze*' clearly has none of its wartime significance, but is associated rather with speed. A month earlier, on 10 April 1937, Stanley had written: 'The Japanese are mightily pleased with the achievement of their flight to London. These things do much good by promoting a feeling of interest and friendship and relieving the tension.'

3

The Incident of 26 February 1936

The year 1936 was marked by an episode of murderous violence far greater in scale and consequence than that of 15 May 1932. The prelude occurred on 12 August 1935, when Lieutenant Colonel Aizawa drove from his provincial barracks to the War Office in Tokyo. He made his way to the office of General Nagata, Chief of the Military Affairs Bureau, and killed him with several strokes of his sword. General Nagata had been responsible for putting into effect a number of appointments and postings designed to lessen the influence of the revolutionary faction among the young officers. General Mazaki, who was regarded by the young officers as their leader, had opposed these changes and been replaced in his post as Inspector General of Military Training. From the time that Aizawa learned of General Mazaki's dismissal, he determined to kill General Nagata.

Aizawa's trial took place in the barracks of the First Division in Tokyo. As in the earlier trial of young officers, it provided an opportunity for the revolutionary ideas current among the young officers to be given a public airing. Once again the counsel for the defence argued that the defendant had acted from the highest motives of patriotism. Once again the court allowed the defendant and his counsel the greatest latitude in proclaiming their ideas. Once again the proceedings received extensive coverage in the press and once again there was widespread sympathy for the defendant.

Aizawa declared that he acknowledged the power of the Emperor alone. The statesmen, bureaucrats and financiers who surrounded the Emperor separated the Emperor from the people. It was they who were responsible for the ills that beset the country. They should return their powers to the Emperor, so that they could be entrusted to those with absolute loyalty to the throne. He had killed General Nagata because General Nagata had plotted with statesmen close to the throne for the dismissal of General Mazaki.

His counsel for the defence, Lieutenant-Colonel Mitsui, brought that motive to the fore: it was unacceptable for statesmen to interfere with army affairs; the army should be free of outside influence; the army should be answerable to the Emperor alone. He argued that conservative forces near the throne were acting in ways harmful to the army and began to call into question the motives and actions of many of the highest in the land. As murder trial turned to witch hunt, the court martial was interrupted by events of the most dramatic kind.

In the early hours of 26 February 1936 a military rebellion broke out from the barracks where the trial was being held. Some 1500 junior officers and their men left their barracks, some to attack the homes of elder statesmen and some to occupy prominent buildings near the Palace. The Prime Minister, Admiral Okada, escaped death, for his brother-in-law was killed in mistake for him. Two former Prime Ministers, Admiral Saito and Mr Takahashi, were killed, as was General Watanabe, who had succeeded General Mazaki as Inspector General of Military Training. The Grand Chamberlain, Admiral Suzuki, was wounded but recovered and was later to become Japan's last wartime Prime Minister. Count Makino, formerly Lord Keeper of the Seals, had the narrowest of escapes, while Prince Saionji was moved to a safe place before the murder squad arrived.

The rebels attempted no further violence but remained in occupation of the buildings they had seized in the vicinity of the Imperial Palace. Here the rebels and the Imperial Guards faced each other but around them life went on. Dr Shaw unwittingly walked right into the midst of the trouble. 'I found myself facing barbed wire and machine guns near the Palace grounds, but of course could not tell which was the revolutionary and which the Government side. I was treated with courtesy by the officers, who allowed me to proceed to my destination and return by the same way.'

A friend of my parents, Kay Stockdale, left for work as usual on the morning of the insurrection and was surprised by the number of soldiers on the streets. She too had to pass by the Palace grounds and she too was allowed to continue on her way. But when she arrived at work, her colleagues were horrified that she had made such a journey, which they felt to be most dangerous for a foreigner. Kay's abiding memory of the day was that the tanks surrounding the Palace had their guns pointing inwards. From this she concluded that the Emperor was, in effect, a prisoner of the military.

For four days the rebels remained in occupation of the area around the Imperial Palace. They had carried out their plan: they had killed some of the most prominent statesmen in the land and now they waited for the army chiefs to take the reins of government into their own hands. While they waited, they distributed a manifesto. This declared that politicians, financiers and bureaucrats were responsible for Japan's problems and that in taking direct action they were performing their duty as subjects of the Emperor.

The Emperor, for his part, was appalled by the uprising, declaring it to be mutiny. Nor did the army chiefs respond as the mutinous officers had hoped. Instead, martial law was declared and extra troops and armaments brought in to surround the area occupied by the rebels. The army generals were working to bring the incident to a close without further bloodshed. An appeal was made to the soldiers over the heads of their officers: the Emperor himself ordered them to return to their barracks; if they failed to obey they would be traitors; if they obeyed they would be pardoned. Tokyo was shut off for the rebellion to be brought to an end: trains, street-cars, telephone exchanges and telegraph offices were all shut down. Groups of soldiers began to give themselves up. One officer shot himself. The other officers surrendered. The insurrection was over.

My father sent a cable to the missionary society in London: 'SPG[8] workers all well Tokyo normal inform families.' Two days later my father wrote more fully of the crisis:

> I sent a cable on Sunday to SPG to let you know that we are all well in Tokyo after an exciting and to some extent anxious time. On Thursday and Friday we were quite uncertain who was in charge of the city and Saturday only seemed to make matters worse, for all traffic in the centre of Tokyo was stopped. We were certain that there would be street fighting and it was only as the radio announced the surrender of bands of rebel soldiers that we realised that the situation was in hand. General Kashii, in charge of martial law, deserves the utmost credit for subduing the rebels and restoring order without more than a few shots here and there.
>
> Saturday's and Sunday's newspapers brought news of wildly exaggerated reports of the uprising in the foreign press. Apparently people in Shanghai could not believe that the announcements over the radio were true and that outside the very small area affected … the city was perfectly normal and everyone calm.

---

[8] Society for the Propagation of the Gospel.

The insurrection brought to an end the government of Prime Minister Okada. He had headed a cabinet which was moderate and bureaucratic. Now what would follow?

> We are waiting anxiously for the appointment of the new premier and the constitution of the new cabinet. Behind the present outbreak there is a feeling of deep discontent among army men with the way the capitalists are treating the country. One hopes for a government that will really tackle the problems of economic distress in the countryside but will not yield to the forces of militarism. It will not be easy for the new cabinet to keep the balance fairly between the conflicting claims of the services, the bureaucrats and the capitalists, but we hope for really statesmanlike leadership at this critical time.

Both my father and Dr Shaw reflected on the uprising when writing their annual reports for the missionary society. Dr Shaw wrote:

> The year 1936 will go down to Japanese history as one of the critical years in the life of the nation. The long continued depression in the agricultural community, the sense of isolation in the world and the extremely rapid growth of population were at the back of what has come to be known as the 'Incident of February 26th'.

My father also saw 1936 as a critical year for Japan:

> The crucial date is February 26th, the day on which a group of young officers carried out a wholesale series of assassinations and attempted assassinations on leading public men, especially those 'near the Throne'. The 'Incident' deeply shocked the Japanese nation and the people, who had condoned a similar series of murders in May 1932 on the grounds of the assassins' patriotism, felt that they had been dragged to the edge of an abyss.

My father set out to explain the background against which such an incident could occur: Japan was neither an autocracy, as Italy and Germany were at that time, nor a democracy as England was. The real power was divided between the services, who were by the constitution directly responsible to the Emperor and not to the civil government; the bureaucrats, i.e. the Cabinet and the permanent officials who initiated and directed policy; and the financiers. (Though the Diet acted in some sense as a curb, its part was very secondary.) The services, the officers of which were largely recruited from the countryside, were very conscious of the sufferings of the peasantry and resented both the corruption of politicians and the profiteering of industrialists. The bureaucrats worked for a strong foreign policy, which they desired the army to conform to and the capitalists to support financially. The financiers believed that Japan's hope of salvation lay in economic expansion and were prepared to sacrifice the agricultural industry to the exigencies of Japan's export trade.

Conflicting aims thus mark these groups, each of which seeks to buttress its position by having around the Emperor officials who are sympathetic to its aims. Hence life in Japan has an uncertain background. Will the services ultimately gain the day and establish a regime not dissimilar ... to that of Fascist countries today? Will the liberals, who are now in eclipse, come back again and restore some of the lost freedom of thought and outlook?

But freedom of thought and outlook continued to be eroded, as the authorities sought to control thought as well as action. In a dozen centres 'thought controllers' were appointed to watch all developments of thought which the government regarded as unwelcome and to 'guide into right channels' those suspected of entertaining such thoughts.

My father quoted the Home Minister:

It is gratifying that the people have come to a realisation of the absolute nature of respect for the gods and ancestor worship, side by side with clarification of the national polity and enhancement of the national spirit. I believe it is urgently necessary to encourage this tendency in the light of the existing situation in this country. I trust that you will leave nothing to be desired in providing guidance for the Shinto ritualists to strengthen the conceptions of the people of the gods and their ancestors in accordance with the wishes of the government.

While the authorities sought to control thought, the power of the military continued to grow. In the new cabinet, formed after the insurrection, the most powerful voice was that of the Minister of War, General Terauchi. The cabinet's declaration of policy insisted that foreign

4

On Furlough

A year after the 'Incident of February 26th', in the summer of 1937, our family returned to England on furlough. My parents had sailed to Japan as a newly-married couple in 1932. Now they were returning to England with two children and another on the way. My brother, Christopher, was three and a half, I was just a year, and my mother was expecting my sister, Helen, who would be born during furlough in England.

The five years my parents had spent in Japan formed part of what has been called in Japan *kurai tanima* or 'dark valley', the 'dark valley' that was to lead from Japan's invasion of Manchuria in September 1931 to Pearl Harbor in December 1941. My parents had sailed for Japan within a few months of the invasion of Manchuria. Now we set sail for England on 3 July 1937 and only four days later the first shots were fired in what was to be war between Japan and China.

This time our family did not take the sea route by Suez, which took six weeks, but the sea and land route by America, which took a month or so. The quickest route was by the Trans-Siberian Railway, but that was closed to our family, for no Christian missionaries were allowed on Soviet soil.

We travelled in company with a young Japanese woman, Ineko Kondo, who was about to embark on a doctorate in English literature at Cambridge University. Family tradition has it that on one occasion she saved my brother's life. Christopher had climbed into a perilous position, from which he looked likely to fall headlong into the Pacific Ocean, when Ineko Kondo caught up with him and snatched him back to safety. He had a picture book of Bible stories and one picture showed the fishing boats on the Sea of Galilee, so he was craning out to try and see the fishing nets over the side of the ship.

For the year of furlough our family would be based partly with my father's parents and brother in Bristol, but mainly with my mother's widowed mother and aunt in Wormingford, Essex. All our grandparents were in straitened circumstances and all lived to some extent as dependent relatives.

The financial problems of my father's parents dated back to the time of the Russian Revolution. My grandfather, Cyril Sansbury, had worked for an insurance firm specialising in shipping between Britain and the Baltic. The Russian Revolution caused this company to go into liquidation and although my grandfather was able to find new employment, he never again earned a good income. In the summer of 1935 my grandfather was due to retire and this necessitated selling the house where they were living in Copley Park in Streatham, as they did not own the house outright and would no longer be able to keep up the mortgage payments on my grandfather's very meagre pension. But selling the house proved difficult and the likelihood of their being able to afford anything desirable on the proceeds seemed remote.

It was in these circumstances that my father's younger brother, Quentin, who worked in Bristol, came forward with a proposal. He suggested that he should rent a house or flat in Bristol and that his parents should join him and pay whatever they could afford towards the cost of their keep. My father tried to reassure his parents that this arrangement would be for the best: 'You will certainly have to make allowances for his ten years' independence and for his being affected by modern ideas. Quentin is genuinely and generously anxious to help you and for himself he is desirous of a proper home instead of everlasting lodgings. He will value what you can give him, so long as he feels that you are not using too narrow a "yardstick". He will respond, I believe, to a generous, uncensorious home life.' Although my father addressed his remarks to both his parents, they were certainly directed to his mother, who kept a strict eye on all her three sons.

And it seems that the arrangement did work for the best. After visiting Bristol during those months of furlough, my father wrote:

> For me the time has been specially valuable, because I have been able to come back into the home atmosphere again. When we went to Japan before, you were in that not very nice house in Copley Park and there was still something of the financial strain – and those things inevitably affected my memory of 'home'. Now – thanks largely to Quentin's generosity – you are living in a much more comfortable place and district, you are free from that former

anxiety and you both seem freer and happier in yourselves. The memory of 'home' for me is consequently enhanced.

My mother's mother had also lived on a very small income ever since she had been widowed more than twenty years previously. My grandfather, Philip Wamsley, had been a captain in the merchant navy but he had died of tropical fever in 1913 and was buried in the English cemetery in Rio de Janeiro. My mother had a childhood recollection of playing with a wooden trainset while visiting her father's ship in Hamburg, but her memories of her father were hazy, for she was only seven when he died and he had spent long periods away from home on voyages to the Far East and to South America.

Once my grandfather had died, my grandmother, Ada, and her three young children went to live with her unmarried sister, Flo Illingworth. Aunt Flo had talents as a musician, artist and linguist and ran a school in Scarborough in Yorkshire. Following the bombardment of Scarborough during the First World War, Aunt Flo moved her school to Hexham in Northumberland and with her moved my grandmother and her children. While my mother and her older sister, Eileen, were pupils in the school, my grandmother helped with the housekeeping.

Aunt Flo was still running the school in Hexham House at the time of my parents' engagement, but by the time my parents married, she and my grandmother had left Hexham and moved to the village of Wormingford in Essex. The Vicar of Wormingford, Mr Vaizey, was a bachelor and he had been sharing his house with his unmarried sister. Now his sister had died and my grandmother and Aunt Flo moved into the Vicarage to look after the housekeeping. Mr Vaizey had no close relatives himself and it seems that he was happy that their relatives should come to visit. And so it was that we stayed for prolonged periods in Wormingford Vicarage during that year of furlough.

My father was not always with us at Wormingford, for being on furlough did not mean having a year of holiday, but involved travel round the country on deputation work, speaking, preaching and attending conferences. Now that war had broken out in China, there was much hostile coverage of Japanese aggression in the press. Audiences wanted to know how the Japanese themselves viewed events in China and whether any questioned the actions of their military.

My father explained that the Japanese public saw only a heavily censored press. They knew nothing of the unceasing provocation by their troops in North China, nothing of the deliberate attempt to undermine

China's financial stability through smuggling, nothing of the iniquities of the traffic in drugs. All they heard was of continual incidents in North China, for which the Chinese were always responsible, of the 'insincerity' of the Nanking government, of the ominous spread of Communism through an increasing number of Chinese provinces. For the Japanese people, therefore, the war was a crusade, a holy war, for the deliverance of the suffering Chinese people from rulers so wickedly pro-Communist and anti-Japanese, and for the uniting of their two nations in lasting brotherhood and peace.

The war had strengthened the forces of nationalism and religious patriotism in Japan. Ever since the 1931 Manchuria Incident had led to Japan's withdrawal from the League of Nations, international ideals had been at a discount. Patriotism, whole-hearted dedication of oneself to the service of Japan, cultivation of the 'Japan spirit' were being instilled into the Japanese people through the press, wireless, lectures and every other means of propaganda. The forces of liberalism, which had been fighting a rearguard action, were now silenced.

Religious patriotism was being promoted as the foundation of the nation's spiritual life. At the heart of religious patriotism was Emperor-worship. In the late twenties, a writer had spoken of a time when some Japanese 'even claimed divinity' for their Emperor. Now school books had been re-written to present as fact that the Emperor was divine, the Son of Heaven, descended in an unbroken line from the Sun Goddess, Amaterasu. It was the Sun Goddess who had bestowed on Japan a divine mission to bring the whole of Asia under the Emperor's beneficent rule, 'The Four Corners of the World under One Roof'.

If religious patriotism was being promoted by the government, how did this affect Japanese Christians? My father explained that Christians were a tiny minority – less than half of one per cent of the population – and they were subject to all the same propaganda as their fellow citizens. They too felt loyalty to their country and found no conflict between their Christian faith and the idea of a special vocation for Japan in the twentieth century. They were ready to go to the utmost limit, therefore, in meeting government requirements, in bowing to the Emperor's portrait and in attendance at Shinto shrines. In fact, there was a growing feeling among both priests and laity that it was possible to have a Japanese Christianity, a synthesis of all that was unique in the Japanese character with all that was most acceptable in the Christian religion.

This nationalist spirit was leading in the churches to a reaction against western influences and a desire for Japanese control. Although the majority of clergy might be Japanese, much church funding and leadership still came from the West. But now western missionaries were finding doors closing against them. The leadership was passing into Japanese hands and the daily pastoral work was more and more being undertaken by Japanese clergy. The missionary as a foreigner was held to be unable to understand the present situation. His advice was not encouraged and his criticisms, if expressed, were bitterly resented. A few of the senior missionaries – by reason of their long service and their personal and official authority – could exercise a little influence at times. But generally the power of foreign missionaries to alter attitudes within the churches was nil.

In these circumstances should my father return to Japan after furlough? And if he did so in what role? For the last three years his lecturing at the Central Theological College had been his primary work. In addition, he had taken the services at the English church of St Andrew's in Shiba, while once a month he had given oversight to a new Japanese church in Kofu. Now his principal work could no longer be among the Japanese.

At this point a decision was taken to revive the position of chaplain to the British Embassy in Tokyo and my father was offered the post. This could be combined with his work as chaplain at St Andrew's Church in Shiba, so that his English chaplaincy work would become his principal role. Meanwhile his work as lecturer at the theological college could continue, though in a more limited way, while his oversight of the Japanese church in Kofu would cease altogether.

Bishop Heaslett urged my father to overcome his misgivings and return to Japan on this basis: 'I hope you will remember that in your position as Chaplain to the Embassy you would be fully protected and be able to carry on your work under circumstances where it would be difficult for an ordinary person to work. You would have diplomatic privileges.'

My parents decided to accept this new situation and to return to Japan in the summer of 1938. This decision caused much alarm among our relations: 'How can you take three small children to Japan when Japan is a country at war?' To which my parents would reply: 'Japan is at war but the fighting is in China. The fighting is as far away from Japan as Greece is from England.' Yet they knew that there were ominous signs for the future both in Asia and in Europe.

* * *

The sequence of my father's letters home had broken off in March 1935. Now the sequence was resumed – for a few months at least. My cousin in Bristol was looking through some of our grandparents' possessions when she came across a brown leather handbag that had belonged to our grandmother. Inside were a few letters from my father's youngest brother, Graham, in South India, a postcard from my father showing the SS *Samaria* and written 'somewhere in Missouri' on 10 August 1938, a letter written on the SS *Hikawa Maru* somewhere between Seattle and Vancouver on 12 August 1938, and a dozen letters written after our arrival in Japan. The last letter is dated 28 April 1939.

* * *

Of all the family none was more eager to return 'home' to Japan than Christopher. For him the year of furlough had been an unsettling time. This was partly due to our moving between relatives in different parts of the country, but more it was due to our father's comings and goings on deputation work. Always Christopher had idolised his father. Even when he was six months old, our father had to stay out of the room when Christopher was being fed, for otherwise Christopher's gaze just followed him round the room and he would not eat. Now, on furlough, Christopher became wildly excited whenever our father came home, stricken with grief whenever he left.

The first day out of Seattle on the SS *Hikawa Maru*, a large dish of Japanese rice was placed on the table for the children's tea. Christopher exclaimed with pleasure, 'Ah, real food!' and took the whole dish for himself. Once we arrived at our house in Ikebukuro Christopher asked for scrambled egg on toast for his tea. This had been his favourite dish at Wormingford. He ate the whole plateful in silence, then turned to our mother and said solemnly, 'We will never go to England again, will we?'

But the longed-for homecoming proved painful. Before we had left Japan, Christopher was speaking Japanese quite unself-consciously. As he turned three, my father commented: 'Christopher acquires Japanese at an enviable pace. He even indulges in Japanese songs in bed!' When we went to England, my mother took simple Japanese story books to read with Christopher, but Christopher had never spoken Japanese to our parents and refused to look at them. He just said, 'I'll speak Japanese when we go back to Japan.' Only once was he startled into speaking Japanese. We were in a cable car at Scarborough when the *Royal Lady* came into view round the cliffs. Christopher was always fascinated by trains and in his excitement he burst into Japanese, much to the astonishment of his fellow passengers.

Now, in Ikebukuro, David Woodward was waiting eagerly for Christopher's return. In this he was encouraged by his parents, who wanted David to have an English playmate once again. As soon as we arrived home, David rushed to our house and began to speak to Christopher in Japanese. Always they had spoken in Japanese together in the past, but now Christopher became very upset and screamed at him to speak in English. He could not understand what David was saying, for we had been away for almost fourteen months and he had lost the language. Now he could not bear for David to play with the Japanese children in the compound and only felt safe if they were playing in the garden and speaking together in English. But this created difficulties for David, for he had been playing with the Japanese children while we were away and he could not suddenly stop.

David himself had had a difficult experience while we were away on furlough. He had begun to attend the kindergarten of a Japanese school. Reminders of Japan's war were never far away, for there was a military barracks nearby and military planes also flew overhead. Each time a military plane flew over, the children had to stand up and bow to the east. Because David was English, he had to stand on a table so that he could be conspicuously seen to be bowing to the east. One day some of the children threw him in the school's fish pond because he was English and the teachers did nothing to stop them. David began to play truant. Once he was delivered to school, he would slip away to the railway station and return to school in time to be collected at the end of the day as if nothing had happened. One day he was picked up by the police at the station and returned home. Then the truth came out.

Clearly some new arrangement must be made. Nearby lived another four-year-old boy, John Caiger, whose father taught at the Peers' School in Tokyo. So once we returned from furlough, on two days in the week Christopher and David would go to John's house and on two other days David and John would come to our house and here they would have their own kindergarten. Christopher would set off very proudly with his new satchel to John's house or as proudly welcome David and John to our house. There was nothing of the 'creeping like snail unwillingly to school'. He thought holidays were hopeless.

But it was not only Christopher who gave some anxiety on our return:

I think Audrey is the one of whom we have to take most care.

She wants to grasp everything that is going on, and the novelty of everything, the use of Japanese by the staff, the standard set by Christopher, which she wants all the time to reach, are a real strain on her. She needs keeping very quiet and it is not always easy.

So it seems it was only Helen who gave no cause for anxiety: she was always the healthy, contented, happy baby, the admiration of all beholders.

Five months after our return, on 26 January 1939, a telegram arrived for my father from Bristol: 'Dad passed on peacefully this morning Quentin.' For my father the news was numbing in its suddenness, for it was only a day or two since a letter had arrived from his father and indeed one or two more letters in his father's hand would arrive after the news of his death. Yet he was not altogether surprised. His father had seemed very fragile during that year of furlough and my parents were told of frightening fainting fits, which made them wonder if death might come suddenly without any lingering illness.

My father thought of how he remembered his father:

There was the old cheerful Dad of the early days, then the silent, anxious Dad of the years after the War, then the hollow-cheeked, ill Dad of 1926 – do you remember how we stood in the morning room that May evening, wondering what the nurse would say? – and then last year once again the cheerful Dad, who seemed to have got lost in the years between our childhood and our return from furlough. It is a most varied series of memories and to it last year came as a splendid climax. The struggles and anxieties were past and the setting associated with those difficult times changed for a new and better one. It seemed as though Father's life had reached a splendid golden autumn after a summer of thunderstorms and lightning.

My father drew a parallel between the death of his father and the death of George V:

Do you remember how fitting we all felt it that the King was kept for his Jubilee year and then taken in the following January? Do you remember how I wrote at the time that I couldn't help feeling there was a real likeness between him and Dad? Both were simple, loyal souls with no frills and no fuss, but with a strong sense of devotion to what they felt was right. Of course, dear old Dad in his humility denied it, but I think it was not a fanciful parallel. And now the likeness has continued further. Both had miraculous recoveries from illnesses that nevertheless left a deep mark on them. Both were kept through their 'year of fulfilment' and both were taken in the January of the following year.

In the following weeks my father began to think of his mother, Sophie's, future. Her youngest son was in India, her eldest son in Japan. Might she not consider making a trip out East? She could make the journey via Suez for no more than £150. She could, perhaps, leave England in the autumn of 1939 and stay with Graham in India until the early summer of 1940 and then come on to Japan and stay with our family until the spring of 1941. It might be worth considering...?

The Japanese Pre-War Empire and Advances into China – adapted from AL Strong, *China Fights for Freedom* (Lindsay Drummond, London, 1939)

136

5

War in China

By the time our family returned to Japan from furlough, war had been raging in China for fourteen months. Matters had been brought to this crisis by the actions of Japan's military in north China, actions designed to bring that region, with its economic importance, under increasing Japanese control. But the Nationalists were determined that Japan should not take over north China, as it had taken over what was now Manchukuo, and Chiang Kai-Shek reached an agreement with the Communists to resist Japanese incursions. On 7 July 1937, fighting broke out near Peking between Japanese and Chinese troops. Both sides brought in reinforcements and the fighting escalated. By early August both Tientsin and Peking were occupied by the Japanese. Fierce fighting began in Shanghai, involving first the Japanese navy and then the army. By the autumn undeclared war raged both in the north and in the region of Shanghai. In Japan it was not given the name 'war', however. Rather it was known as the 'North China Incident' and later as the 'China Incident'.

That summer of 1937, while our family was travelling towards England, Larry and Caroline Rose were holidaying in Nikko with their daughter Peggy, who would be two in the autumn. The strange thing about their stay was that there were scarcely any other visitors. Nikko, with its magnificent temples and shrines, was usually a magnet for visitors, but this year there were few foreign tourists, while the Japanese seemed to be taking no holiday trips at all. Even the spectacular Kegon Falls was deserted. Larry and Caroline received news of the outbreak of war from *gogai* or 'extras', and from then on *gogai* were delivered every morning or afternoon by little boys who came running from door to door jangling their special little bells and delivering small sheets covered with great characters at every house where there was a subscriber. The papers spoke of Japan's bold 'self-defence', in extravagant quotations. They had to read between the lines and on the inside among the insignificant-looking articles to try to find the real story.

The effects of war were felt at once, for troops and munitions were being moved up and down the country and schoolchildren were lined up at the stations to show their loyalty whenever the troop trains went through. One day Larry and Caroline invited neighbours for dinner at noon, but twenty-three young men of the village had been ordered into the army on twenty-four hours' notice and all the delivery boys were seeing off the soldiers. The uncooked chickens were not delivered until nearly eleven o'clock.

Larry attended a summer camp for boys. A Chinese boy was at the camp for the first two days, was handsomely welcomed and was happy to be there, but the person responsible for him grew panicky and decided he had better get him safely out of the country as soon as possible.

Larry sent a telegram to one of the graduates of the *Shingakuin*, congratulating him on his ordination as a deacon. That student was booked on a ship leaving Yokohama later in the month for America, where he was to spend a year at a School of Social Work in Cincinnati. Larry received a reply, thanking him for his telegram, but saying that he would not be going to America, for he had received orders to report at the front in China immediately.

Larry and Caroline returned to Tokyo in September and found 'refugees' from China parked in all the houses of western staff at *Rikkyo* and the *Shingakuin*. These were mostly people returning to China from furlough or on their way to take up new posts. Having reached Tokyo, they were halted with orders to take up what work they could there.

A letter arrived at their house from Tientsin addressed to 'Mrs Garrett'. The letter was from her husband, Norman Garrett, who was somewhere in the interior. It was no surprise, therefore, when a telegram was delivered in the evening announcing her arrival from Kobe the following morning and saying 'inform Rose Fowler'. But the Fowlers already had one 'refugee' and Larry and Caroline had all the baby paraphernalia, so Caroline said firmly, 'That's Henrietta and the baby. We will have them here.'

So the following morning Henrietta arrived with the baby, to Peggy's great delight. The baby was called Norman Duncan, but was known as Dee-dee (a Chinese nickname meaning little brother). They were to stay for possibly six weeks or until it was certain whether they must proceed to the States, whether Norman would join them, or whether they could return to Wuchang.

Poor Henrietta kept thinking of the contrast with the time she was in Ikebukuro as a bride. She hated the separation but was not really anxious for the safety of her husband. Meanwhile the Chinese bishops were asking the single men to stay on. An American called Father Wood came to Ikebukuro for a few hours en route back to Wuchang via Hong Kong. Each time a visitor came through there was a gathering of hosts and 'refugees' to discuss the pros and cons, while Henrietta would slip away to the typewriter to write a letter to Norman that had a prospect of certain delivery. The danger was in risking the round-about trip and in the shortage of foreign foods, of canned goods including milk, and of fuel, which made it unwise for the women and children to remain in any part of China.

In other ways there were fewer evidences of the emergency in Tokyo than Larry and Caroline had expected. Trains were less full, dancing and certain comic entertainments were taboo, but movies and theatre performances were still crowded. Then, for five days and nights, there were rehearsals for air-raids. Restrictions against lights in the evenings were very strict, while Larry had to attend faculty meetings to listen to long lectures on protection against bombs and poison gas attacks. Meanwhile Caroline had to learn about local food resources, for prices of imported foodstuffs and drugs were soaring. There was no more cinnamon to be had and soon they would have to do without foreign canned goods entirely.

The most insistent reminders of the emergency were the shouts of *banzai* coming from the station at all hours of the day, as farewell parties accompanied the soldiers setting off for China. One morning a procession of departing troops went by at five o'clock in the morning, waking even the children with their forced cheer. It was pouring with rain but a long queue of friends and members of the patriotic associations followed the men with umbrellas held over their banners. This was during a week when a tremendous number of boys and men were called out. Streets and railroad stations everywhere were crowded with farewell parties. There were no tears shed, but the aspect was nonetheless grim. There was an outspoken finality about all the goodbyes, summed up in the monotonous patriotic song with its first line, 'We'll never come back alive'.

As autumn set in, the American consulate gave permission for Shanghai missionaries who had been marooned in Japan during the summer to return to their homes and jobs, while several of the men quartered at *Rikkyo* were ordered back to Shanghai for the opening of St John's University on 18 October. Their wives were left in no enviable position.

Neither the consular service nor the bishops would encourage their return to China, but no one seemed empowered to refuse them outright when they insisted on accompanying their husbands.

Henrietta knew she could not return to China with her baby and decided to leave for America on the earliest possible boat. She might obtain a passage within the next week or two, but would probably not be sure of the passage until a day or two before the boat sailed, so there would be a last-minute rush whenever the summons came.

Meanwhile the students returned to *Rikkyo* and the *Shingakuin* for the autumn term. Members of the English Speaking Society visited Larry and Caroline to ask for their help in producing an English pamphlet to be published as propaganda for circulation among students abroad. This put them in a delicate situation, for it was difficult to mention either facts or opinions outside the government-prescribed circle of rationalisation. Although different groups of students were assigned to the different subjects covered, all had dealt with what Caroline described as 'the same nauseating rehash'. Larry and Caroline tried to suggest to the students some of the fundamental questions that students abroad must be asking: 'What is the basis for the anti-Japanese policy in China?' 'What sort of government does Japan really want in China?' But the students admitted that it was quite impossible for them to express themselves until the government itself outlined its policies publicly.

Work at the *Shingakuin* was going particularly well in that autumn of 1937 and students were studiously courteous to foreign members of staff. What their true feelings were was difficult to know. On 5 October in London an event took place that aroused bitter anti-British feeling in Japan. This was a meeting held at the Royal Albert Hall to protest against Japanese bombing of civilian targets in China, a meeting at which the Archbishop of Canterbury took the chair. This meeting was described in the Japanese press as 'anti-Japanese' and was put forward as proof that Britain favoured the Chinese cause and was hostile to Japanese aspirations in China. The involvement of the Archbishop led to bitter words in the *Nippon Sei Ko Kai*. Bishop Matsui of Tokyo exploded: 'This is the end of our connection with the English church!' Bishop Heaslett calmed the atmosphere by saying: 'We English missionaries are only here to help you. As soon as you wish it we will go.' It seemed that day could not be long.

Meanwhile the fighting in China spread up the Yangtse from Shanghai to Chiang Kai-Shek's capital of Nanking. The city was taken from the Nationalist forces on 13 December 1937 and was sacked by the Japanese

Imperial Army among scenes of such indiscriminate killing, of such brutality and bestiality, that the episode became known as 'The Rape of Nanking'.

News of the atrocities was kept out of the Japanese press and the seizure of Nanking was hailed as a triumph. Schools in Tokyo were given a holiday and the streets were thronged with cheering students marching to the Imperial Palace and in the evening with lantern parades. Larry and Caroline were appalled:

> We are in favour of a stiff boycott as the only possible protest on the part of all peaceloving powers. It will mean suffering for many innocent friends here, but we do think it is high time people of this nation assume responsibility for their army's behaviour. Meanwhile, the actual news reports make us sick.

'The Rape of Nanking' was to be the most notorious instance of atrocity in the war between China and Japan, but it was not only in Nanking that the Chinese were suffering. Larry went to Yokohama to meet a missionary who was en route from Soochow to America: 'The evils in his area are not worse, but much more widespread and generally prevalent than we had imagined. The horrors are literally unspeakable.'

As Japan felt increasingly isolated in the world, so it seemed that the time for foreigners in Japan was growing more and more limited. In May 1938 the Synod of the *Nippon Sei Ko Kai* was to be held in Kyoto and as the time approached different groups within the church were outdoing each other in the proposal of patriotic resolutions to be presented to the convention. Some of them seemed quite inappropriate to church proceedings, but it would be a bold voice that dared to say so out loud. The crucial business was the passing of a resolution in relation to the war. The first draft was for the *Nippon Sei Ko Kai* to give a straight expression of gratitude to the troops for their actions in China. It became clear that this would not be accepted by the foreign bishops. This realisation caused something of a furore, as the place was stiff with army police and any failure to support whatever patriotic resolution was put forward could mean trouble. Eventually all sections agreed on a resolution which expressed emotion at the gallantry of the Japanese troops, urged the need for increased loyalty to the Emperor and expressed sympathy with the Chinese people, and especially with Chinese Christians, who had suffered loss. Even this would not be well received abroad, but in view of pressure from the nationalistic environment it was the best that could be hoped for. Afterwards some of the clerical and lay delegates expressed themselves as grateful to the foreign leaders that a moderate resolution had prevailed. It seemed that the time for a showdown was not yet.

This was a second crisis for the *Nippon Sei Ko Kai*. The first was the Archbishop's presiding at the protest meeting in the Royal Albert Hall, and either could have led to British missionaries having to withdraw from Japan. So, in returning to Japan at the end of August 1938, my parents knew they were returning to a very uncertain future.

As they arrived back in Tokyo, their first reaction was: 'Is this really the capital of a country engaged in war?' There was so little to recall the hardships and privations of life in a European capital between 1914 and 1918. Shops and department stores were full of goods and customers; theatres, cinemas, baseball matches and wrestling contests were all well attended; neon lights blazed out as brightly as ever. People seemed to be going about their business as usual and there seemed no obvious shortage of young men. The Japanese people, who had never had to stand in a queue for food and never had to experience an air-raid, seemed to have little conception of the reality of modern warfare. Yet reminders of the war were never far away. At Tokyo's railway stations there were troops being seen off with much flag-waving and many a *banzai* to the front, high officers being welcomed home, and wounded soldiers surrounded by groups of wide-eyed Japanese, for whom a wounded soldier's crutch or stick might be the first tangible evidence of the devastation of war and of the fact that Japan was not having everything her own way.

There were signs too of the great economic strain Japan was undergoing. Japan's export trade had fallen off drastically and to avoid insolvency imports had been severely curtailed. The packed trams and trains in Tokyo bore witness to the strict rationing of gasoline, which meant that bus services had been cut back and so caused other means of transport to be crowded. For the same reason taxis were practically double in price and in outlying parts of Tokyo, such as Ikebukuro, not easy to find. Foreign films were scarce. Woollen and cotton goods were becoming unobtainable, replaced by goods made of staple fibre, which shrank and went yellow in the wash. Boots and shoes were rationed to save leather. Prices had risen of butter, milk, meat, cereals, charcoal, anthracite, and also of canned goods, because of the scarcity of metal to make the cans. Staple Japanese foods, such as rice, fish and vegetables, had gone up very little, so the Japanese were less affected than foreigners. Always shoppers were urged to buy substitute articles made in Japan rather than goods imported from abroad.

As for the general atmosphere, it was safe to say that not all the nation had supported the army's handling of the 'Incident' at the start, even if there was no channel through which to express disapproval openly. But now the attitude seemed to be: 'It's no good arguing whether we were right or wrong to take the step we did, for since that step was taken the whole international situation has changed and we must stand together for the very existence and safety of our country.' There was anxiety concerning the future, doubts as to the wisdom of this or that step, but beneath that a real sense of national unity.

Japan was confident of final success but the Japanese were being prepared for a long struggle. Following the loss of Nanking, many Japanese thought that Chiang Kai-Shek would capitulate, but he refused to accept the harsh terms proposed by the Japanese and retreated along the upper reaches of the Yangtse River to set up a new capital in Chungking. The fall of Hankow, which had been declared to be imminent for the past three months, would not be the end of the struggle and five or six years was now being talked of as the time needed to bring matters to a successful conclusion.

On 26 October 1938 my father wrote home:

It has been a momentous week here in the Far East – first the fall of Canton with surprisingly little defence put up by the Chinese and now we await any hour the announcement of the fall of Hankow. The next few days are likely to be decisive, for it must become clear almost at once whether Chinese resistance is going to crumble completely or whether the war will be carried on merely one stage further back from the coast.

To this letter he added a postscript: 'Last night we were at the Kabuki theatre when the news came through that Japanese troops had entered Hankow...'

On 28 October he wrote again:

Well, Hankow has fallen. The news was broadcast through the city at night by siren and people were soon out (our students among them) with lanterns to celebrate the capture. Today schoolchildren are going to the plaza before the Imperial Palace to pay respects to the Emperor and in universities and colleges it is a holiday. There is a thanksgiving service in the chapel of the university over the road, but attendance is voluntary and none of us foreigners is attending. Afterwards the heads of departments (our own Principal included!) are going to pay their respects at the Meiji and the Yasukuni Shrines.

The Meiji and Yasukuni Shrines were the most important nationalist shrines in Tokyo. The Meiji Shrine was dedicated to the memory of the Emperor Meiji, who had guided Japan from feudalism to the status of a world-power during his reign from 1868–1912, while at the Yasukuni Shrine the spirits of those who died in battle for Japan were enshrined. Here, at the annual festival, relatives from all over the land gathered to hold communion with their departed and to worship them as now exalted to be guardian spirits of Japan. When going into battle, Japanese soldiers would encourage each other with the cry – 'We'll meet again at the Yasukuni Shrine!'

The whole nation had been taught that its highest duty was to serve the Emperor and its highest privilege to die for him. The corollary of this was that the deepest disgrace was to be taken alive as a prisoner in battle. An example of this attitude, so alien to westerners, was given by a Major Koga who, in 1932, committed suicide in Shanghai. He had been taken prisoner by the Chinese when wounded and unconscious. After being released he was, in accordance with military law, court-marshalled by the authorities but exonerated as he was captured when unconscious. He felt, however, that for a Japanese soldier, under whatever circumstances, to have been taken prisoner was such a disgrace that he could only clear himself by committing suicide. The Minister of War praised his act, saying that this was universally received as the unwritten rule of the Japanese army.[9]

At the end of November 1938, the annual service of re-dedication for Tokyo members of the Brotherhood of St Andrew, a student Christian group, was held in the chapel of the *Shingakuin*. During the service the names of the hundred members now serving in the army and navy were read out. A moment of silence was observed in memory of Lieutenant Paul Seitaro Koizumi, a former *Rikkyo* student, who had been killed in China on 7 September. When he heard of his death, his godfather, also an army officer, had written: 'I am very anxious to know how he died. As I write this letter his figure of past days looms in front of me – a

---

[9] Susan Ballard, unpublished report to SPG for 1932, Rhodes House Library, Oxford.

young officer on the battlefield. He was such a faithful fellow! He must always have acted most bravely. My sorrow is great.'[10]

But it was not only the Japanese who were mourning their losses in Tokyo in that year of 1938. Earlier in the year Larry and Caroline were invited to a luncheon at the home of American friends, Dr and Mrs Reischauer. Dr Reischauer was a professor at one of Tokyo's universities, the *Meiji Gakuin*, and the luncheon was to mark the birthday of their son Bob, who had been killed in Shanghai in the previous year. Caroline wrote, 'They are carrying on so courageously, doing the things with their friends which they have always done.' Their son Edwin was at a later date to become American Ambassador in Japan. He dedicated his book, *Japan: The Story of a Nation*, 'To My Brother Bob, the first American casualty in World War II, Shanghai, August 14, 1937'.[11]

Meanwhile, in China, suffering was on a vast scale. Missionaries gave their reports: 'I come from a land where fully a million fighting men are living in the countryside, where 30,000,000 people have fled from their homes, where roads are trenches, bridges burned, where internal and external commerce are paralysed and finance is chaotic, where seed-time and harvest have ceased, for all seed grain has been eaten' ... 'In this area they have finished eating all the leaves of the trees' ... 'The district has been in a state of famine. The floods destroyed the crops and they have been feeding an army all this year. Many people are homeless owing to frequent burnings of villages' ... 'Conditions in the village districts are not good. The peasants suffer much. Banditry is rife.'[12]

The Japanese government issued its declaration on 'The New Order in East Asia':

> What Japan seeks is the establishment of a new order which will ensure the permanent stability of East Asia. In this lies the ultimate purpose of our present military campaign. This new order has for its foundation a tripartite relationship of mutual aid and co-ordination between Japan, Manchoukou [Manchuria] and China in political, economic, cultural and other fields. Its object is to secure international justice, to perfect the joint defence against communism, and to

[10] Elizabeth Anne Hemphill, *The Road to Keep: The Story of Paul Rusch in Japan* (Walker/Weatherhill, Japan 1969, USA 1970), p. 37.

[11] Edwin O. Reischauer, *Japan: The Story of a Nation* (Charles E Tuttle Co, Tokyo, 1970).

[12] *The Church Undaunted* (SPG report for 1939; undated), p. 47.

create a new culture and realise close economic cohesion throughout East Asia.[13]

The 'new order', painted here in such glowingly unrealistic terms, was not to be realised. The Japanese won victories, gained control of towns and cities and of the lines of communication, the roads, rivers, canals and railways that connected them, but large areas of the countryside were never under their control and here a variety of Chinese forces continued their resistance. The war in China was neither lost nor won.

---

[13] JM Maki, *Conflict and Tension in the Far East – Key Documents 1894–1960* (Seattle, University of Washington Press, 1961), pp. 78–9, cited in RHP Mason and JG Caiger, *A History of Japan* (Melbourne, 1972), p. 292.

6

War in Europe

'Well, things look about as black as they could be internationally and the odds seem pretty heavy on our being at war by the time this letter reaches you – if indeed it ever does.' So wrote my father on 28 September 1938, just one month after our return from furlough.

There seems general agreement between ourselves, France, Germany and Czechoslovakia on the question of ceding predominantly Sudeten areas of Czechoslovakia to Germany. There is no doubt they have real grievances, though equally there is no doubt that those grievances have been exploited by the Nazis and passions inflamed by the bitter anti-Czech campaign in the German newspapers. The question now seems to be 'how' and 'when'. Hitler, who has not made one single concession or contribution to peace during the whole controversy, says 'October 1st or we march in'; Czechoslovakia says 'No dictation about dates and what about non-Sudeten minorities in the areas to be ceded?'; Britain and France say 'Any more rough stuff from Hitler and he is for it.' So someone has to climb down in the next three days. Either Hitler has to postpone his date, October 1st, or Czechoslovakia has to yield to his demands, or England and France have to back down from their offer to help Czechoslovakia, if attacked. One or other of these things must happen, if war is to be avoided. Otherwise there is bound to be a European conflagration – and one cannot but feel that that is the most likely solution.

If war were to come, then the attitude of Japan was going to be of very personal concern for our family. The extremists were all in favour of going in with Germany from the start and joining forces with them against Soviet Russia. What Japan's attitude to Britain would be was uncertain: with the war in China and trouble likely from Russia, Japan would have her hands full and would probably not care to attack, say, Hong Kong, to add to her burdens. If Japan should declare war on Britain, then of course diplomatic relations would be severed and all the Embassy staff, our family included, would return home, though other people might face internment 'for the duration'. My father urged his parents not to worry about us, for our new position would protect us, though it might not be pleasant for our friends.

On all hands one feels a horrible uncertainty and insecurity, not knowing what may happen in the next few months or weeks – or even days. It is not very good for one's work, for it is difficult to settle to anything with anything like full attention and as for plans for next week it simply does not seem worth making any.

A week later, on 6 October, my father wrote again:

Well, it has certainly been a dramatic week. Last Thursday we practically gave up hope and Bishop Heaslett and I spent the evening working out various plans (a) in case Japan didn't come in and (b) in case she did. The four-power conference came as a tremendous relief from the war tension and the credit for its being held seems to be due (a) to Chamberlain for his last-minute appeal to Mussolini (b) to Mussolini who, I think, saw the red light, despite all his bombastic utterances round Italy and (c) to Hitler, who had enough sense to yield on matters of time and method when his main objective was granted. It has all been rather a dirty business, with Hitler exploiting genuine grievances for economic reasons and imperialist expansion, and I am not nearly so sure that we have reached the new age of peace and cordiality as some people seem to imagine. Nevertheless, it is a great thing to be free from the threat of immediate war and to feel that one can carry on normally for a time.

Three weeks later my father's doubts seemed to have grown:

I have had *The Times Weekly Edition* of October 6, recording the sense of relief and thankfulness felt everywhere after the Munich agreement. It was a natural reaction, but I don't feel convinced about the 'new era of peace' and all that. For four great powers to settle the minority problem of a small nation over her head, because one of the great powers wants the problem settled that way and is prepared to act the bully to get it, doesn't seem to me to augur well for the future.

And, indeed, within six months, Hitler was to prove how false were his words at Munich, his assurances that he had no interest in Czechoslovakia beyond the Sudeten lands, for in March 1939 German troops marched into Prague and Germany took control of a Czechoslovakia left defenceless by the terms of the Munich agreement.

Stanley Woodward expressed the general astonishment:

We are all staggered at Germany's behaviour these days and the wanton threat it presents to world peace. We wonder how much further the democratic powers can allow it to go. The Japanese are cultivating friendship with Germany and Italy and have publicly justified Germany's action, but it has rather taken their breath away and, I should imagine, set them thinking what sort of allies they are linking themselves up with now.

Germany's seizure of Czechoslovakia finally destroyed Chamberlain's trust in Hitler's assurances. He knew now that it would only be a matter of time before Hitler turned his attention to Poland. On 31 March 1939 Chamberlain announced in Parliament that he had given to Poland an historic undertaking: if any threat should be offered to Poland, then Britain would give Poland all the support in its power.

My father wrote:

What a change British policy has undergone! Till now there has been a real cleavage in feeling between those who supported the Prime Minister and those who felt that Anthony Eden and Winston Churchill had a much more realistic grasp of the situation. Since Munich I have been emphatically among the latter and the continued retreats of England before the totalitarian powers has made me feel ashamed of being an Englishman. The policy might be called 'appeasement', but along with a genuine desire to maintain peace there has also been a lot of national selfishness, a refusal to face unpleasant issues squarely, a foolish optimism that somehow we would muddle through, a preference for dividends over principles. It has been a disquieting six months. Now all that is over. Everyone, whether a Chamberlain-ite or an Eden-ite, is united in the belief that we must stand firm for decency, for the independence of small nations, for the elimination of the international blackmail practised by Hitler. I only wish we had taken this line a year ago and so perhaps saved Czechoslovakia, but that can't be helped now. Our future line is clear and I hope indeed that thereby peace may be saved. Whether it is so or not depends on the next few weeks and months, I think.

Japan continued to cultivate friendly relations with Germany. Larry and Caroline Rose had experienced one manifestation of this when staying in Karuizawa the previous summer, for thirty men and boys of the Hitler Youth were staying there during a visit to Japan, while thirty of Japan's youth were on a reciprocal visit to Germany. Caroline reported:

The Germans are handsome as can be. To the amazement of their hosts not a single one wears glasses. We can hear their singing – they have dozens of brisk marching tunes to use every time they go anywhere and we cannot help feeling proud of the very splendid impression they are making throughout the country. I am afraid that Peggy and the amah have given a good many *heils* and *banzais* in their enthusiasm.

Meanwhile, as 1939 progressed, Britain was made the scapegoat for all Japan's misfortunes. As the China Incident dragged on without any immediate prospect of a victorious conclusion, as the strain began to tell on Japan's economic life and the living conditions of Japanese people, as the desire of more extreme elements in Japan for a total military alliance with the Axis powers was frustrated by more moderate elements, so frustration was vented on Britain, and Britain was made out to be the cause of every misfortune, external and internal, that had befallen Japan.

This hostility was expressed, both in Japan and in China, by anti-British demonstrations and processions, by the pasting up of posters denouncing Great Britain and demanding her withdrawal from East Asia, and by the publication of fiery articles in the press. That Japan, from her point of view, had legitimate grievances against Britain could not be denied, for Britain's conduct at Tientsin, for instance, where there was a British concession, had been anything but neutral. But that Britain was responsible for all Japan's troubles was obviously an absurd exaggeration, a psychological compensation for frustration in other directions. Nor was there any indication of spontaneous feeling among the Japanese against Britain or against British people. In one summer seaside resort an anti-British demonstration was held. Afterwards the mayor called on a Canadian, a leading member of the foreign community, to say that the demonstration meant nothing, that it had been ordered from outside, that it had had to be held, but that the people of the resort held no hostile feelings towards the British. All this created a difficult atmosphere in which to live and work and one fraught with apprehension. No one could tell when the situation might take a sudden turn for the worse, when diplomatic relations might be broken off or even war declared. People talked half-jokingly about the possibility of internment camps and were nervous of going far from home during the summer.

Then, towards the end of August 1939, came the sudden announcement of the Soviet–German Non-Aggression Pact. Japan had looked upon Germany as an ally in opposing Soviet Russia. In 1936 Germany and Japan had signed the Anti-Comintern Pact to resist the spread of Communism and the activities of the Third International (the Comintern), an organisation of Communist and socialist parties willing to follow Moscow's line. Now there was disgust at Germany's double-dealing. The extremists were discredited and the anti-British campaign faded away. A friend of my father's, who went to Haneda (then Tokyo's international airport) to see off the round-the-world plane, reported that a number of Japanese officials who had been looking through him or pretending he wasn't there for the last few months came up and shook him warmly by the hand. The Italian air attaché said that he and his colleagues were expecting a present of Japanese swords with which to commit *hara-kiri* on account of the treachery of their German ally! Meanwhile, those of the British community most devoted to Japan were already talking of the possibility of a renewal of the former Anglo–Japanese alliance.

Our family and the Woodward family were spending the summer at the seaside resort of Takayama, north of Tokyo near Sendai. As the international situation grew ever more tense my father returned to Tokyo, for only there could he hear the most up-to-date news. Each day my father wrote to my mother. She kept those letters, folded together in a small envelope printed with the words 'The Sanno Hotel, Tokyo, Japan'.

The first letter was dated 27 August 1939:

Here we are on Sunday afternoon still holding on and wondering what will happen. Friday's paper looked pretty black and then yesterday there seemed a gleam of hope with Hitler's message sent suddenly to Chamberlain. It looks as though he has got cold feet, which is a good sign, but the various reports of the contents of his message are not very encouraging. They seem to be roughly 'give me the things I want in Danzig and the Polish corridor and we can call the war off.' He doesn't seem ready to make any concessions at all himself. Parliament is meeting in emergency session again tomorrow and that looks as though it will be the crucial day. War can only be avoided if Hitler climbs down – for to let him get away with this crisis is merely to postpone the inevitable disaster to a worse time. Either he must back down on his demands on Poland or fight – that is the flat issue and at the moment the odds seem to me in favour of the latter.

It is a grim situation and one still hopes for the best. The very delay is encouraging, because it means that Hitler has not taken advantage of a sudden surprise attack immediately after the conclusion of the pact with Russia, but has given England and France time to get fully mobilised. He probably knows Germany can't stand a war and is trying a spot of 'appeasement' of the Munich type. I hope to heaven Chamberlain is proof against that. War would be, I am sure, a lesser evil than allowing Hitler to get off scot-free with the swag again.

On 28 August:

Another 24 hours gone by and still no final decision. The midday news announces that Hitler's demands of Poland are Danzig and an alteration in various places along the border – sufficiently little to tempt the appeasement instincts in all of us! It also announces the dispatch of a German messenger to Chamberlain and there are reports of an invitation to another 'Munich' conference! Beside all that, the resignation of the Cabinet here seems a very minor matter!

On 29 August:

Still no decision! Henderson, the British Ambassador to Germany, has flown back to Berlin with the Government's reply to Hitler's message and now it seems up to Hitler to decide for peace or war. It seems the British reply has been a flat refusal of Hitler's proposal to take over Danzig and the Polish corridor, and to make various boundary adjustments, combined with an invitation to further negotiation which prevents it from being an ultimatum. What will be the next step? I alternate between a realisation of all the tragedy that war would involve and a feeling that Hitler will have to be mopped up sometime and that now is the best opportunity.

In the evening I went to the Embassy and listened in to London relayed from Hong Kong. It was a good example of British fairness. Practically all the part I heard was a résumé of Hitler's speech!

On 30 August:

It looks today as though we are being granted a few days' grace, at least. Hitler seems in no mood to turn down the British answer to his message and there is every likelihood of a few days' more talks and conferences before everything is settled. The general feeling at the Embassy this morning is that Hitler has bitten off a bit more than he can chew and cannot get out of his fix without fighting or backing down – if the mixed metaphors may be excused!

Last night I took my food along and ate with the Paasches [German friends from *Rikkyo*]. She especially is very worried about the situation, though both said that many in Germany hope that Britain and France will remain firm and fight, if necessary, as it is the only hope they have of deliverance from Nazi rule.

On 31 August:

Things are still dragging out in Europe. The midday news announces Henderson's return to Germany with the British Government's reply to the German answer to the British Government's communiqué in reference to the original German proposal – I think that is the right number of missives! Whether we are near the final débâcle remains to be seen; Chamberlain's words to the Commons were not very reassuring, but one continues hoping if only because of the length of the negotiations.

On 1 September:

Today's paper and the midday broadcast suggest that the sands are running out. One thing that astonishes me is the fact that Poland is apparently now only partially mobilising – I should have thought she would have mobilised fully immediately after the signing of the Soviet–German Pact last week.

This evening the Paasches and Hamish [Hamish Sutcliff from *Rikkyo*] are coming to supper – we shall be an interesting foursome.

On 2 September:

Well, the fat's in the fire now. Fighting has broken out along the Polish–German border, the German troops are invading Poland and German planes bombing every Polish city possible. Poland has appealed for aid, Great Britain and France are fully mobilised and we shall all be in it in a matter of hours. It is a tragic business, but it seems the only way to deal with Hitler – and that's all that can be said about it.

I couldn't help feeling the appropriateness of our dinner party last night – the Paasches, Hamish and myself. Four Christians – two Germans and two English – facing together this crisis of their nations and able to do so with complete friendship and bringing their evening to a close with prayer. It was a great experience.

This morning I have been down to the Embassy, where our official relations with Germany are declared to be strained!

On 3 September:

The European situation is strange. We are deluged with blaring headlines about Germany's invasion of Poland, we remember our 'automatic' guarantees and expect the balloon to go up in a matter of hours – and nothing happens! Later accounts make one doubt the extent of the fighting, accounts of the bombing of Warsaw are conflicting, and Chamberlain still goes on talking the language of negotiation. Henderson is told to ask Germany whether she has aggressive intentions towards Poland (of all stupid questions!) and no time-limit is set for the answer. So much at least for the Prime Minister's statement on Friday in the House. Last night's statement seems to have been stronger, if I got the gist of the midday radio right – an immediate stopping of the fighting and a five-power conference, the German acceptance of these demands to be into London before 12 noon (Tokyo 8 p.m.) today. There seems to me real danger of mucking about with futile negotiations, while Poland loses the corridor, instead of going to her aid at once. Possession is nine points of the law and Hitler has every chance of getting what he wants (for the moment) if he can spin out his acceptance of an invitation to a conference until his troops are in possession. Our two-days' delay is to me quite incomprehensible.

I hate and loathe war, but as things are I can see no alternative course but for us to stand firm by our pledged word and resist Hitler's attempt at world domination. Another 'Munich' and we can put up the shutters on the old British Empire as preferring dividends to honour – and become isolationist citizens of the USA with no truck with Europe!

This was the last letter my father sent to my mother in Takayama, for at this point the Woodwards' younger son, Peter, fell ill, David was placed in quarantine and my mother decided to return with us to Tokyo. I was myself running a temperature and so my mother's first action on hearing that Great Britain and Germany were at war was to call round to borrow a thermometer from the German doctor staying next door.

7

Time to Leave – But Where to Go?

'A volcano that is likely to erupt at any moment is not perhaps the best site to choose for writing an annual report.' So my father began his report for the missionary society on 10 October 1940. Yet at the beginning of that year it had not seemed clear that Japan would become involved in the European war. The German–Soviet Pact signed in the previous August had been regarded as a betrayal of Japan and it was still difficult to see how the war would develop and who would eventually win.

In January 1940, the stopping of the Japanese steamship, the *Asama Maru*, by a British warship and the forcible removal of twenty-one out of fifty German sailors on board led to another flare-up of anti-British feeling. Stanley Woodward commented:

> The point which angers the Japanese is the fact that it was done almost within sight of the coast of Japan – they consider it an insult and a blow to their national prestige. We cannot help feeling that the incident is being greatly worked up and magnified in order to distract attention from the difficulties of economic life and the opposition to the government. But the fact remains that it was a tactless and unimaginative act on the part of our Navy. They could probably have prevented German combatants travelling on Japanese ships by diplomatic negotiations, instead of doing it in quite such a high-handed way. But our Navy, of course, has been irritated by Japanese actions off the China coast and were probably quite ready to have a bit of their own back.

Then, in April, May, June 1940, came the 'blitzkrieg', Germany's lightning invasions of Denmark, Norway, Holland, Belgium and France, and it was this apparently unstoppable run of German successes that brought the decisive shift in Japanese policy. The collapse of France's renowned army, in particular, made an enormous impression in Japan, where military achievement counted for more than anything else. It sealed the fate of all liberal and democratic sections of opinion in Japan and led to Japan's aligning itself definitively with the Axis powers.

Ever since the start of the war, British residents had been called to the Embassy for positive pep talks about the splendid progress of the Allies and the certainty of a British victory. Now it seemed that invariably as they emerged from these talks the newsboys would be ringing their bells to announce that Hitler had overrun yet another country. Caroline wrote, 'Our distress over the daily headlines seems moderate compared to the great anxiety among our British neighbours.' My father and Stanley read the Japanese headlines as often as they saw them and grew increasingly proficient at reading the articles inside, to squeeze out of them the last items of news that might not be reported in the English language papers.

Larry and Caroline held a party for an American, Dr Scott, and his French wife, who were leaving Japan for New England: 'Luckily we didn't know about the occupation of Paris until the next morning.' Several other parties had been arranged in their honour, but Mrs Scott was so completely sunk over the fate of her country that she did not attend any of them.

Caroline wrote:

Our life goes on here through the usual round in spite of the nightmare of the war. We notice that in Tokyo there is a more normal social activity than during the first year or two of the China Incident. And now, since our British friends are so apt to be preoccupied with worry for their country and families, there is a more firm determination than ever to carry on as long as we can. Neighbourhood tea parties are held on every possible pretext.

Yet arranging these tea parties required some ingenuity, for many foods were now scarce and of poor quality. Sudden shortages arose, either because the government was controlling prices, or because the dealers were going on strike against low prices by refusing to supply goods until the government consented to a rise. Thus there was a sudden sugar famine, then a shortage of eggs, then of fuel, then matches disappeared, then rice became scarce and precious. These things always appeared again in a short time, but usually at an increased price. Butter, the better kind of tinned foods and to some extent eggs were permanently scarce. The

Woodwards had an arrangement to get butter – five pounds at a time – through a firm in Hokkaido. The price, though, was abominable.

Water was a serious problem. At the beginning of the year Stanley had written: 'We have been able to procure a little fuel for heating the bath and heating the children's room if necessary. No rain or snow has fallen this year yet, and the reservoirs are getting so low that to add to all our war-time economies, we shall have to economise on water.' And two weeks later: 'We have had no rain or snow all January – it is the last day today – but it has been very cold – a fine dry cold. The water shortage is rather serious. There is dust everywhere and dust storms whenever a wind springs up. And owing to the dryness there have been some disastrous fires.'

One such disastrous fire broke out in Shizuoka. Owing to a wind that changed direction constantly and the lack of water, a fire that started in a small house near the centre of the city spread until six and a half thousand buildings – the whole of the business centre of the city including the main post office and the railway station – were burned and thirty-six thousand people left homeless in the cold. The fire spread on both sides of the railway line and the main line connecting Tokyo with Osaka was cut for thirty-six hours. Though only two people lost their lives and only eight were seriously injured, property insured to the value of twenty-five million yen went up in flames besides a vast number of smaller, uninsured dwellings.

By May the water shortage was growing acute and Larry and Caroline were having to set their alarm for two or three o'clock in the morning to fill their pails when the water was trickling through. Then there was a week when they could get no water upstairs at any hour and Larry had to fill the pails downstairs and store the water in the bath tub upstairs. Then the girls had to drag it downstairs as they needed it through the day. Once, for thirty-six hours, they could not get a drop of water anywhere in the house. 'Even the Japanese editorials are reprimanding the government for short-sightedness in so greedily enlarging the city of Tokyo without adequate planning.'

In early June things began to improve, for they could count on filling the bath tub from the upstairs tap at five o'clock in the morning and the girls were encouraged to do the laundry before the water went off downstairs by nine o'clock. Then water rationing was introduced and they actually had pressure enough to brush their teeth in running water if they rose at 6.30 in the morning. Rationing was introduced too for sugar and matches. The red tape and nuisance of procuring them took a lot of time but it did ensure that they received their allowance in the end.

The Rose family were spending the summer in Karuizawa, where the annual garden party was held as usual. Milk, sugar and charcoal were solicited in small lots from several households, in addition to sandwiches and whatever could be invented in the way of fruit tarts or plain cookies. The sugar ration for Karuizawa residents was one pound per person per month but the rationing tickets ran out before the Roses secured theirs. They just hoped some more would become available in time. And indeed the garden party proved a success: 'One Embassy person sent a box of fudge sufficient for the crowd of sixty! It was the most generous gesture I have known for a long time!'

Throughout that summer of 1940 the question that was occupying the minds of the British was whether, now that France had fallen, Hitler would attempt an invasion of Britain. Larry and Caroline held a tea party for their neighbours in Karuizawa: 'Our At Home was a fair success in spite of the wordless preoccupation of our English guests.' Our family and the Woodward family were planning again to spend the summer in Takayama, but it looked as though my mother and Gwen would have to go alone with us children, for neither my father nor Stanley wanted to leave Tokyo at all. Yet my father and Stanley did both come up from time to time to Takayama. On one of those occasions the police went through our house and took my father's camera. Fortunately he had checked his photograph albums earlier and destroyed any photographs that might be thought of as suspect.

The holiday houses in Takayama were situated on the cliffs. One day my parents watched helplessly as a fishing boat was dashed to pieces in strong waves and all the fishermen drowned. Each evening the missionary families gathered on the cliffs for evening prayers and each evening Christopher asked for the hymn 'Abide with me'. The line 'Fast falls the eventide' must have seemed to the adults more apt than my brother knew. My mother used to go for walks along the cliffs and look at the sea and think of the two islands – Britain and Japan. The sea was a defence for Britain, but could it save Britain from a German invasion? The sea was a defence for Japan, but might it turn Japan into a prison for our family?

During that summer, following Hitler's dazzling run of successes, the existing political parties in Japan were dissolved, a new mass national party was formed and a new national structure announced, on Fascist lines, from which all traces of democracy would be eliminated. In this structure all the stress was laid on 'oneness': one central authority, one political party, one system of thought and life and action. One type of suit for men (the civilian uniform) was to be introduced and one type of outfit for women was planned. In line with totalitarian philosophy, individual initiative and freedom were curbed and the ideal of the ant-heap was held up for admiration.

Then, at the end of September, Japan signed the Tripartite Pact with Germany and Italy. My father continued his report:

Thereby Japan has wagered her future on the victory of Germany and Italy and has placed in Nazi hands the ultimate decision as to whether she will enter the war. Hitler, not the Emperor, will settle that question. We are indeed sitting on a volcano that may erupt at any moment – if not over the Burma Road question next week, then when Berlin gives the order.[14]

Stanley commented:

The latest change in the situation is the alliance of Japan with Germany and Italy. It was announced two days ago and caused much excitement among the foreigners and Americans in particular. A few are packing up to go already and how much longer we shall be here we don't know. Of course, nothing may happen after all, but October is bound to be a critical month.

These events brought a new crisis for the *Nippon Sei Ko Kai* and indeed for all Christian churches in Japan. My father later wrote to the missionary society:

Since 1931 and the Manchuria affair and the Lytton Commission, anti-English feelings have been having full play. They swelled up into an ugly chorus in 1937 when the Archbishop of Canterbury took the chair at an anti-bombing-of-open-towns meeting; they rose again to fever pitch over Tientsin[15] and the *Asama Maru* affair; and

---

[14] The Burma Road was an important supply line for foreign military equipment to reach the Nationalist Chinese in Chungking. Under pressure from the Japanese the British agreed to close the Burma Road for three months from 18 July 1940. By the autumn Britain was no longer prepared to submit to Japanese pressure and so it was reopened on 18 October 1940 and shipments to Chungking resumed.

[15] In June 1939 Japan blockaded the British concession in Tientsin. All who entered the British compound were subjected to a search. Japan justified this action by citing the need to suppress anti-Japanese terrorists operating out of the concession and anti-British feeling was whipped up in Japan. Japan's real intention was to humiliate Britain and damage her standing in Asia.

we were all considering war and evacuation and concentration camps over the Burma Road incident; but that from an apparently fair sky this bolt should fall, no one expected that. By the act of arresting and intimidating the Japanese leaders of the Salvation Army all mission work of all churches came, in mid-August, to the last scenes in the drama of Christian missions from foreign sources in Japan.

All Christian churches were now under suspicion. Anti-British and anti-Christian posters appeared outside churches and warnings to 'Beware of silver-tongued Japanese, who are under the influence of foreigners. They may very easily be spies.' Missionaries met with the same friendship as ever from their people, but were asked not to visit them, for every visit would be followed by a call from detectives and unpleasant questioning. The Salvation Army, with its military name and titles and uniforms, incurred special suspicion. It was compelled to change its name, forego foreign funding and dismiss its foreign workers.[16]

It was clear that the *Nippon Sei Ko Kai* would soon receive attention and so the Japanese bishops approached the authorities to ask on what terms it would be allowed to continue its work. The answer was that no foreigners should hold positions of authority in the church and no foreign funds should be accepted for its support. As a result all the foreign bishops resigned in October 1940 and oversight of the whole church was entrusted to five Japanese bishops. As for the foreign priests, some were retired, some kept on in very uncertain circumstances. The attitude of the Japanese bishops differed: some valued their foreign staff and wished to retain them; others regarded them as an embarrassment and wished for them to be withdrawn. Women missionaries, though not directly affected by any official action, still felt the influence of official decisions. Some, but not all, were asked to give up their work, some were so restricted as to make continuance of their work impossible, one had her house stoned and could not even return after the summer to pack up her things, while one, who was in charge of the leprosy hospital in Kumamoto, had her house searched and both her secretary and the hospital chaplain detained for questioning.

As for the three foreign staff at the *Shingakuin*, Larry Rose, Stanley Woodward and my father, they were told that they could not remain after the end of the academic year in March 1941. For my father's part, he felt that it was an act of grace that he, who was tarred with the

---

[16] Onward: *a survey of the mission field in war-time* (SPG report for 1940; undated), p. 20.

Embassy brush, was allowed to stay at all. Yet the scope of their teaching was now restricted, for new legislation stated that foreigners could no longer teach anything influencing thought and specifically not religion. My father wrote:

> It must be recognised that while for us and the missionary societies the question of what place, if any, will be available for the foreign worker in Japan in the future is a matter of immediate concern, for most Japanese Christians it is already a closed issue. It was settled in August and we are little more, in their eyes, than the relics of an age that is now over, waiting only for the final adjustments before we disappear from the scene.

There was another issue of immediate concern and that was the official demand for a union of the Christian churches. In government eyes it was intolerable that there should be so many Christian bodies. The attempt of each to get itself registered under the recently enacted Religions Control Bill was causing the clerks of the Religious Department of the Education Ministry an immense amount of work. Why not save them the long hours they were now compelled to put in, and also come into line with the new national structure with its emphasis on 'oneness', and amalgamate in a single organisation for the government to deal with? And furthermore, as a great united Christian demonstration of thanksgiving for the glorious 2,600th anniversary of the founding of the Japanese Empire, to be celebrated on 17 October, why not try and get the scheme accepted by then?

This request from the authorities fitted in with a good deal of feeling towards union that had existed among Protestant churches for years. Many of them wished to amalgamate, rather than dissipate their resources as at present, so they had less difficulty in complying with the official request. The Roman Catholic and Orthodox Churches would not enter into such a united church, of course, even though the authorities got the Methodist Bishop to approach them. But what of the *Nippon Sei Ko Kai*? They were small in comparison with the combined Protestant churches, but had a distinct, more Catholic, tradition. Larry wrote in his diary: 'Oct 17, 1940. A critical day for the *Sei Ko Kwai* (2,600th anniversary of founding of Empire!). Oct 15, church standing committee voted not to join *Go Do*.[17] Today the union may be proclaimed and

---

[17] The *Go Do* was the government-sponsored United Church.

Sei Ko Kwai left out. What will the future be? Will government permit *Sei Ko Kwai* to exist?' But the government refused and so the church had to go underground and attempt to survive as a hidden church through the war years.

Foreigners were kept under surveillance. Larry went to the corner tobacco shop to buy a pack of cigarettes. The shopkeeper apologised and said that his brand was not available. 'Well then,' said Larry, 'let me have another brand.' 'But I think you wouldn't like them,' protested the shopkeeper. 'That's all right,' said Larry, 'I'll try them anyway.' But the tobacconist was becoming increasingly embarrassed and Larry realised what the problem was: the *Kempeitai* or Secret Police had asked the man what brand of cigarette Larry smoked and now, if Larry were to be seen smoking another brand, the shopkeeper would be in serious trouble.

In the streets children would point at foreigners and call them spies. Usually the college compound was a safe haven but David Woodward had one nasty experience. The students did military training and one day a student was standing in the compound holding a gun. David was examining the gun with interest when the student said, 'One day I might have to use this gun to kill somebody, and if our countries go on being enemies, David, then one day I might have to use it to kill you.' Electrified, David fled home, expecting every moment to be hit by a bullet in the back. As an adult he wondered if the student was saying that such terrible things happen in war, but as a six-year-old he just ran for his life.

Most Japanese were friendly. Stanley wrote: 'In our daily life we meet with nothing but kindness – extra kindness in many cases. Today, as we went to St Andrew's Church, people were almost fussily ready to give up seats to Gwen and the children in the trains and trams.' Furasawa-san had to stay at her own house on certain days to practise air-raid precautions, but her neighbours teased her: 'You'd be no use in an air-raid – at the first bomb you'd be off to those English children of yours!' Our milkman left messages with the cook – whatever happened, he would see that there was milk for us children. The Woodwards received their potatoes from a farmer in Takayama. During the summer they had ordered a sack of potatoes and paid for it. They received a message from the farmer: a new law forbade the supplying of potatoes outside the district except to relatives, so please would they understand that a sack of potatoes addressed to 'Watanabe' was intended for Woodward!

Rationing was tight. People had to queue for tickets to get bread or potatoes, as these were rice substitutes, and then queue again for the goods themselves. Furasawa-san would take me with her to collect these rations. She would then return to queue again and would be surprised to be told, 'You've been here before'. She didn't realise how conspicuous it made her to be accompanied by a small, fair-haired child! The patriotic thing was to eat only a 'Rising Sun' lunch at noon. This consisted of two cold rice balls with a sour plum or other red pickle in the centre. The Japanese were encouraged to accept the shortages of food and the growing discomforts of life gladly, for they were all in loyalty to the Emperor.

As winter approached, the girls in a class my mother was teaching expressed their happiness at having unheated classrooms, as in this way they could share the hardships of the soldiers at the front. David Woodward, John Caiger and Christopher began to attend a new kindergarten, and after a while I joined the kindergarten too. We have a photograph of the teachers and children standing outside the kindergarten which has always puzzled me, for it shows nearly all the Japanese children dressed in neat white shirts and dark shorts or skirts, while Christopher, David and I are dressed in thick winter overcoats. Could it be that the Japanese parents were happy for their children to share the hardships of the soldiers at the front and that our parents were not?

Certainly the children like the adults were being prepared for war. The previous autumn Stanley described the annual air-raid practices to his parents, who were themselves enduring war-time conditions in England:

We are taking it very seriously this time, as though under war conditions. Like you, we live practically in darkness after daylight fails and drills of all kinds take place. The College is organised for the purpose. Today we had an air-raid warning at 8.30 a.m. and in five minutes they had cleared out over six hundred children from the neighbouring primary school and brought them on to the College compound. Then, until the 'All Clear' at 9.30 am, they held demonstrations of how to deal with fire, with various kinds of gas, etc. The College boys took part in all this, and the members of the staff, including myself, were organised into an emergency fire brigade.

As yet there was little positive news of the war, yet sometimes there were moments of encouragement. One day Stanley was in Tokyo's central post office sending off a telegram. He was kept waiting a long time, as it was the time of day when international cables were usually sent off. Shortly after he joined the line, a foreigner came up and stood just behind him. He was very large and fair-haired and Stanley wondered if he were one of the enemy. However, there were some telegraph forms nearby, so Stanley motioned to pass one to him, when he said in guttural broken English that he had only come to ask the clerk a question. He then turned to Stanley and said, 'Are you American?' Stanley replied, 'No, I am English', at which he let out a great guffaw. Stanley wondered what it meant and whether he were German or not. He turned to Stanley again and said, 'What do you think of this war?' Stanley said that he thought it was going quite well and that the tide was definitely beginning to turn in favour of Britain. He then asked, 'Do you think you will win?' Still not knowing which side he was on, Stanley said, 'Of course we shall win – in the long run!' At this the stranger let out another great laugh and said, 'Well, the confidence of you British is most extraordinary. I can never get over my astonishment!' Then, seeing Stanley's perplexity, he said, 'Yes, it is all right, I am an Estonian and I do not like the Nazis. It would be a disaster for the world if they won. But when France fell, I said, it has come, it is all over. The world is to become Nazi. But you British are the astonishing thing. You do not know when you are beaten. It is your confidence which causes me to hope again. After the fall of France, the first ray of hope I had was when I was travelling on a neutral ship to Hong Kong. As we came near, we were boarded by a British naval detachment. The young British officer came on board that ship as if he owned it!' Stanley laughed and said he was afraid that was a fault of the British. They did tend to walk about the world as though they owned it and no doubt it was annoying to others. 'Oh no,' said the Estonian, 'it was magnificent. It gave me hope again. No man belonging to a defeated race could come aboard a ship like that!'

One memorably happy event took place during that anxious autumn of 1940. That was the wedding of my godmother, Kay Stockdale, to Hamish Sutcliff. Though both Kay and Hamish were British, the wedding took place at the American church, Holy Trinity, where Kay attended the services and Hamish sang in the choir. To our great delight Peggy Rose and I were the small bridesmaids (or flower girls as the Americans called us) and we were each given a powder compact with Mount Fuji engraved on it as a present. The older bridesmaid was Kay Spackman, whose father was chaplain at Holy Trinity. A difficulty arose over the cake. Eggs were in short supply. Perhaps there were dried eggs? Certainly there was dried milk, known as

KLIM. But a Chinese cook could always provide what was necessary and a Chinese cook produced eggs for the wedding cake. Caroline, Gwen and my mother each baked a tier of the cake in their ovens. As Kay and Hamish were having a church wedding they had to have three wedding ceremonies – first in the Japanese registry, then in Holy Trinity, then in the British Embassy. There it was solemnly announced that the marriage was valid in all countries of the world except Turkey!

An elderly missionary died and Stanley was asked to sell her effects. He did so just in time. The government had already forbidden the sale of luxury articles of thirty yen value and over (thirty yen equalled three pounds), and as from the following month certain articles classified as 'luxuries' could not be sold at all. Some of this missionary's things might come under the heading of 'luxuries', as the list was pretty wide. Stanley took a suitcase of her books to sell at a Christian bookshop – about fifteen books in all and much of it old theology – and was astonished to be given thirty-five yen for them. Books in English were selling for enormous prices, as it was almost impossible to import them.

One evening Stanley was conducting a prayer meeting at St Andrew's Church. He set off in good time and took with him some of this missionary's old gold teeth fillings to sell at a jeweller's shop on the way. Gwen followed and came into the meeting room with a large *furoshiki*[18] bundle containing a kettle, a toast rack, an elaborate Victorian silver-plated tea-pot and some other odds and ends of hardware, and dumped all this ironmongery with a clatter on the floor. After the meeting she tried to sell all this stuff to the assembled company and was indeed very successful. She told how she had set off in a great hurry from home and when waiting for the bus discovered that she had in her purse only one button and two moth-balls to pay the fares. So Gwen and Stanley were teased about going out to prayer meetings expecting to pay their fares with buttons, mothballs and old gold teeth! Fortunately for Gwen, my mother had joined her at the bus stop and paid her fares. Otherwise she would have had to pawn a kettle on the way. A story was going round in Tokyo about a group of British people from one of the Baltic states, returning to England via the Trans-Siberian Railway and Canada. One man arrived in Moscow with no money at all, but was able to acquire a ticket for the opera for the price of one old woollen sock!

---

[18] My father explained a *furoshiki* in a letter of 1932: 'The Japanese always carry everything in a *furoshiki*. It is something like the red handkerchief an English workman carries his lunch in, only more artistic!'

Stanley was asked to clear out further boxes containing possessions of former missionaries. Some of these things had to be sold and some sent back to England: 'No end of a job, but there is less and less to do in other directions. I shall go into the pawn-broking trade when I get back to England after the experience gained here in the last few months!'

For all three foreign staff at the *Shingakuin* there was less and less to do within the college. This was partly because of the laws the government had passed preventing foreigners from teaching anything influencing thought, but it was also because the number of students was diminishing and would inevitably continue to diminish almost to nothing.

On 17 October Larry wrote in his diary: 'The date finds me struggling with one of the most difficult decisions of my life. No use here after March 1941. Had decided to go in December when Dr Sugai (the Principal) asked me to stay – wait and see – be ready for a new day.'

On 19 October:

Conversation with Bishops Reifsnider and Binsted yesterday helped clear the atmosphere. I find that gradually the decision to leave Japan has slipped up on me during this week – 10 days of doubt and feeling that foreigners' presence here may handicap the *Sei Ko Kwai* in days ahead gives a grain of balm to my conscience. If I stayed I should not have a real job, of course, and it would always be possible for suspicion to be excited by that very fact. Dr Sugai, kneeling here beside me, dear man – what does he face? He wants me to stay. He will be loyal. I can't face the risks involved for Caroline and Peggy, Judy and no. 3. [Caroline was expecting their third child, Frances.] God forgive, if He would have me stay.

On 21 October:

How can the channels be kept open for the *Sei Ko Kwai* to maintain fellowship and receive help from America? The Bishops will all probably leave soon. A very few women will stay on for a time – and one or two teachers at *Rikkyo*. Pitiful. It would still be pitiful if I were to stay, of course.

On 25 October:

I must tell Dr Sugai today. Waiting for something to happen to allow a clear cut decision, can't go on indefinitely and the decision has made itself. I have let it. It is perhaps a cowardly, weak, selfish choice. I could teach Latin 3 hours at *Rikkyo*. I might be able to teach 2 hours of Christian doctrine (emasculated) and might not. I could study the language to fill up the time and preach and lecture occasionally. What might open in the future no one knows. Students here at *Shingakuin* will dwindle to practically none. It would be a gloomy prospect – but yet I might be able to perform a service – just keeping channels open. Anyone could do it. Am I the one who ought to?

On 29 October:

Told Dr Sugai final decision last night. He was not impressed with the reasons, seemed really to want me to stay, but could give me no more assurance that there would be anything for me to do next March and after. It is going to be hard to get a passage. SCW [Stanley Woodward] decided to go in January – no space on boat.

On 9 November:

The die is cast now and Dec 12, 1940 we sail for San Francisco, on the *Cleveland*. Will mission work in Montana be our work? So be it. I shan't go pining for 'larger fields' nor moping about for academic work.

On 4 December:

Official farewell – moving speeches genuine expressions of regret.

On 10 December:

Three requests from Bishop Binsted turned down. How can one know that one is right in such decisions? Can't, I guess.

Bishop Binsted had asked Larry to consider work in the Philippines. Caroline commented: 'It is tempting socially and financially but we have our faces pretty well turned homewards and it does not seem the proper direction to take a family in this year. We might have to move even sooner than April if naval operations should open up in those regions.'

The Binsteds, the Spackmans from Holy Trinity and other Americans went from Japan to the Philippines. Most were interned in prison camps when the Japanese occupied the Philippines a year later.

On 13 December:

Our last day in Japan. Someone asked yesterday – Mr Grew it was [Joseph C. Grew was American Ambassador in Japan] – whether the six years were wasted 'apart from what you have given'. No. It would be a sad confession if one had to say there was no personal gain, growth, enrichment of mind or spirit from such a period. I have learned much from the Japanese. I admire the race and love many individuals.

On 14 December:

God bless this chapel and all those who worship in it – this *Shingakuin*, this *Sei Ko Kwai* and people.

On 9 November Larry had written that they would be sailing for San Francisco on the SS *President Cleveland* on 12 December. But sailing dates were not predictable and on 19 October Caroline had written, 'If we cannot get space on the *President Cleveland* leaving Yokohama December 5, we will try for an NYK boat[19] direct to Seattle'. On 27 October Larry and Caroline were in Yokohama getting first-hand information about steamships and freight possibilities. Their passage was not yet confirmed but they were confident of getting on one boat or another during December.

On 10 November Caroline wrote, 'We have felt so restless and unsettled until we could hear definitely about our sailing. Now we know that there will surely be a cabin for us on the *President Cleveland*. We reach San Francisco on 26 or 27 December.' But on 28 November she wrote, 'The *President Cleveland* is delayed again – not leaving Yokohama until December 14.'

Meanwhile, Stanley and Gwen, together with the Hutchinsons from Fukuoka, had started to enquire in September about the possibility of work in Jamaica. Early in October Stanley wrote:

---

[19] *Nippon Yusen Kaisha*: Japanese steamship company.

Things here are drifting from bad to worse. People who can leave
are beginning to go and we don't know when our turn may come,
but meanwhile we are waiting and seeing 'in a condition of alert'.
If we get fixed up to go anywhere definite, we shall send a cable
to you and from that time you should write to us at the new
address.' Where that might be was still unclear. Would it be Jamaica?
... or Australia? ... or Canada? 'If we are sent home to England,
well, that will be the best of all, and you won't need to write!

By the middle of October there was still no news from Jamaica. Canon
Hutchinson was now staying with the Woodwards, having come up to
Tokyo from Fukuoka. He had written to the Bishop of Jamaica by air
mail in September, applying for a position for himself and asking for a
cable in reply. Shortly afterwards he had written again, on Stanley's
behalf, but had said that Stanley might not be available until the end
of the academic year in March 1941. Now he sent a cable: 'Woodward
self available immediately Hutchinson'. At the end of the month Canon
Hutchinson received a cable from the Bishop of Jamaica: 'Kingston
Jamaica considering offer awaiting reply from CMS[20] about salary will
cable when received.' This applied only to Canon Hutchinson, so he
sent another cable to the Bishop: 'Woodward also available immediately
Hutchinson.'

Meanwhile, on 25 October, all British subjects in Japan were advised
by the Embassy to leave as soon as possible, while they were still free
to choose their own ship and destination. Stanley and Gwen knew that
the time might come when they would have to be evacuated at a
moment's notice, leaving all their possessions behind and going where
they were sent rather than where they wanted to go. If such an emergency
evacuation were to take place they would almost certainly be sent to
Australia, which was in the sterling bloc, rather than to Canada, which
was in the dollar bloc, for it was easier for money to be transmitted
from England to sterling bloc countries than to dollar bloc countries.

The boats were filling rapidly and it was necessary to book far ahead,
so Stanley booked provisionally on the *Tatsuta Maru*, leaving Yokohama
on 18 December for Los Angeles. He had tried all the boats going direct
to Panama, where they could change for Jamaica, but they were all full
until the middle of January. The only alternative was to go to Los
Angeles and then either change to coasting vessels for Panama or else

---

[20] Church Missionary Society.

go overland to New Orleans and proceed by ship from there. The Canadian Pacific line would land them too far north and was in any case booked up a long time ahead. The American President line was quite booked up by Americans and was, in any case, very expensive. Meanwhile the *Tatsuta Maru* was reputed to be one of the best Japanese ships on the Pacific.

In the middle of November Canon Hutchinson received the expected cable about Jamaica. It had been sent, not by the Bishop of Jamaica, but by the Church Missionary Society in London. Canon Hutchinson in turn sent a cable to Stanley from Fukuoka: 'Barclay cables Jamaica welcomes Hutchinsons Woodwards stop please confirm bookings Hutchinson.' The last part referred to the provisional bookings Stanley had made for the *Tatsuta Maru*. So Stanley confirmed the bookings and they expected to sail on 18 December and to reach Los Angeles on 3 January. 'We shall be very sorry to leave many of our friends in Japan, but it will be a relief to depart from a country where one is obviously not wanted.'

For my father there was less sense of urgency, owing to his position as chaplain to the Embassy:

I plan to stay by the old ship till the end, as we now have diplomatic status and so would be among those evacuated with the Embassy in a crisis. If America is involved we should probably be evacuated to Mexico – the only country likely to be neutral (barring Siam) for miles around! I am writing to the Archbishop of New Westminster, the Bishop of Argentina and my old vicar in the West Indies, to see if there would be any chance of work in those areas if the balloon goes up. I am also planning to write to Australia and perhaps New Zealand. One doesn't want to be landed in some odd spot with no contacts and nothing in view. Personally, I should like to get back to England and do something in East London or elsewhere, where there is so much loss and suffering, but the family would have to be left somewhere en route and the question of their support would arise and so I fear that course is impossible.

My father wrote of these possibilities in a letter accompanying his annual report of 10 October 1940. He knew that this would almost certainly be his last report from Japan, for it looked only a matter of time before the European and Far Eastern conflicts would become one with America involved in both. So he concluded his report with his impressions from more than eight years spent in Japan:

First, a deep thankfulness for the opportunity of serving in this country. The clouds have been growing darker and the opportunities becoming more and more restricted, but in the first five years at any rate, in Numazu and Tokyo, the work was fully worthwhile. It has been a great privilege to serve in a land so beautiful, among a people so naturally kind and courteous, and to see the Church in action in the mission field.

Secondly, a sense of anger that a people so naturally kind and hospitable should have been led by military leaders with an unbounded lust for power into the present pass. The country has been drained of its resources, food has grown in many ways scarce and of poor quality, clothes have deteriorated to the most temporary kind of ersatz. And then they dare to speak of this poverty-stricken country and the ravaged and desolate land of China as a 'co-prosperity area'.

But worse than that is the poisoning of people's minds, the staging of spy trials, the inculcation of suspicion against foreigners. In the sixteenth and seventeenth centuries Japan was open for about eighty years and then came the seclusion of the Tokugawa period.[21] Now again, after another open period of eighty years, Japan is losing her nerve and is seeking in something akin to seclusion (this time a closed East Asia) refuge from a world too complex for her to cope with and opportunity to absorb (and often reject) what she has received in the great days of the Meiji era.[22] It is indeed a sad day for those who have admired Japan's fine achievements to see the disastrous course she is now following.

My father was able to write so frankly because his letters and reports were sent to England by the diplomatic bag. Bishop Heaslett added a note to the report: 'In articles and so on founded on this my name must not appear. I'm staying on for a while.'

So, at the end of the year, the Roses and the Woodwards sailed for America and our family moved from our house in the *Shingakuin* compound to a house in the compound of St Andrew's Church. My father continued to teach New Testament Greek at the *Shingakuin* (language, not ideas!), but his relationship with the students could now

---

[21] The Tokugawa shoguns ruled Japan as a closed country until the arrival of Commodore Perry and his 'black ships' in 1853.

[22] The Emperor Meiji ruled Japan from 1868–1912, during which time Japan moved from feudal state to modern world power.

be little more than formal. His principal role was to serve and help, as best he could, an anxious and unsettled British community.

In January 1941, a further notice was sent from the Embassy to British subjects:

> In October of last year, British subjects were advised to consider leaving Japanese or Manchurian territory at an early date. Since then the international situation has shown no signs of improving and all British subjects are therefore once again advised by the British Government to leave Japan or Manchuria. It would be wise to take advantage of existing transportation facilities because, should an emergency arise, it is unlikely that the provision of shipping for evacuation would be practicable. British subjects who ignore the advice now given do so at their own risk.

The British subjects to whom this notice was addressed included both British residents in Japan and British people arriving in Japan from China. For many it was not easy to choose a destination and not everyone made good choices. Just as many Americans were considering the Philippines, so many British people were considering Singapore or Hong Kong. Indeed, there had been much talk of sending women and children to Singapore or Hong Kong for safety in the event of a crisis. When my father said he did not think that either would be safe, people looked at him in surprise and said, 'What a pessimist you are!'

Foreigners were under increasing suspicion. Old and respected residents were arrested. It was sometimes said that the least probable people were charged with spying to prove to the public that no foreigner could be trusted. One large delivery of letters to our house gave my parents an unpleasant jolt, for they were all addressed to a journalist who was in prison. It indicated that the mail for our house was going through the same censor's office.

The Japanese continued to be kind to us as children. The Sisters of the Epiphany had a house in Tokyo. Furasawa-san had grown up in their orphanage and girls from their embroidery school came to our house to do sewing or to look after us. One day I decided I should like to see the Sisters' house, so I got on the bus with the girls and refused to get off. No Japanese would touch me to make me get off the bus, so I saw the Sisters' house, my father was telephoned, and I returned home well pleased with my adventure. On tram rides my brother liked to stand by the conductor and sing out the names of the stops as we approached. One day my father heard sounds of mirth coming from a barber's shop near the compound. When he looked in he saw seven-year-old Christopher telling the Japanese inside that it would be much better for Japan to support England in the war and not Germany, at which all the Japanese present were doubled up with laughter.

Although food was becoming increasingly scarce, we ate quite well during those last few months in Japan, for more and more people were leaving and many bequeathed the contents of their store cupboards to us, who were still staying on for a while. People were also leaving behind possessions they could not take with them. As it was not possible to take money out of the country, my father spent what money he could on things that were not too bulky to pack – Japanese prints, silks, bronzes, china, lacquer. In fact, it has always seemed astonishing that, with the world falling apart, my parents set off into an uncertain future with such a cargo of fragile objects.

At last, in May 1941, the day came for us to leave and we took the train for Yokohama to board the NYK ship, the *Hie Maru*, bound for Seattle and Vancouver. We stood on the ship's deck, looking back towards Japan, and there they were on the quayside, Furasawa-san, our amah, and Takahashi-san, our cook, two Japanese women in their kimonos, with tears streaming down their faces. My parents and my brother would all see Furasawa-san again after the war but, although my parents tried, they were never able to trace Takahashi-san, and so they feared she might have died during the terrible bombings of Tokyo in the final months of the war.

We went down to our cabin and as we stood on the threshold I gasped, for the cabin was filled with flowers. I have two other memories of the voyage. In the first I am walking with my father and another man in the hold of the ship between rows of piled-up packing-cases. One packing-case had a nail sticking out which gashed my leg. There must have been blood and tears, but I do not remember those. I still have the scar on my knee. In the other I am sitting at an oblong table with other children. It is my fifth birthday party and there is party food and streamers flying across the table. But was it really my birthday party? The dates don't seem quite right. Perhaps it was a children's party and I remember it as my birthday party because my birthday was coming quite soon.

For luncheon and for dinner on the ship there were elegant menu cards with reproductions of Japanese prints. On one dinner card is a picture of a Japanese castle. We were all three allowed to draw on this card. Helen was three and she has made bold marks, up and down, to and fro, with coloured pencils. I have drawn what might be a ship with faces staring glumly out of the portholes. Christopher has also drawn a ship with the words 'NO 6 LIFE BOAT' and underneath a row of Japanese characters.

Did we sense our parents' anxiety? Our family had left it very late to leave Japan. The *Hie Maru* was the last Japanese passenger ship to cross the Pacific in that summer of 1941. Each morning my parents looked out of the porthole to make sure that we were still sailing in the right direction, that the sun was still on our starboard side. One of the most beautiful sights they had ever seen was that of the American destroyers in Puget Sound. We had made it!

In staying so long, my father was relying on his connection with the British Embassy to provide us with some measure of protection. Yet, had he stayed, this would not have protected him, for he was later told that his name was on a list of foreigners set down for solitary confinement. Perhaps the fact that he had connections with the Embassy, combined with his connections with St Andrew's Church and the *Shingakuin*, made him all the more likely to arouse suspicion, for these meant that he moved both in foreign and in Japanese circles. So, had he stayed, he was marked down for the experience that Bishop Heaslett was about to endure – time in a Japanese prison.

PART IV

And Afterwards

1

From a Japanese Prison

In December, 1941, only a few missionaries remained in Japan, carrying on such work as they could under great difficulties. Suddenly, without warning, they found themselves enemy aliens, liable to internment. But, with one outstanding exception, they were well treated by the Japanese authorities, and all received most touching proofs of affection and continued trust from their Christian friends. The one exception was the man whose forty-two years of service to the country should have ensured for him the respect and trust which Japan traditionally gives to 'Elder Statesmen'.[23]

The 'one exception' was Bishop Heaslett. He was indeed an 'Elder Statesman' of the church in Japan, for he had gone to Japan in 1900 at the age of twenty-four and, apart from three years spent with the Chinese Labour Corps in France during the First World War, he had served in Japan through the whole of his career. He became Bishop of South Tokyo in 1923 and eleven years later Presiding Bishop of the *Nippon Sei Ko Kai*. Though the foreign bishops resigned in October 1940, Bishop Heaslett stayed on as bishop-in-charge of European congregations. His wife had died in 1936 and his only son was now a man, so he felt that he should stay on, to keep channels of communication open and to give help and support where he could.

He was not, however, strong for the ordeal he was about to face. In December 1937 Caroline Rose wrote: 'Bishop Heaslett's eyes are failing him rapidly so that he cannot read now without a magnifying glass. He is preparing to learn braille.' In January 1938 she wrote again: 'Last Sunday there was great excitement when the Japanese papers published Bishop Heaslett's picture with a three-column account of his resigning as Presiding

---

[23] *In This Sign* (SPG report for 1942, published 1943), p. 8.

Bishop. The only basis for this report is that because of very seriously failing eyesight he has given up some of his committee chairmanships.' In September 1938 my father wrote: 'This week there are the Bishops' meetings here at Ikebukuro and we have Bishop Heaslett staying with us. He is remarkably well considering everything and the knowledge that his eyes are not likely to get worse has cheered him a great deal.'

But it was not only his failing eyesight that gave rise to anxiety. October 1940 was a month of crisis for the *Nippon Sei Ko Kai* and on 17 October (a National Holiday for the 2,600th anniversary of the founding of the Japanese Empire) Stanley Woodward wrote: 'Bishop Heaslett, who has had a time of great strain recently, had a heart attack last Tuesday and spent most of last week in bed. I saw him on Sunday afternoon when he got up for the first time. Then on Monday and Tuesday he held his last Diocesan Synod before retirement.'

That Bishop Heaslett had no expectation of the harsh treatment he was about to receive is clear from his own account of his arrest and imprisonment.[24] He was arrested on 8 December 1941, the very day on which Japan declared war on America and Great Britain.[25] At about 10 a.m. he heard, to his amazement, the announcement on the radio of a state of war. He had earlier been informed by the Tokyo police that whatever happened he had nothing to fear, so he expected confinement to his house with restricted liberty to be his fate. The thought of arrest and gaol never entered his mind; internment with others in a camp was the utmost limit of his ideas. He was in a state of bewilderment, quite unable, on that first day, to adjust his mind to the idea of Japan at war. When, therefore, at 4.30 p.m., four men in civilian dress appeared in his front hall, he could only think that they had come to warn him and give him instructions as to his new mode of life. A new mode of life opened for him, in a sense he had never dreamed of, when the senior of the four men read out to him, in English: 'You are arrested on suspicion under the provisions of the Safety of the Realm Act.' Even then his mind did not take in the meaning of the words. He thought: 'Oh, am I to be interviewed?'

The officials were very considerate; they seemed to be sorry for him, a fact that added to his bewilderment. On their advice he changed into his

---

[24] Samuel Heaslett, *From a Japanese Prison* (Student Christian Movement Press Ltd., London, 1943).

[25] The Japanese air attack on Pearl Harbor, the American naval base near Honolulu, took place on the morning of Sunday 7 December. In Tokyo, across the International Date Line, it was already Monday 8 December.

warmest winter suit, put on an extra sweater and filled a suitcase with such things as might be necessary in a cold concentration camp. To questions from him as to where he was going they gave only vague and evasive answers; 'a little fear entered my mind for the first time when one of the men – a detective – ran his hands over me in professional style to make sure that I was not carrying any firearms; that shade of little fear grew day by day until it nearly swamped my mind and became a terror.'

He was told to pick up his suitcase and go out with the biggest of the four men to an unknown destination. The detective took him away; the others remained to search the house. 'As I stepped out of the door to begin my four months of exile, the elder and senior of the party said to me: "God bless you." I suppose he was a Christian. I have often thought since that a more appropriate farewell salutation would have been "God help you" if he knew where I was heading for.'

It was a shock he would never forget when he was taken into a police station in Yokohama and told to wait in a large office full of uniformed police officials. He was left with his thoughts and his suitcase in the main office for about twenty minutes, then was ordered to pick up his belongings and was led into the inner part of the station, through heavy doors, and so ushered into the presence of the two policemen in charge of the cells. 'So I left the world I knew and passed completely into an unknown world that had existed hitherto but vaguely in my thoughts, and I became a member of the criminal classes...'

To the right of the entrance was a cell containing four boys, to the left a cell containing four women. Opposite the entrance, in a straight line along a corridor, were five cells for men, each it seemed full, though later he would come to realise that, however full a cell might seem, there was always room for one more. At the end of the long corridor there was an open window, two washbasins and a toilet.

When the time came for Bishop Heaslett to be examined, he had first to empty all his pockets. Everything was taken from him, even his braces. All this was done in full view of the forty-odd prisoners in the cells, and of course to their intense interest. He was the only foreigner in the station. Standing there shoeless, holding up his trousers with one hand, while the police counted his money and tied up all his belongings in his hat, he must have been to them a novel sight. He was allowed to keep all his clothes, even his heavy overcoat, and his spectacles. This last, so vital to him, was a great concession, he learnt later.

His examination being finished, the policeman opened the door of cell three and pushed him into the midst of its four occupants. 'There is no more horrible sound than that of the key turning in the lock of a prison cell by an official standing outside. I shall never forget that, my first experience of it; it reminds me now of "abandon hope all ye that enter here".' Complete with clothing, but minus all else, he turned to face his new companions, all Japanese. They eagerly questioned him as to what he was in for, but as he did not know himself he could only reply that he supposed his arrest had 'something to do with the war'.

The cell was nine feet long and five and a half feet broad. The floor was of wood covered with pieces of thin matting, the walls were of concrete, a light shone high up overhead day and night. Though it was December, the cell was full of mosquitoes, and the walls were covered with the bloody remains of mosquitoes slaughtered by the inmates. In the far corner near the window was a heavy iron lid that covered the toilet. This could, on request, be flushed from a tank controlled by the superintending policeman. The flushing of the toilet seemed the one redeeming feature in the squalor of cell life.

Shortly after this abrupt introduction to life in the police station, the command to prepare for bed was issued. One person from each cell went to the room where the *futons* were kept and under the policeman's gaze carried one *futon* for each prisoner into the cells. 'Our cell had five of these – two were spread on the floor and formed our common bed, three were spread over our bodies. The previous occupants of the cell, being accustomed to rules and methods of keeping warm, made the bed. My position in the row was on top of the toilet lid.'

The bedding was filthy, lousy and bug-ridden. The *futons* were taken from a pile in a nearby room and in the evening they were handed out just as they came to hand and were never the same on two consecutive nights. Bishop Heaslett felt he escaped fairly lightly with an unpleasant skin disease, which later yielded somewhat to medical treatment after he was removed to prison. One of his companions contracted a venereal disease.

That cell, or a similar one, was home to Bishop Heaslett for thirteen days. Silence in the daytime was not compulsory. So gradually he got to know the affairs of his companions. No one was reticent about the reason for his presence in the station. Of the four who occupied the cell he was first pushed in, the youngest was a lad of about eighteen years of age, who had stolen money from his employer in a country town and come up to Yokohama to spend it. Another had transgressed the trading laws. The third was a brothel-keeper who had been caught, with three others (all in the station in different cells) gambling. The fourth, 'a most interesting young man', was in to be examined for 'dangerous thoughts'. He was a member of a banned Society of Students of Esperanto and had written in their magazine an article on freedom. He was expecting to receive a sentence of three or four years in gaol.

Their numbers received additions every night, such as intoxicated men, people of feeble intellect found wandering in the streets, night prowlers, thieves. These stayed one or two days and then disappeared to unknown fates and destinations. Bishop Heaslett was treated with consideration by his companions, and they had many a long conversation on religion, social life and English life and manners. The only remark on the war was made by the brothel-keeper, and his idea of the end of it was that the USA should deliver all her ships and pay an indemnity of $1,000,000,000 to Japan.

Several incidents relieved the darkness of the thirteen days spent in the police station. The most amusing was supplied by the happy-go-lucky brothel-keeper. It was not his first visit to that police station and he knew the value of keeping in the good graces of the officer in charge. He looked after the *futons* morning and evening, brushed the corridor, washed down and dusted the desk of the policeman. As a reward he was allowed to sit by the fire-box for an hour or so, and given tea to drink and an occasional cigarette by the policeman. Twice, after they had settled down at night, a stealthy hand was passed over the shoulder of each occupant of the cell and five Japanese sweet-cakes pressed into each hand. Bishop Heaslett asked the brothel-keeper how he managed to get the cakes. It came out that, in order to curry favour with the policeman on duty, he had got his friends outside to send in at his expense a present of these cakes. So, when he was resting after his self-imposed labours and when the policeman was away from the desk, he had stolen a quantity of his own cakes and passed them on to his companions in the cell.

Two small incidents involving women in the police station helped to renew his waning faith in human nature. Both were young women of education and both were under arrest for harbouring 'dangerous thoughts'. One morning, on going with the other members of the cell to the cold-water tap for the usual wetting of his hands and face, he met one of them just finishing her own washing. She had a small piece of soap in her hand. After a short, whispered conversation, he said, 'You're lucky, having a piece of soap,' and she at once replied, 'I'll lend it to you.' After ten days of dirt, of isolation, of irritating restrictions and searchings, he broke down at this first human touch of kindness. 'Consider this – an open window, a cold December wind blowing in, a water tap running, a dirty, unshaven man in *déshabillé*, a girl with a sense of comradeship in affliction, and a small piece of scented soap. I've often smiled at the scene since, but it has been a wry smile, yet not ungrateful.'

The other incident occurred on the day he left the police station. That day he was ordered to dress, all his clothes being handed back to him. 'If you've ever had to hold up your trousers by hand day by day and you've been losing weight all the time, you can understand the feeling of security when braces are once more in place!' As he sat by the entrance waiting for his escort, he saw an opportunity and seized it. There was a pair of nail cutters among the policeman's pens. He summoned up courage enough to ask him to allow him to use them. The policeman was in a placid mood and nodded agreement. Japanese scissors are not easy to use, so he soon took the skin off a finger and was about to give up in despair. The girl was nearby, mending some torn bedding. She saw the blood and his efforts to staunch it and sympathised. Then he did a bold thing. 'Would you,' he asked, 'please cut my nails?' She was somewhat taken aback, but the policeman urged her and she shyly took his hand and in the end, to his great comfort, cut his nails closely, neatly and effectively.

Bishop Heaslett quotes a Japanese proverb: 'Even in Hell there are angels':

> I endorse it from my own experience in the police station. The sense of being in the grip of a heartless system; the tight hold on one's person and things; the finality of the sound of the turning of the key in the cell lock from outside; the sordid atmosphere of the place, with its accumulated dirt, its vermin, its noise, also the constant comings and goings of prisoners, the beating of bodies and the bullying of bewildered men, the absolute authority of the guards, the hopelessness of all of it – these made the place a Hades, and yet, in the midst of it, from companions in fear and misery, there came sympathy and help. Truly in every man-made hell one can find angels, and they are a blessed company.

Bishop Heaslett was held in the police station from 8 to 20 December 1941. On the tenth night of his detention he touched the depths of despair:

> The uncleanness of body, the soiledness of mind, the hopeless isolation; the complete identification of myself with thieves, gamblers,

suspects, men who trafficked in women; the ruthlessness of the machine in which I had been caught and in which I was as helpless as a small fly in a large spider's web; above all, what I thought of as being the failure of my friends and their abandonment of me: the accumulated shame and weight of all this brought me that night to bitter tears and the verge of a breakdown. I felt, as I lay there, that I had reached a limit beyond which I could endure no more. I was, in a word, an abandoned, hopeless, helpless speck in the crime world of Japan and in the close grip of the law.

It was at this point, as he touched bottom, that he had a spiritual experience that transformed his state of mind:

Then at what seemed the limit of endurance there came a message to me almost as if spoken in my ear. The words of the message were: 'He was numbered with the transgressors.'[26] ... A flood of light and illumination came upon me in the moment. For the first time and through my own experience I knew what our Lord had suffered from His arrest until His crucifixion, as far as the human mind can fathom His experiences.

It was later that his thoughts developed along this line, for at the moment the relief was immediate and full. Sympathy takes varied forms. There is the 'long-range sympathy' of the well-to-do person, who subscribes money to a society for the aftercare of prisoners. There is the deeper sympathy of the men and women officers of such societies, who devote their lives to assisting men and women after they are released from gaol. There is the yet deeper sympathy that leads people to assume life as tramps to gain insight into the realities of such lives. But even these persons are kept from sounding the depths of degradation and horror by the knowledge that, at any time, they can escape and return to comfortable conditions.

But in the experience expressed in the Old Testament words, twice applied to our Lord in the New Testament narrative: 'He was numbered with the transgressors', what a fundamental difference there is between ordinary sympathy and that! He became, He was, a criminal, forsaken, abandoned, helpless. That night as I had in

---

[26] *Isaiah* ch. 53, verse 12 (*AV*).

weakness cried, so weakness being changed to strength, I cried in gladness of heart...

On 20 December, Bishop Heaslett was handcuffed – at that moment, he said, 'the iron entered into my soul'[27] – and taken in a public taxi to the detention section of a large prison in a suburb of Yokohama. On the way the taxi stopped at another police station and took in one of the leading foreign businessmen of the city. In spite of the plight of both of them, Bishop Heaslett was glad to see him. It was his first contact with the outside world and his first intimation that he was not the only foreigner who had been arrested. The satisfaction increased when he found in the prison more than forty British, American and men of other countries. There was comfort in numbers, he found, when in trouble.

The prison was a fairly modern building of steel and concrete. It was divided into four: the prison proper, with about a thousand prisoners – mostly men serving a two- or three-year sentence; and three detention sections, for men, women and boys respectively. Bishop Heaslett was given cell No. 12 in a corridor having twenty cells, and all these, as well as a corresponding number in the upper storey, were filled with foreigners. In each cell there was a low bed with bedding; also a wash-stand and toilet, both with running water in abundance. There were two spaces, a small one where he could keep his surplus clothing when it came and another which he used as an exercise ground. This was two yards long and one-and-a-half feet broad. The cell was scrupulously clean and also the bedding. Any sickness among the thousand men was a serious problem – hence the care.

On arrival, he was ushered into a room full of gold-braided officials and there he and his suitcase were subjected to a rigorous search. As in the police station, braces and belts were taken away, also all knives and things with cutting edges, to prevent suicide attempts. Money, watch, hairbrush, razor, books and medicines were all taken away, but he was allowed to have soap, towels, toothbrush, toothpaste and a comb. On the physical side the detention house was paradise compared with the purgatory of the station. Washing his body with water and soap morning and evening helped to clear up the skin disease he had contracted in the police cell and so enabled him to live more comfortably and to sleep.

---

[27] *Psalms* 105, verse 18 (*BCP*).

The prisoners were supposed to be completely isolated and a long list of forbidden things was stuck on the wall on a typed sheet in English. Among forbidden things were whistling, humming, singing and talking. However, Bishop Heaslett soon found out who were his companions on the right and left and gradually the news spread as to who was in what cell, until he knew the names of all the forty-odd Americans, British and other nationals who were on that side of the detention section. He was happy in having near him men whom he had known in Yokohama, with whom he could exchange greetings in the morning and even make enquiries as to their health and progress of their police or gendarme examinations. After the manner of prisoners in all ages they took risks and delighted in outwitting their wardens and ignoring prison rules. A high wall ran along in front of all the cells, dividing the foreign prisoners from the prisons proper. This acted as a sounding board and by speaking slowly with well-filled lungs they could make themselves heard at quite a distance. Bishop Heaslett used it to announce services in his cell.

By unlawful ways he let it be known that he said Morning and Evening Prayer daily and also that he held a celebration of the Holy Communion every Sunday and Saint's Day. The manner of his Sunday celebration was this. He kept back a small piece of white bread from his Saturday's ration. Wine he had none, but the water in the washstand was drinkable. So he spread out on the lid of his washstand a sheet or two of Japanese soft paper; on this he laid his scrap of bread and into a small aluminium cup he ran a sip of cold water, and he propped his Service book against the back of the washstand. On Easter Sunday he announced the beginning and end of the service by three taps with the heel of his shoe on the wall so that his neighbours could join in. He had announced on Saturday as loudly as possible through the window that there would be a service at 6 a.m. Those who cared to do so could follow the service silently in their cells. The absence of wine troubled him at first, but he got over that difficulty in a manner by composing a new prayer. The opening words were: 'O Thou, who at the marriage feast in Cana of Galilee didst turn the water into wine...' He discussed this point with a Roman Catholic priest on board the repatriation ship. The priest thought that he had not celebrated a valid sacrament because of the absence of wine, but wound up by saying, 'God does sometimes work miracles.'

One cold day the warden on duty opened the cell door and ordered Bishop Heaslett to fetch his bucket and bring it and his washing-rag outside into the corridor. 'Wash the doorstep, the posts and the outside of the door!' he shouted. The water was ice-cold, the Bishop's hands were frozen and he went about the business slowly and reluctantly. 'You're not good at this work,' said the warden. 'No,' replied the Bishop, 'I don't usually do this kind of thing; somebody does it for me.' The warden looked at him for a moment and then said, 'You're a Christian, aren't you?' Surprised, the Bishop answered, 'Yes.' 'Didn't your Master wash His disciples' feet?' Not quite sure what he was after, the Bishop said hesitantly, 'Yes, He did.' 'Well then,' said the warden in triumph, 'surely you ought to be able to wash a door!'

On his first day in gaol, just after noon, Bishop Heaslett was sitting in the sunshine in his cell feeling forsaken, desolate, hopeless and abandoned by all his friends. The cell door was opened and a warden brought in a large basket and a thermos flask. He had just eaten as much as he could of a Japanese meal supplied by the prison. He opened the basket and flask. There, to his astonishment, he found a large quantity of sandwiches and good home-cooked food and hot coffee. These had been brought from Tokyo, a two-hours' journey away, by his faithful Japanese cook. That was his first contact with the outer world since arrest, his first intimation that his friends knew where he was and cared, and his first sight of ordinary food. Knowing that he was not forgotten, he laid his head on the cover of the washstand and wept. From that day until he was released four months later, his loyal cook and her daughter brought food daily from Tokyo (a return journey of four hours) and never once – in rain or snow or storm – did they miss. They were rugged north-country folk. In spite of rationing difficulties and with the assistance of countless friends, every day they came with good food and warm drink.

One thing only spoiled the food situation and that was that the authorities insisted on dividing the day's supply into open boxes. It was bitter weather and so the food arrived in the cell stone cold. The Japanese officials had strange ideas of division, so sometimes the fish would be covered with custard sauce and the spinach be mixed with stewed fruit. But the liquids were always hot. There was a rigorous rule against sharing. The men who brought round the food were prisoners from among the sentenced men. For them it was a great opportunity to get a bit extra: 'Bread they loved and begged for; Japanese cakes they almost wept for, and anything in the nature of fish or meat was a godsend to them. All against rules; but what could one do when the peep-hole into the corridor was darkened by a face and a voice said: "*Danna* (Master), have you any spare bread?"'

On 10 January Bishop Heaslett began to undergo examinations in

Japanese by the police, which continued for about six weeks. He had twenty examinations in all and they averaged an hour or so each. But, at the beginning, on several days, he had six-hour examinations with intervals for meals and rest. He was never examined at night. Sometimes the policeman was alone, sometimes he had assistants, but there were never more than four men in the room at once. For the most part the assistants were silent and took notes. The examinations were conducted in special rooms and he was allowed to sit during each session, whether it was long or short. In examinations he had to face the light, while the examiner was in the shade. There was, in his case, no physical pushing about or beating. There was no courtesy or consideration shown: all was in the shortest possible and rudest language. He felt from the beginning that he was on trial as much as anyone who had robbed or murdered.

The usual procedure – a somewhat naïve way, and easy to see through after one or two experiences – is to open the examination session with a time of general gossip and pleasant exchanges on your health, your family, your work, and so on. Then the prisoner, convinced of the friendliness of his examiner, and sure that he will – as assured – soon be released, is suddenly confronted with a changed being, who hurls accusations at you, browbeats you, bellows at you, and calls you a liar in several forms of speech. He sees evil in all that you have ever done, believes only what fits into his preconceived notions, and in general treats you as a guilty person who must be in some way persuaded to accept the police estimate of your life, and then sign a statement that the formal indictment is true.

Bishop Heaslett had two chief examiners. The first was efficient in the above methods, and so twisted all that he said that he was sometimes sure he was heading straight for a life sentence as a spy. The examiner had no conscience, saw no truth in his denials and made large mountains out of small molehills. He was, in the Bishop's estimate, an evil person. The second was more reasonable and saw sense in his friendship with Japanese people and his life's work in the country. But even he held the belief that, under the cloak of religion, the main work of the Church was collecting and forwarding information on economics, thought, and army and navy affairs, and that churchmen were, in effect, agents of the Archbishop of Canterbury or servants of the British Ambassador.

Bishop Heaslett's first examination, when the exchange of civilities had ended, was a tirade on the subject of spies, the cruelty of the British towards native races, and the treachery of the British soldiers in the war. Contrasted with this, Japan was a righteous nation, wishing only to lead weak nations by the hand to prosperity, and the Japanese army was imbued with the lofty spirit of *bushido*.

So under the cloak of religion I was a spy: the British Ambassador, all diplomats, consuls, merchants, teachers, and missionaries, more spies. He said: 'We have proof of your spying activities, and unless you confess you will be handed over to the gendarmes,' who would, he said, treat me much more severely than the police. 'You now belong to Japan, your body and all your possessions are ours, and we can do what we like with you.' When I objected to this, and advanced proof, his reply was: 'You're a liar. You tell lies only.' That was his usual answer. I was called a liar that day more times than I could count, and certainly more times than I deserved. It was a tiring and tiresome business. It raised simple despair in the mind. Answering was so hopeless. To keep one's temper was vital whatever the provocation, but to be called a liar in the loudest and rudest language by an uneducated underling who, in the ordinary custom of this polite country, would have addressed me in very humble language – this was a real occasion of provocation.

Bishop Heaslett concluded that the real difficulty was that their minds were working on absolutely different levels. While the examiner's was on the level of suspicion and distrust and a determination to make a good case against him, his own was on the level of trust, openness and belief in a man's words and acts, and some desire to get at the truth. He had determined at the beginning to be open about all his acts and connections. He felt he had done and said nothing of which he was ashamed and, as he said, would have done anything lawful to avert war between their two countries. This statement appeared in the police report presented to the procurator with the word 'anything' underlined. Here was evidence of guilt!

After three long periods of concentrated questioning, he had a rest. During one of these sessions he had suffered another heart attack, which frightened the examiner, so that after that he gave him shorter sessions. His house was thoroughly searched and his servants questioned and threatened, his Japanese colleagues questioned and their houses searched, and all papers dealing with the diocese taken from them for closer examination. The effect of this on the examiner was that he became less brutal and more considerate in a minor degree:

There were many official photographs in my house showing me in robes welcoming members of the Imperial Family to official services in Tokyo, St Andrew's Church; and my colleagues gave me a good character too, I suppose! Though some of them said unwise things in their examinations.

Examinations were carried out on the following scheme: (1) We have printed evidence that you were an active member of the official British Information Committee. That was a specimen of the lie direct. It was untrue in all respects. (2) We suspect that you talked to your friends, especially Japanese, on Japanese food problems, the war in China, etc. That was the lie suggested. (3) Because you have been in Japan so long, know the language, and have travelled widely, you must have given information to the Ambassador on points you know. We believe this, therefore you must be a spy. Here was the lie lying at the base of all the examinations. Nothing could change this belief in the minds of the police. In the end it became clear that to know that there was a food shortage, a war in China, soldiers coming and going, indeed everything extraordinary, was a suspicious, nay, a criminal act. Indeed, if anyone lived in Japan, unless he could prove he was blind, deaf and dumb, he could be arrested and punished.

It was on 12 January, during his second long examination, that Bishop Heaslett had a second saving spiritual experience. He was in a room alone with a police official. He was still groping in the dark, both as to the reason for his arrest and the purpose of the severe questioning. It was one of the most grilling experiences that he had had. He knew that a small slip in answering a question might open a new line of questioning, or involve his friends, or give a wrong impression as to the motives for his actions. All through the session he prayed steadily that the officer's questions and his answers should be guided by the Holy Spirit, but he did not receive the divine aid that he hoped and prayed for. Moreover, at the end of the day, he was so exhausted mentally and spiritually that he had his one heart attack while in prison and had to be assisted back to his cell.

But towards the end of the session, when my cry became 'O God, end all this!', quite suddenly relief came, and in a wholly unexpected way. There came into the room a Presence. There was a Presence behind me on my right hand, and a message, 'My Grace is sufficient for thee and My strength is made perfect in thy weakness.'[28] There was a Presence and a message as real and definite as if an embodied Spirit had appeared in the room, and there was light where the Presence stood. (This is to me inexplicable, but I could not and cannot doubt its reality.) It stayed with me, having, as it were, a hand on my shoulder, until the session ended. So having reached my limit, I was not allowed to collapse physically and mentally. There was no insurge of strength. There was power given to endure – just that. That was the unexpected, promised Presence, the answer to my prayers, the mitigation of my fears.

On another night Bishop Heaslett lay in his prison bed, comfortable and warm in body, tortured in mind. It was the night after a severe examination. The net seemed to be closing round him, and the only question that remained was what was to be the kind and quality of his punishment. Escape seemed impossible. He knew that he was innocent, but his most innocent acts and words took on a sinister meaning when the police officer's mind worked over them. As he lay there he was obsessed by fear of the coming unknown. The effect of constant and reiterated and hammered-in questionings was to begin to raise doubts in his own mind about himself. It seemed that a concocted story and a confession that would satisfy his examiners and bring his weariness to an end might be the best way out of all difficulties.

Suddenly I saw light, real seeing of real light. Mental illumination came in a way I have never before known. It had an almost physical quality. I saw, with a clarity almost frightening, all my personal affairs. My mind seemed to be afire and my vision penetrating. My arrest, the official plan against me, the purpose of the whole episode, lay clearly before me. And, in addition, the future also lay revealed. It took this form: 'There is a plan of God for your life, and it cannot fail.' 'The plan cannot fail.' 'The plan cannot fail.'

So I saw this clearly, that there was plan and purpose in my life in Japan, in this end of my missionary service in Japan, that nothing happens by chance; that there is a guiding Providence, and all man's efforts to twist or turn God's ways with us men are simple folly.

---

[28] *2 Corinthians* ch. 12, verse 9 (*AV*).

Let things happen; none can change the ultimate result. So, come imposed guilt, come judgment, come prison, all can be fitted into and used to forward the plan. This may seem personal presumption, but it's not. For every morning at daybreak in prison I was awakened by the chatter of sparrows in the trees outside, and our Lord's words, 'Ye are of more value than many sparrows,'[29] often gave me personal assurance. There has never been more real experience than this in my life.

Bishop Heaslett wrote later that, when relating his experiences to friends, he was uneasily conscious that he might be making much of little and that, after all, the experiences might not have been so bad:

I cannot, even now, five months after, understand why these police and gendarme examinations terrorised and affected us so deeply. Speaking personally, they drove me to the edge of despair, and there were many times, especially during sleepless nights, when death would have been a welcome relief. I have abundant evidence that others suffered just as I did. I believe that the whole atmosphere was charged with evil. Even the rooms of examination were full of menace. They were the abodes of evil and malignant influence, if not presences. The officials who examined us became the visible agents of a world of evil. The atmosphere was hostile and threatening. Strong men who had occupied the highest business positions were frightened; some broke down. I know of two who committed suicide.

At the end of February, in the midst of a snowstorm, Bishop Heaslett had his last examination and signed a statement that he had seen and heard read the police report. On the way back to his cell, his second examiner gave him a hint that he was not to be accused, that there was no case against him and that he would soon be released and allowed to live in a more comfortable place.

I shall not forget our walking side by side along the open snow-wet corridor, he waving the cell key while he explained that my case was 'not a question of right or wrong, but a question of patriotism'. 'Patriotism,' he said, 'is above questions of right and wrong.' He told me that he had had a talk with the Procurator in

---

[29] *Matthew* ch. 10, verse 31 (*AV*).

charge of my case and that his report was favourable. So that night's sleep was peaceful.

A few days later Bishop Heaslett was called to the office of the Procurator. He learned later that pressure from outside – private and official – had already secured his release and that this interview was routine. The atmosphere of the Procurator's office and the interview was well above that of the police level. Though it was official and in that sense hostile, it was judicial in tone and not merely hostile. The Procurator began by saying 'I am going to ask you four questions. Answer "Yes" or "No" to each.' The questions surprised him, for they had little relationship to the subject matter of his examinations. Bishop Heaslett concluded that these questions were the real grounds for his arrest:

(1) Has the Archbishop of Canterbury ever asked you to make any investigation into any aspect of Japanese life, and report to him?
(2) Has any British Ambassador, especially Sir Robert Craigie, ever made to you a similar request and demanded an answer?
(3) You have lived a long time in Japan, have travelled, and in trains, trams, buses, and shops must have heard many things and opinions. Have you ever compiled a report on your experiences and presented it to the British Ambassador?
(4) Did you, on such a day and in your home, to a certain person criticize the conduct of the Japanese Army in China?

It was not difficult to say the required 'No' to the first three questions; the fourth was somewhat difficult, for he had, on the request of a Japanese friend, explained why the Archbishop of Canterbury had taken the chair at a meeting of protest in the Albert Hall. That involved criticism of the Japanese army. He explained that, and his explanation nearly wrecked the interview. But in the end the Procurator accepted his assurance that he had not then or on other occasions to his Japanese friends criticised their country's doings in China, merely giving him the Archbishop's reasons for presiding at the protest meeting. So he was dismissed.

On 8 April, Bishop Heaslett was called out of his cell to the Procurator's office at noon. The Procurator told him that, although he had broken the law in several points, on account of his long service in Japan, he was going to be released that day. He cautioned him about his future conduct. The Bishop heard all this in silence and at the end said, in accordance with Japanese custom, 'I have caused you much trouble and anxiety.' And so he returned to his home in the compound of St Andrew's Church in Tokyo, and three-and-a-half months later, on 30 July 1942, sailed from Yokohama on a repatriation ship. He had been in custody for 120 days.

2

Scattered and Returned

My father wrote to Bishop Heaslett on 18 December 1942 from the RCAF station at Exeter in Ontario where he was now based:

> Sorry to hear of your four months' solitary confinement – in the next cell to Stagg of the Hong Kong Bank who *The Times* reported had committed suicide. Mrs Stagg was in Toronto last winter looking very distraught and it is good to know they are all together again. We do hope you have had a chance to recuperate and that you are now back in your usual health and spirits.

Bishop Heaslett had planned to end his days in Japan, but that plan was now impossible. He returned to England by ship and became assistant bishop in the diocese of Sheffield. The church and people of Japan remained his chief concern and he never missed a chance of saying in public that there was another Japan very different from its military rulers. He longed to see that other Japan built up again, to see an end to warfare and hatred, and expressed his hope for a better future in the phrase, 'I keep my eyes on the horizon'.

Bishop Heaslett was not the only one of our acquaintance to return to England by sea during the war years. The Woodwards arrived in Los Angeles from Yokohama in January 1941. They had no money and no means of earning money, though Larry Rose was able to arrange some financial support for them through an American church charity. They were living in an apartment block where the other residents were unfriendly. The English were not popular in America, for public opinion was against America's getting involved in the European war. David still spoke Japanese to Peter, but Peter began to whisper back: 'Don't speak Japanese. People will think we're spies.' And so their Japanese gradually faded away.

197

It was difficult to keep the children quiet, but if the children made a noise the neighbours complained. In the apartment there was a door with a strong spring. One day David got his finger trapped in the door. The pain was excruciating but he knew he must not make a sound. He kept quiet till he fainted on the bathroom floor with blood pouring from his crushed finger and broken fingernail. He recovered consciousness to find his parents leaning over him. His first words were, 'I didn't make a noise, did I?'

Stanley obtained a post teaching classics in Jamaica, but he was trying to get back to England. One day, in the middle of a lesson, a message came through that there were places for the family on a ship sailing for England within 48 hours. Stanley told the headmaster and never returned to his class. Their ship was sailing in a transatlantic convoy escorted by American destroyers. That convoy would become famous for, at 5.25 a.m. on 31 October 1941, one of the American destroyers in their escort, the *Reuben James*, was hit by a torpedo from a German submarine and sank off the coast of Iceland. Of the crew 44 survived and 115 died. The loss of the *Reuben James* created a tremendous impression in America, for it was the first American ship to be lost in the Second World War and its sinking off Iceland made clear that President Roosevelt was providing escorts for British transatlantic convoys, even though America was not yet officially at war.

My father too made the transatlantic crossing during the war. We had left Japan in May 1941 and spent our first summer in Canada on Toronto's Centre Island. But that autumn we moved into a rented house on the outskirts of Toronto and my father became a chaplain in the Canadian Air Force. He spent the first eighteen months on air bases in Ontario and then, in May 1943, he sailed from Halifax, Nova Scotia, on the SS *Beaverhill*, and for the rest of the war he was based on Canadian bomber stations in Lincolnshire and Yorkshire.

My father always kept a record of the talks and sermons he gave. That record survives in linen-bound exercise books, now very worn and much repaired. The pages were marked in columns for day, time of day, date, occasion, place, text (if a sermon), subject and remarks. Through all the war years, whether in Canada or in England, he gave talks on Japan, sometimes illustrated by lantern slides, sometimes not. Some talks he gave many times: 'Life and Problems of Japan'; 'The Church of Japan in Crisis'; 'Japan and the West – Past and Future'; 'Japan and her Nationalistic Creed'; 'Japan in the Far-Eastern Crisis'; 'Japan – Measuring our Opponents' Strength'. Once he came to England, the talk that he gave over and over again to audiences of Canadian airmen was entitled at first 'Knowing Our Enemy – Japan', and later, 'Knowing Your Enemy – Japan'.

While our father was away in the Canadian Air Force, we children stayed in Toronto with our mother. In the letter our father wrote to Bishop Heaslett in December 1942, he reported that we were now settling down to our new way of life, but clearly the early stages had not been easy:

> Christopher had a bit of a rough patch at first, for the change and the new surroundings tended to increase his nervous shyness, especially as his English accent and his Japanese origin got picked on at school ... Audrey is in some ways the trickiest of the three to bring up. She reacts so much to atmosphere and craves attention. And if she can't get it by being good she gets it by being bad ... Helen is a less complicated person – she goes her own happy way without caring what people think or reacting much to atmosphere.

And so the war went on. Behind our house there was a field. One day I sat down in the field and looked up at the sky and thought: The war is like the sky. I don't remember when it began and I don't know when it will end. It's just there, over our heads, all the time. We didn't fit in in Canada. Of course we did not. Our father was not with us and besides we were not Canadian. We could not go back to Japan, that was impossible. But one day the war would end, one day our father would come back. Then we would go to England and there we would fit in, because we would be together again and, after all, we were English.

Of course, nothing could have been further from the truth. One day the war did end, and on VE Day in 1945 our father did come home, but he had been away for nearly four years, a huge proportion of our lives. We did not know each other at all. We came to England and arrived at the house where we were to live. Two elderly ladies in black came down the stairs. I thought: Are they the maids? But we were told they were our grandmothers. A family tea party was held in London to welcome us back to England. Uncles, aunts and cousins came. Great-uncle Arthur wore a top hat in honour of the occasion. But all I knew was that they were all strangers, that I could not relate to any of them.

And England. What was England? On the radio in Canada I listened to Vera Lynn singing, 'There'll be blue birds over/ The white cliffs of Dover/ Tomorrow, just you wait and see' – 'blue birds'? 'white cliffs'? was that England? We had a book, *The Children of the New Forest* –

'New Forest'? What did it mean? At primary school in Lincoln we learnt a song with the line 'You've never smelled the tangle o' the Isles'. 'The Isles'? What were 'the Isles'? On the ship from Canada we had travelled with a girl who was going home to the Channel Islands. That must be it, I thought – 'the Isles' must be the Channel Islands. One day we were given an essay to write on 'fish and chips'. Helen did not know what 'chips' meant, but she wrote an essay on fish swimming about in the sea. For me it was the last straw. I laid my head on the desk and wept.

My father's brother, Quentin, came to live with us. He had been in the East too, for he had been on Mountbatten's staff in India, but now he was demobbed. For my eleventh birthday he gave me a bicycle. I was not well that summer. My mother thought I was suffering from anxiety over my eleven-plus exam and wished we were not kept waiting so long for our results. I did not know what was the matter. All I knew was that cycling round and round and round helped to soothe the throbbing in my head.

Always there were divided loyalties. The Reischauers' son, Edwin O Reischauer, was now Japan expert for the US Army Intelligence Service. He was credited with protecting Kyoto from the atom bomb:

> On the shortlist of targets for the atom bomb, in addition to Hiroshima, Kokura and Niigata, was the Japanese city of temples, Kyoto. When the expert on Japan, Professor Edwin O Reischauer, heard this terrible news, he rushed into the office of his chief, Major Alfred MacCormack, in a department of the Army Intelligence Service. The shock caused him to burst into tears.[30]

When the first atom bomb fell on Hiroshima there was jubilation in Britain, a sense that victory could not be far away. Eleven-year-old David Woodward could not share in that joy. He thought: The next one will fall on Tokyo. And he knew that he did not want that.

For us there were two Japans. At home my parents remembered the years spent in Japan with warmth and affection. Friends from Japan days – Bishop Heaslett among them – came to stay and the talk was of the Japan they knew and loved. Our most treasured family possessions

---

[30] Robert Jungk, *Brighter than a Thousand Suns: A personal history of the atomic scientists* (NY: Harcourt Brace, 1958) p. 178. Reischauer refuted this story in his book *My Life Between Japan And America* (NY: Harper & Row, 1986) p. 101, saying: 'I probably would have done this if I had ever had the opportunity, but there is not a word of truth to it.'

were woodblock prints, lacquer bowls, bronze candlesticks, kimonos, boys' and girls' festival dolls. But outside our home the talk was of military Japan and especially of the brutal way in which the Japanese had treated their prisoners-of-war. A word that seemed charged with hatred and bitterness was 'Japs': it always hurt us to hear it. 'Japanese' was a neutral word: the 'Japanese' were a people. 'Japs' was a hostile word: the 'Japs' were the enemy. For three years I went away to boarding school. We did not have a school chapel and on Sundays the girls from my boarding house cycled out to attend the morning service in the village of Leckhampton. The Vicar was the Revd Eric Cordingly. We all knew that Eric Cordingly had been on the Burma–Thailand Railway in the war and we all knew that this was a dark and terrible thing. It was spoken of almost in whispers.

It was not long after the war that friends and members of the family began to go back to Japan. The first was Bishop Heaslett, who returned in May 1946. He was one of the four members of the Anglican Commission sent to Japan from America, Canada and Britain after a break of five years. The purpose of their visit was to convey the greetings of their Churches to the *Nippon Sei Ko Kai*, to assure them of their desire for a renewal of friendly relations, to learn of their situation now hostilities were over, and to discover what help they could provide towards reconstruction. Bishop Heaslett wondered what reception they would be given, for they were making these overtures to a Church that had dismissed them, that had supported its government in the war against them, and that was divided against itself, for one-third had joined the government-sponsored United Church, while two-thirds had stayed outside.

Bishop Heaslett had experienced similar misgivings when he came out of prison four years earlier. Would the fact that he had been in prison make his Japanese friends wary of associating with him? His fears at that time proved unfounded, for in the three months between his release from captivity and his leaving the country a steady stream of visitors called to see him. They all apologised for the treatment he had received, expressed their sympathy and brought presents of food, fruit, flowers, tea and coffee: 'Their minds seemed to run on lines somewhat as follows: "We consider that he is a martyr. What do martyrs most require and how can we show our sympathy?" The invariable answer they arrived at was "Martyrs require food!" and they brought it in abundance.' They were, if possible, even more friendly than they had always been. Again and again men and women came with their children, to see him and to say goodbye to him as their bishop: 'To the end I was their bishop.

My body was rested and strengthened and my spirit healed in their friendliness and sympathy. It is impossible to exaggerate what their love meant to me in the atmosphere of war, boasting, and exultation rampant in Tokyo against the Allies, and after my gaol experiences.'[31]

Once again Bishop Heaslett wondered how he and his fellow members of the Anglican Commission would be received and now again all his doubts and fears were swept away by the warmth and friendliness of their reception. People did not dwell on the broken past but at once returned to the earlier spirit of co-operation, friendliness and unbroken unity: 'They took us to their friendship, renewed their spiritual communion, showed by every possible sign that, whatever had been broken, their union with their fellow Anglicans throughout the world had not been, indeed, could not be, broken. ... So we spent ten weeks among them with never a cloud between us. People offered their hearts.'[32]

The *Nippon Sei Ko Kai* had suffered greatly during the war, with church buildings destroyed by bombing, clergy impoverished and sometimes imprisoned, lay people scattered. Yet it had survived and even showed signs of vitality. Now the arrival of the Commission gave an opportunity to look to the future. Church leaders made it clear that they wished to abide by the resolution of 1940 that the Church should be self-governing and self-supporting. Yet it was taken for granted that America, Canada and Britain would want to help the Church in the aftermath of war, just as they had helped before in the aftermath of natural catastrophes.

Bishop Heaslett was heartened by what the Commission was able to achieve in helping the *Nippon Sei Ko Kai* to move forward, to overcome internal divisions, to re-establish links with the outside world. Above all, he was heartened by the warmth and affection shown to him and to his fellow members of the Commission. The Japan that he knew and loved had survived the war and he had been welcomed home. He returned to England tired but happy. In the following year he died.

Of the three families who had lived next door to each other in the *Shingakuin* compound, the first two to return were David Woodward and then my brother Christopher, for both returned within a year or two of leaving school. Those were the days when most young men spent two years in National Service. David spent three years instead in the Merchant Navy. The ship he was serving on sailed to Yokohama and

---

[31] Heaslett, *From a Japanese Prison*, pp. 49–50.

[32] Printed leaflet: Japan Church Aid, Guild of St Paul, November, 1946.

there he received a warm welcome from Japanese who had known his parents before the war. He appreciated their kindness all the more, as he knew that they had had a hard time during the war and that life was still a struggle for them in this post-war period.

When Christopher was due to be called up for National Service he was given a form to fill in saying what he would like to do. He wrote that he would like to do anything that would let him get back to Japan. He trained as an education instructor and when four volunteers were required to serve in the Far East his hand shot up double quick. He was sent to Hong Kong and from there he took leave in Japan. The Korean War had only just finished and there were British troops still stationed there. Christopher was able to hitch a lift on a troopship from Hong Kong to the base camp at Kure on the Japanese Inland Sea. From there he returned to Ikebukuro, where he was kindly welcomed and shown round. Our house and the *Shingakuin* had both been hit by bombs but much of that part of Tokyo was little altered since our time. The surroundings were familiar and yet Tokyo did not feel like home. Just as when he returned to Japan from furlough as a child, so now again his longed-for 'homecoming' was painful. The war had intervened, Japan had changed, he had changed, and once again he did not speak the language.

It was 1959 when my parents returned to Japan to attend the Centenary celebrations of the *Nippon Sei Ko Kai*. They were glad not to have returned sooner. It would have been painful to go back to a Japan defeated and humiliated, but by 1959 Japan was on the way to recovery and was taking its place once again in the company of nations. As he began his address Bishop Yashiro, the Presiding Bishop of the *Nippon Sei Ko Kai*, acknowledged the dark night through which the Church and the nation had travelled:

At the end of the war, when almost all Japanese people were conscious of the crisis in our nation and working daily with heavy hearts and dragging feet as though tied by chains, a certain poet, Daigaku Horiuchi, wrote a very simple poem of just three lines in Japanese: 'Be thankful. Today I am still alive!' Although this little poem is very short, and our emotions in great confusion, it reached the hearts of the people in those weary days. Everybody who read it found comfort in it. Now, as I stand here with you all to celebrate this great occasion of the Centenary of the commencement of Protestant missionary work in this country, on this day of April 8, in the year 1959, I should like to say with you, 'Be thankful. Today I am still alive.'[33]

Of our three families from the *Shingakuin*, it was only Peggy Rose (now Peg Webber) who returned to live in Japan. Her husband was rector of a parish in New York. One day he came home and said it had been suggested he become Rector of St Alban's Church in Tokyo. During the war, the English St Andrew's Church and Holy Trinity Church had both been destroyed by fire, and for ten years afterwards the Japanese congregation shared their building with the English-speaking congregation. Then St Alban's Church was built to provide for a mainly American congregation. Peg's response was unhesitating: 'When do I pack?'

So, in 1966, Peg returned to Japan with her husband, Chris, and stayed for six years. They already had three children when they went out to Japan, just the youngest being born in Tokyo. And their children experienced that same need to fit in, to belong, that we had all experienced in our childhoods. Each morning Chris would take their youngest daughter to kindergarten and each morning he noticed, as they approached the kindergarten, that his daughter showed signs of anxiety. He did not understand the reason until one day she said, 'Daddy, maybe if you weren't so tall, the other children wouldn't know I'm not Japanese.'

It was not until 1990 that I returned. I knew it was time to go back and yet there were still questions. Japan was associated in my mind with such a sense of grief and loss, would it be all right to go back? And, having gone back, would it be all right to come away again?

Yes, it was good to go back. And for one reason. We did not go back as tourists or outsiders, but everywhere went to Japanese people. In Tokyo we met my parents' friends: Paul Sekiya, whom my parents knew even before they went out to Japan in 1932 and who was my brother's godfather, and Ineko Kondo, who had sailed with us from Japan to England in 1937 when she was a doctoral student and we were travelling to England on furlough.

But it was fifty years since my parents had left Japan and it was a family friend, Mary Chandler, who helped us most with our travel plans. As a young woman Mary would have liked to go to China, but there was no place for Mary in the People's Republic of China, so instead she volunteered for Japan. Her interviewers almost flung their arms round

---

[33] From typescript copy of Bishop Yashiro's address.

her in delight. They said, 'Japan is crying out for English teachers and because of the war nobody will go.' So Mary went to Japan and stayed there for more than thirty years. She had not long returned to England. It was she who made sure that everywhere we went we stayed with Japanese hosts. And for that reason it was good to go back. And, having gone back, it was good to come away again, for the way was now open and I knew I could always return.

There was one other question in my mind. My memories of Japan were so slight, so fragmentary, so unsatisfactory, but when I went back, would memories return? Would things forgotten seem familiar? Twice I did experience a strong sense of recognition. The first time was at Gotemba in the Fuji National Park. We were staying in an old wooden house with a veranda. Other wooden houses and a wooden church were scattered among the pine trees, and my thought was, 'Why, this is Canada!' The second time was at Lake Towada in the north of Honshu. We were staying by the side of the lake, boats were drawn up on the lakeshore and each morning the boats set out across the lake to catch the fish for the day. It was autumn, the maple leaves were in brilliant colour, and again my thought was, 'Why, this is Canada!'

Five years later we returned to Japan. By then both my parents had died. My brother and sister and I gathered to discuss how we should share their possessions. I walked in the garden with my brother and asked about certain ornaments in the drawing room. He said, 'I don't so much mind about the things. What I should really like is to go back to the East.' So the next year we set out again: Singapore, Hong Kong, Japan.

Our father had been Bishop in Singapore from 1961 to 1966, the last English Bishop of Singapore and Malaya. So my parents, who had spent the early years of their married life in Japan, returned to Asia after twenty years to serve in a place that had suffered so greatly at the hands of the Japanese. We had none of us been to stay with them there. Air travel was still very expensive. My brother was a curate, my sister and I were both newly married: we could none of us afford costly fares to the East. So, when my husband and I visited Singapore in 1990, it was for the first time. Now we returned with my brother. Again we visited St Andrew's Cathedral, again we visited Bishopsbourne, where our parents had lived, but this time we went on to visit Changi Gaol.

Changi was still a working prison, but outside the prison walls there was a museum commemorating the lives and deaths and sufferings of thousands of Allied prisoners-of-war, and beside the museum building a chapel, a reminder of the chapels within the wartime prison camp. In the museum was displayed a newspaper article concerning the Revd Eric Cordingly, whose church I had attended when I was at school, and the return to Changi by members of his family of the Changi Cross.

Eric Cordingly was an army chaplain who had already experienced defeat at Dunkirk before arriving in Singapore only nine days before its capitulation. Once the supposedly impregnable fortress of Singapore was seen to be at risk, British troops en route for the Middle East were diverted to join the Singapore garrison forces from Australia and India, but they arrived too late to have any effect on the rapid Japanese advance through Malaya, and on 15 February 1942 Singapore fell.

Thousands of shocked and bewildered men were herded into Changi camp and Eric Cordingly sought to minister to them as a chaplain. He found there 'an impressive little mosque' which had been abandoned, and set about converting it into a chapel. Many men willingly gave their help and this chapel became a centre of spiritual activity within the camp. Temporary furnishings were replaced by beautiful objects made in makeshift workshops.[34] Pre-eminent among these was the altar cross:

> We have designed a cross which has now been made from the brass of a 4.5 Howitzer shell case, and some bits of brass from an ordnance gun shop. The RAOC have mounted the cross on a half shell case and there are four trefoils, one at the end of each arm, and a craftsman from the Sappers has engraved on the trefoils the badges of the four regiments in this 'parish'. The cross is finished and its workmanship is first rate. Our altar is now most dignified.[35]

The chapel was dedicated to St George and a few months later the Bishop of Singapore, Bishop Leonard Wilson, came to the camp and confirmed 200 men. Bishop Wilson was himself to become a legend in the Far East for the courage with which he endured the most appalling physical and psychological torture. Three years later he gave an account of his experiences and what it was that helped him to endure:

> I looked at their faces as they stood around and took it in turn to flog, and their faces were hard and cruel and some of them were evidently enjoying their cruelty. But by the grace of God I saw

---

[34] EWB Cordingly, 'Captive Christians' in G Moir (ed.), *Beyond Hatred* (London, 1969), pp. 127–9.

[35] Typescript extract from Eric Cordingly's Changi prison camp diary, March 1942. Kindly loaned by members of Eric Cordingly's family.

those men not as they were, but as they had been. Once they were little children playing with their brothers and sisters and happy in their parents' love, in those far-off days before they had been conditioned by their false nationalist ideals, and it is hard to hate little children...[36]

In April 1943, Eric Cordingly left Changi with 'F' Force, a force of 7,000 men who, with the earlier parties, were to be responsible for completing the construction of the railway from Thailand into Burma. There they faced cholera, starvation and death:

Men had suffered so much that death became a casual thing, but we were able in a short time to instal a decent and seemly procedure for funerals and these became impressively simple and moving... Men were stunned and apathetic, but slowly the spiritual side revived and flourished as never before. Men had been so near death – life for them had been stripped of its veneer, stark reality had faced them, they expected to be met on these terms. They talked about death, and many is the time at the bedside of a dying man he has asked me to pray for his death, for his peace, for release from his present misery.

On the route of the railway, volunteers helped to build a second St George's Chapel – 'a very attractive little shrine of bamboo and mats' – and there the cross, which had been brought from Changi, was set up once again on the altar. Nearly two-thirds of 'F' Force died building the railway and three of the eight chaplains were buried in Thailand: 'We were stunned by the horror of that year. Yet amid all that mud and misery, the countryside, with its mountains and beautiful sunsets, helped us to pull through.'

In April 1944 their camp was dismantled and they returned to Singapore to spend the next seventeen months under the shadow of the gaol walls in Changi. These were grim months with rations at starvation level and the men growing ever more gaunt and haggard. A third St George's Chapel was built in the camp and Eric Cordingly continued his work of ministering to the troops: 'The thin veneer of civilization, of reticence, had been stripped from men. We were all down to bedrock. One saw people as they really were. There was no reason for humbug or cant;

---

[36] Cordingly, 'Captive Christians', p. 129; R McKay, *John Leonard Wilson: Confessor for the Faith* (London, 1973), p. 33.

many men had no use at all for religion, but great numbers had – and these men were no longer shy about the faith which they had found.'[37]

Their captivity ended in September 1945 with the arrival of paratroopers following the Japanese surrender and Eric Cordingly returned to his Cotswold parish of Leckhampton. He took with him the cross from St George's Chapel in Changi and kept it in his study until his death in 1976. In 1992 two members of his family returned to Singapore and brought with them the cross that stands now on the altar of the present chapel, the fourth St George's Chapel.

Eric Cordingly became Bishop of Thetford and is buried in Norwich Cathedral. On his gravestone are inscribed WH Auden's lines:

> In the deserts of the heart
> Let the healing fountain start,
> In the prison of his days
> Teach the free man how to praise.[38]

So we left Singapore and continued our journey to Hong Kong and then Japan. Paul Sekiya had died but we visited his brother John. During our conversation John Sekiya expressed sorrow at the actions of the Japanese during the war and spoke of a visit that he and his wife had made to one of the great military cemeteries scattered through south-east Asia. There he saw a young man standing beside one of the graves. He approached and asked whose grave it was. The young man replied that it was the grave of his grandfather. 'I was so moved,' said John Sekiya, 'by that young man standing beside his grandfather's grave.'

My mother's friend, Ineko Kondo, we had seen the previous year in Cambridge. As a young woman Kondo-san had not been able to complete her studies in Cambridge, and as war came to Europe she returned to Japan by the sea and land route across Canada. She was later awarded her doctorate, and once air travel became easier she made regular visits to England. She invited us to lunch in Cambridge and afterwards asked if we could take her to Grantchester, as she wished to visit the grave of a don's wife who had been kind to her while she was a student. She explained that during her time in Cambridge hostility was growing towards the Japanese, but this don's wife had shown her great kindness and so whenever she had the opportunity she liked to go to Grantchester to visit and tend her grave.

---

[37] Cordingly, 'Captive Christians', pp. 129–35.

[38] From *In Memory of WB Yeats*.

From Grantchester we drove to Long Melford, where my brother was Rector, to visit the house and the grave of Edmund Blunden. From 1924 to 1927 Blunden was Professor of English at Tokyo University and won the regard and affection both of students and fellow academics. He returned in 1947 to a Japan defeated and demoralised and received an astonishing welcome:

> Immediately on arrival he embarked on a kind of royal progress through the country from Asahigawa in the north of Hokkaido to Kogoshima [*sic.*] in the south of Kyushu, when everywhere enthusiastic audiences (mostly students) packed in their hundreds – on at least one occasion in their thousands – into university lecture theatre, school assembly hall, civic building or Buddhist temple, to hear him talk on a variety of literary subjects. He found them eager to discover western culture and hungry for intellectual stimulation.

In *Edmund Blunden: A Tribute from Japan* Mikio Hiramatsu wrote: It has often been said that the greatest merits of the occupation period in Japan were the dispatch of General MacArthur from the United States and Professor Blunden from the United Kingdom. True it was. I could be a living witness for it any time.[39]

The year after our visit to Japan, I was to receive a letter from Kondo-san: 'This year is to celebrate Edmund Blunden's centenary.' Kondo-san went on to list the events to be held in his honour, in Westminster Abbey, in the Imperial War Museum, at Christ's Hospital and in Long Melford. So once again my husband and I set out to join my brother in Long Melford. We attended a service of commemoration in the magnificent church and stood beside the gravestone inscribed 'Edmund Blunden 1896–1974 Beloved Poet' interwoven with the opening lines of his poem *Seers*:

> I live still, to love still
> Things quiet and unconcerned.

Then we joined the throng making its way down past the green to Blunden's home, Hall Mill. There a plaque was unveiled, speeches were made and tea was served in the garden. One of the speeches was given by a Japanese professor, who spoke of Blunden's gift for engaging with

---

[39] B. Webb, *Edmund Blunden: A Biography* (New Haven and London, 1990), p. 275.

Japan and its people. Blunden himself wrote: 'I am haunted by a sense of the spirit of Japan – by Japan in her human expression; of the Japanese scene. I cannot go for my walk in England without seeming to be in one moment or another in Japan as well.'[40]

In Tokyo we returned with Kondo-san to the chapel at Rikkyo. Once again the chapel was filling with students. This time Christopher and I were asked to stand up and say something of our association with this place. Around the walls was an exhibition of photographs showing the devastation wreaked on Tokyo by the terrible bombing raids of 1945. It was 1995, the fiftieth anniversary of the end of the war.

Christopher was invited by Kondo-san's nephew, Keizo Hoshino, to a reunion lunch of their kindergarten class. The group were instructed to meet their hostess at the Metropolitan Plaza. This did not sound like the grey and scruffy area that Christopher remembered. Nor was it. It was all high rise, high tech and bright lights. But then their group turned into a side street which was just as he remembered and he felt, 'I've come home.' They arrived at the *Seikatsudan*, where once the kindergarten, the *Jiyu Gakuen*, had been based. No kindergarten was based there now, but the building had survived the war and was of architectural significance, for it was designed by Frank Lloyd Wright. There the reunion lunch was held and there, after a world war and more than fifty years, two former teachers and nine former classmates gathered to welcome my brother back to Japan.

So twice I made the journey back to modern Japan, first with my husband and then with both my husband and my brother, but even before I made the first of those journeys I knew already that I must make another journey, and that I could only make that journey through writing a book. I did not know what material I had to draw on. I had no coherent memories of my own. Perhaps I was relying on my mother's memories. But then my mother told me of my father's letters that I found in the two box files in the metal cabin trunk in the garage. And David Woodward told me of his father Stanley's letters that he had found in a shoe bag hanging in the garden shed. And Peg Webber told me of her mother Caroline's letters that she had saved from being burnt. And so I set out on that other journey, the journey back to the lost world of my childhood, the world of my own lost childhood. For I knew that it was only through making that journey that I could at last find my way home.

---

[40] Ibid., p. 143.

Glossary

banzai	literally meaning 'ten thousand years', it is the equivalent of 'three cheers' or 'hurrah'.
bushido	'The Way of the Warrior'; military code originally associated with the military class, which was more widely promulgated as a national ethos during the 1930s.
daikon	giant white radish.
furoshiki	a large cloth used to wrap and carry items.
futon	padded quilt used as both a mattress and a covering.
geta	traditional wooden clogs.
Go Do	Government-sponsored United Church.
gogai	special extra editions of newspapers.
hari-kiri	ritual suicide by disembowelling: mode of suicide adopted by samurai when they had no alternative but to die.
hiragana	syllabic script generally employed in written Japanese.
kabuki	traditional form of drama, characterised by stylised acting, gorgeous costumes and revolving stage; all parts played by men.
kabuki-za	theatre where *kabuki* performed.
kaji	fire.
kamikaze	literally meaning 'divine wind', this term was applied to aeroplanes, indicating at first speed and then, in wartime, planes on suicide missions.
katakana	syllabic script usually employed to write foreign loan words and Japanese onomatopoeia; used for official documents.
Kempeitai	Japanese Secret Police.
Nippon Sei Ko Kai	Anglican or Episcopal Church of Japan.
NYK	(*Nippon Yosen Kaisha*) Japanese steamship company.
O Bon	summer festival when people make offerings to their ancestors

	and pray for the happiness of their ancestors' souls in the next world.
onsen	hot springs.
pan	bread.
Rikkyo	St Paul's University, Ikebukuro, Tokyo.
sake	rice wine.
sensei	term of respect generally employed when addressing teachers.
Shingakuin	Central Theological College, Ikebukuro, Tokyo.
sukiyaki	meat and vegetable dish cooked at the table.
tatami	woven mat of rice straw used as a floor covering.
yukata	light cotton kimono often worn in the summer.

Bibliography

WG Beasley, *The Rise of Modern Japan* (Weidenfeld and Nicolson, London, 1990).

Samuel Bickersteth, *Life and Letters of Edward Bickersteth Bishop of South Tokyo*, 2nd edn (John Murray, London, 1905).

Frida H Brackley, ed., *Brackles, Memoirs of a Pioneer of Civil Aviation* (W&J Mackay & Co. Ltd, Chatham, 1952).

Hugh Byas, *Government By Assassination* (Alfred A Knopf, New York, 1942).

Samuel Heaslett, *From A Japanese Prison* (Student Christian Movement Press Ltd, London, 1943).

Elizabeth A Hemphill, *The Road to Keep, The Story of Paul Rusch in Japan* (Walker/Weatherhill, New York & Tokyo, 1969).

Robert Jungk, *Brighter than a Thousands Suns: A personal history of the atomic scientists* (Harcourt Brace, New York, 1958).

James E Lindsley, *He Was The Dean, a memoir of Lawrence Rose Dean of the General Theological Seminary 1947–1966* (General Theological Seminary, 1990).

Roy McKay, *John Leonard Wilson Confessor For The Faith* (Hodder & Stoughton, London, 1973).

RHP Mason & JG Caiger, *A History of Japan*, Cassell Asian Histories (Cassell Australia, Melbourne, 1972).

Guthrie Moir, ed., *Beyond Hatred* (Fortress Press, Philadelphia, 1970).

FSG Piggott, *Broken Thread An Autobiography* (Gale & Polden Ltd, Aldershot, 1950).

Willard Price, *Japan and the Son of Heaven* (Duell, Sloan and Pearce, New York, 1945).

Edwin O Reischauer, *Japan, The Story of a Nation*, 3rd edn (Charles E. Tuttle, Tokyo, 1981).

C Kenneth Sansbury, *A History of St Andrew's Church, Tokyo (English Congregation) 1879–1939* (Kokusai Shuppan Insatsusha, Tokyo, 1939).

Richard Storry, *A History of Modern Japan* (Penguin Books, London, 1960).

Barry Webb, *Edmund Blunden, A Biography* (Yale University Press, New Haven and London, 1990).

Index